The Op

AA100
The Arts Past and Present

Book 2
Tradition and Dissent

Edited by Carolyn Price

This publication forms part of the Open University course AA100 *The Arts Past and Present*. Details of this and other Open University courses can be obtained from the Student Registration and Enquiry Service, The Open University, PO Box 197, Milton Keynes, MK7 6BJ, United Kingdom: tel. +44 (0)870 333 4340, email general-enquiries@open.ac.uk

Alternatively, you may visit the Open University website at http://www.open.ac.uk where you can learn more about the wide range of courses and packs offered at all levels by The Open University.

To purchase a selection of Open University course materials visit http://www.ouw.co.uk, or contact Open University Worldwide, Michael Young Building, Walton Hall, Milton Keynes, MK7 6AA, United Kingdom for a brochure. Tel. +44 (0)1908 858785; fax +44 (0)1908 858787; email ouwenq@open.ac.uk

The Open University
Walton Hall, Milton Keynes
MK7 6AA

First published 2008

Edited and designed by The Open University.

Typeset in India by Alden Prepress Services, Chennai.

Printed by Alden HenDi, Oxfordshire

ISBN 9780749217013

1.1

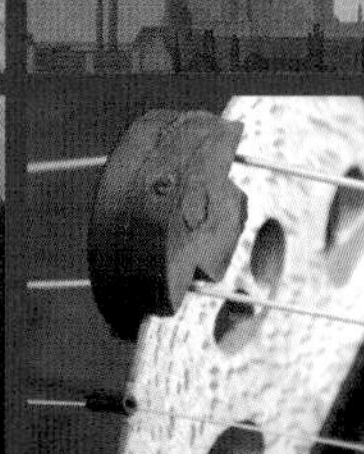

INTRODUCTION
Carolyn Price
page v

1 PLATO ON TRADITION AND BELIEF
Carolyn Price
page 1

2 READING POETRY: *THE FABER BOOK OF BEASTS*
Richard Danson Brown
page 39

3 TRADITION AND DISSENT IN ENGLISH CHRISTIANITY
John Wolffe
page 71

4 PUGIN AND THE REVIVAL OF THE GOTHIC TRADITION
Carol Richardson, Elizabeth McKellar and Kim Woods
page 107

5 IRELAND: THE INVENTION OF TRADITION
Anne Laurence
page 149

6 TRADITION AND DISSENT IN MUSIC: DMITRI SHOSTAKOVICH
Fiona Richards
page 191

AFTERWORD
Carolyn Price
page 226

GLOSSARY
page 227

ACKNOWLEDGEMENTS
page 234

INDEX
page 235

Contents

William Blake, 'Los howld in a dismal stupor', plate 10 from *The First Book of Urizen*, 1794, colour-printed relief etching in ink and watercolour, 25 x 18 cm. Yale Center for British Art, Paul Mellon Collection, USA. Photo: © Yale Center for British Art, Paul Mellon Collection, USA/Bridgeman Art Libray.

INTRODUCTION

Carolyn Price

The first book of *The Arts Past and Present* adopted the theme of 'Reputations', focusing on particular individuals and – in some cases – particular works of art or literature. This second book introduces two broader themes: 'Tradition and Dissent'. While reputations tend to belong to individuals, traditions are shared by a group of people. Traditions bring people together; but, as we'll see, they can also pull people apart.

Moving from a single theme to a dual one complicates things a little. Here we have to think not only about our two themes – tradition and dissent – but also about the relationship between them. I hope you'll find that this additional complexity makes for some rich and satisfying discussions. I'll begin this introduction by picking out some issues that you may wish to keep in mind as you engage with the material in this book.

We might think of a tradition as something that's rooted in the past – a way of doing or thinking about things that hasn't changed for years. But can traditions, like reputations, change and develop? In Chapter 3 on English Christianity, John Wolffe traces the way in which a number of religious traditions rose and matured (and, in some cases, waned and revived) over 200 years of English history. The traditions he describes are far from settled; rather, his story is one of change and controversy. And, as you'll discover later in the book, even the assumption that traditions must be rooted in the past is open to challenge: in Chapter 5 on Ireland, Anne Laurence describes the way in which a sense of tradition may be created at a particular moment in history to serve the needs of the present.

Should we cherish our traditions? In Chapter 1 on Plato, Carolyn Price describes how some philosophers have questioned the value of tradition and have argued that each individual should decide for him or herself what is valuable in life. The potential opposition between shared tradition and the voice of the individual is explored in a number of other chapters too. For example, Richard Danson Brown describes in Chapter 2 how poets such as D.H. Lawrence reject poetic traditions in order to develop their own voice.

But could we really dispense with our traditions without losing something of value? There's no denying the immense political and social significance of tradition: the chapters on English Christianity and on Ireland highlight the crucial importance of tradition in creating a sense of shared identity. But we'll also examine the role that tradition plays in allowing people to share ideas. As well as describing how poets have challenged tradition, Richard Danson Brown explains how poets are able to express ideas by exploiting traditions that people have shared over a long period of time. You'll find a similar idea in Chapter 4 on the architect Augustus Pugin (by Carol Richardson, Elizabeth McKellar and Kim Woods) and in Chapter 6 on the Russian composer Dmitri Shostakovich (by Fiona Richards). Perhaps it strikes you as surprising that a building or a piece of music can be used to communicate an idea – but, as the authors of these chapters explain, Pugin and Shostakovich are able to give meaning to their works by exploiting traditions that people can recognise and understand.

I've mentioned the idea that traditions can be targets for dissent. But can tradition and dissent sometimes go hand in hand? As the authors of Chapter 4 explain, Pugin challenged the traditions and values of classical architecture – not by inventing something novel, but by reviving and adapting an earlier architectural tradition. In her chapter on Shostakovich, Fiona Richards describes how the composer uses references to traditional Jewish music in his work in order to express his dissent from Stalin's regime. As you work through the book, you'll find many illustrations of the ways in which tradition and dissent can connect, as well as clash.

At this stage in the course, you have encountered seven Arts and Humanities disciplines. The first chapter of this book will introduce a further discipline – Philosophy – through a discussion of a short work by the ancient Greek philosopher Plato. In this chapter, you'll develop skills in finding and testing arguments: skills which are crucial to the practice of Philosophy, and which you may find useful in all your studies.

The remaining chapters of Book 2 will take you back to some of the disciplines that you've already encountered: English, Religious Studies, Art History, History and Music. You'll have a chance here to practise and develop your skills in using historical evidence and in analysing texts, visual images and music. But these chapters will also introduce new aspects of these disciplines. For example, in English the focus will move on from drama to poetry; in Art History it will shift from painting to architecture; in Music it will progress from singers and their reputations to the works of a single composer. We hope that this material will help to communicate the breadth of interest and varying perspectives that can be found even within a single discipline.

There will be a chance too to sample the way in which two or more disciplines can work together to produce a more rounded understanding of a topic. For example, there are helpful connections to be found between Chapter 3 on English Christianity and Chapter 4 on Pugin – connections that are highlighted in the DVD ROM material on St Chad's Cathedral in Birmingham. As you move on from this book to the second half of the course, you'll find authors from different disciplines working together in an even more integrated way. But here you'll have your first chance to make this kind of connection across disciplines.

As you might expect, you're likely to find the material becoming more demanding as we move further into the course. So don't worry if the chapters in this book stretch you a little further than the discussions in Book 1, *Reputations*. Tutorials and electronic forums provide opportunities for you to talk through complex ideas and arguments. And remember that you can go to the Study Companion if you need further advice on dealing with difficult material.

Finally, you'll find that many of the chapters in this book make substantial use of material on DVD ROM, DVD Video or Audio CD. Much of this material is linked to the printed material in the book and needs to be referred to at a certain point in each chapter. We hope that this material will help to enrich your understanding of the topics under discussion. But, before you begin each chapter, it's worth checking what you will need, to make sure that you have the right equipment and materials to hand.

1 PLATO ON TRADITION AND BELIEF

Carolyn Price

INTRODUCTION		3
1.1	WHAT IS A TRADITIONAL BELIEF?	3
1.2	PLATO AND SOCRATES IN ATHENS	5
1.3	PLATO'S SOCRATES	6
1.4	SOCRATES' QUESTION	9
1.5	LACHES AND GREEK TRADITION	11
1.6	IS COURAGE ENDURANCE? SOCRATES' ARGUMENT	13
1.7	IS COURAGE ENDURANCE? INTRODUCING DEDUCTIVE ARGUMENTS	14
	Definition of validity	14
1.8	IS COURAGE ENDURANCE? THE CASE OF THE FOOLISH FIRE-FIGHTER	15
1.9	NICIAS DEFINES COURAGE	16
1.10	IS COURAGE THE WHOLE OF VIRTUE?	18
1.11	THE PUZZLE OF THE *LACHES*	20
1.12	KNOWLEDGE, OPINION AND THE STATUES OF DAEDALUS	20
1.13	WHY SOCRATES DOES NOT KNOW THE ANSWERS (AND WHY PLATO WILL NOT TELL US WHAT THEY ARE)	23
1.14	WHY DOES PLATO REJECT TRADITION?	24
1.15	THE SOCRATIC METHOD, TEACHING AND LEARNING	26

REFERENCES 28

FURTHER READING 28

RESOURCES 29

Reading 1.1 29

Reading 1.2 30

Reading 1.3 31

Reading 1.4 31

Reading 1.5 32

Reading 1.6 33

Reading 1.7 34

Reading 1.8 35

Media notes 36

MATERIALS YOU WILL NEED

- Audio CD: Plato's *Laches* – a Discussion with Tim Chappell
- DVD ROM: Plato
- Course website

AIMS

This chapter will:

- introduce you to some skills involved in studying philosophy, including reading a philosophical text, recognising a philosophical question, and analysing and evaluating a deductive argument
- explore some of Plato's philosophical views – in particular, his views concerning the value of traditional beliefs.

INTRODUCTION

In this chapter, we shall read some extracts from the *Laches*, a dialogue written by the ancient Greek philosopher Plato (*c*. 427–347 BCE) (see Figure 1.1). One of our aims in reading these extracts is to discover how Plato uses philosophical argument to question traditional beliefs. I shall start by explaining what I mean by a traditional belief.

Figure 1.1 Bust of Plato, *c*. 427–347 BCE, stone. Vatican Museums and Galleries, Vatican City. Photo: Bridgeman Art Library/Alinari.

1.1 WHAT IS A TRADITIONAL BELIEF?

For many years, I believed that dock leaves are a good remedy for nettle stings. I was told this by my parents, and I imagine that they picked it up from older friends and relatives too. The belief has been handed down from generation to generation, much as a family heirloom might be handed down. I have never tested the truth of the belief for myself. I have simply absorbed it from the people around me, without reflecting on it or trying to check whether it is true. By a traditional belief, then, I mean a belief that has been passed down from one generation to another, and that someone has simply absorbed from other people, without examining it for him or herself.

Many of my own beliefs are traditional, in this sense. They include ethical or moral beliefs – that is, beliefs about the ways in which people should conduct their lives and treat other people. Here are some moral beliefs that I picked up from older relatives when I was young:

> It is wrong to tell a lie.
>
> It is wrong to be sexually promiscuous.
>
> There is nothing wrong with eating meat.

When I was young, I accepted these beliefs on trust. Most of us, I imagine, have picked up some of our moral beliefs in this way.

It is open to us to question traditional beliefs. For example, I might test the truth of my belief about dock leaves by using a dock leaf when I next have a nettle sting. It is not so easy to see how to test the truth of traditional moral beliefs. But one way in which someone might do this is by drawing on his or her own personal experience of applying traditional beliefs to real situations. Alternatively, he or she might use reason to examine traditional moral beliefs – for example, by investigating how well such beliefs fit together and whether they can be explained by more general principles.

Still, examining traditional moral beliefs is likely to be a time-consuming and difficult task. It can be argued that the task is not worth undertaking because it is impossible to improve on tradition as a source of moral beliefs. Here are two arguments that might be used to support this claim:

1. Traditional moral beliefs are shared by the members of a community. As long as all members of the community act in accordance with traditional beliefs, everyone will know what kind of behaviour to expect from everyone else, and so people will get on well with each other. If individuals start questioning traditional beliefs, there will be confusion and conflict.
2. Traditional moral beliefs have a long history: they reflect the experience and wisdom of many generations. So it is unlikely that individuals will be able to improve on tried and tested traditional beliefs, either by drawing on their own personal experience or through reflection.

Activity Take some time to think about these two arguments. Do you find either of them convincing? If you prefer one to the other, try to decide why.

Discussion Different people will react to these arguments in different ways. My own reaction is that both arguments have some merit, but I prefer the second to the first. The first argument appeals to the idea that shared traditional beliefs can promote social harmony, but it says nothing about whether these beliefs are *true*. In contrast, the second argument does provide some reason to believe that traditional moral beliefs are likely to be true: it suggests that this is because they have been tried and tested over many generations. Although I do not think that this argument settles the issue, I do think that it raises a serious challenge for anyone who thinks that it is sometimes right to reject a traditional moral belief in the light of one's own personal experience or reasoning. The challenge is to explain why one's own experience or reasoning should be preferred to the experience of many generations.

The view that tradition is the best source of moral beliefs is called **moral traditionalism**. Whatever the arguments in its favour, moral traditionalism has been rejected by many philosophers. The opponents of moral traditionalism include philosophers who adopt a position known as **moral rationalism**. Moral rationalists argue that we ought to question existing moral beliefs, and retain only beliefs that can be rationally defended and explained. And so they hold that it is reason, not tradition, that is the proper basis for our moral beliefs.

Plato was a moral rationalist. In this chapter we will discover how Plato uses rational argument to question traditional beliefs and we will investigate why he held that we should look to reason, rather than tradition, to ground our moral beliefs.

1.2 PLATO AND SOCRATES IN ATHENS

If you would like to know more about the topics discussed in this section, you can look for entries on Plato, Socrates and Classical Athens in a printed or online encyclopaedia. You might try using Oxford Reference Online, which allows you to search for articles across a range of reference works published by Oxford University Press.

Plato and his mentor Socrates are among the most influential philosophers in the history of western thought. In this section, I will provide some background information about their lives and the social and political world in which they lived.

Plato was born towards the end of the fifth century BCE. His family were wealthy and prominent citizens of the Greek city state of Athens. Athens was governed by a democracy, in which adult male citizens were entitled to vote in the assembly. (It is worth bearing in mind, though, that only a small minority of the adult population could vote: women, slaves, and foreign residents were all excluded from the democratic process.) Democratic politics seems to have fostered a culture of discussion and debate among male citizens, who would meet in public places or at drinking parties to exchange gossip and discuss current affairs. Moreover, at this time Athens was the cultural and intellectual centre of Greece, attracting scholars and teachers from across the Greek world. Leading citizens played host to visiting intellectuals, who would discourse on science, literature and politics, and deliver lectures on how to succeed in life.

Moving in these circles was the Athenian philosopher Socrates (*c.* 469–399 BCE; see Figure 1.2). Unlike Plato, Socrates was of relatively humble origins: his father was said to have been a stonemason or sculptor and his mother a midwife. Rather than pursuing a trade, however, Socrates dedicated his life to philosophical discussion. He seems to have presented himself not as a teacher or an expert, but as someone with a knack for drawing other people into discussion in the hope of discovering the truth. He attracted an entourage of wealthy and influential friends, many of whom were young men, like Plato.

From 431 to 404 BCE, Athens was at war with Sparta, a rival city state. The conflict produced great political and social upheaval, and ended in defeat for Athens. For a time the city was ruled by a vicious puppet government, in which Plato's own uncle played a leading role. Democracy was soon restored, however, and four years later Socrates was put on trial, accused of impiety and of corrupting the young. He was found guilty, suggesting that, for many Athenians, it was plausible to suppose that Socrates' philosophical activities, which had encouraged people to question traditional religious and moral values, had contributed to the downfall of the city. Socrates was sentenced to die by drinking hemlock (a drug that induces paralysis and respiratory collapse). Plato was present at Socrates' trial, though not, he tells us, at his execution.

Socrates left no writings, but Plato wrote many philosophical works. Most of these take the form of a dialogue between two or more people, usually with Socrates as one of the main characters. Plato also founded the Academy, a meeting place for scholars and students interested in philosophy, mathematics and astronomy. The Academy was an important source of philosophical ideas for many centuries after Plato's death, and his philosophical writings are still highly influential today.

1.3 PLATO'S SOCRATES

In his dialogues, Plato portrays Socrates discussing a range of philosophical issues with other people, many of them well-known figures of the time. Most of the dialogues are named after one of the other characters involved. The *Laches*, for example, takes its name from the Athenian general Laches, who plays an important role in the discussion. (Plato's dialogues are usually referred to as 'the *Laches*', 'the *Protagoras*' and so on, rather than just '*Laches*', or '*Protagoras*', much as people refer to Leonardo da Vinci's painting as 'the *Mona Lisa*', rather than '*Mona Lisa*'.) The dialogues do not record actual conversations that took place while Socrates was still alive: they are literary works, not historical accounts. But the earlier dialogues, which include the *Laches*, probably present a fairly accurate picture of the philosophical questions that interested Socrates and the method that he used to investigate them.

Nevertheless, it is important to distinguish between the real, historical Socrates and the character that appears in Plato's dialogues. While the historical Socrates was clearly an important influence on Plato, there is no reason to assume that Plato wrote his dialogues simply as a showcase for Socratic philosophy. It is likely that, even in these early dialogues, Plato had his own reasons for choosing certain topics and following certain lines of argument. For this reason, I am going to assume that the philosophy of the *Laches* is that of Plato, rather than Socrates. And from this point on, I will use the name 'Socrates' to refer to the character in the dialogue, rather than the real person. When I refer to the real person, I will use the phrase 'the historical Socrates'.

Figure 1.2 Portrait statuette of Socrates, *c.* 200 BCE–100 CE, height 27.5 cm. British Museum, London. Photo: Scala, Florence/HIP.

Plato presents Socrates as interested primarily in moral questions. In particular, he is concerned with the qualities or virtues that people need in order to live a good life. In the *Laches,* he is concerned with the nature of courage. In other dialogues, he discusses piety, friendship, temperance and justice. Socrates does not try to answer the questions raised himself. Instead, he proceeds by asking other people what they think. He often picks people who might be expected to know about the issue: in the *Laches*, his question about courage is addressed to two military generals. Once the other person has given an answer, Socrates puts it to the test by asking a series of further questions. Socrates presents himself as adding nothing to the discussion: he simply asks questions without putting forward opinions of his own. The point of these questions is to investigate whether the person's answer is consistent with other things that he believes. (I say 'he', rather than 'he or she', for a reason: all the characters in Plato's dialogues are male, though the *Symposium* includes a long speech reporting the views of a priestess named Diotima (*Symposium* 201d–212b).)

In the early dialogues, none of the other characters manages to give an answer that passes Socrates' test. The dialogues generally end with the other characters baffled and frustrated. Indeed, some of them become extremely annoyed. No doubt the historical Socrates often provoked a similar reaction. Nevertheless, Plato seems to have found the historical Socrates both fascinating and inspiring in his tireless quest for philosophical truth; and in his dialogues he portrays Socrates as stirring love as well as infuriation.

You will decide for yourself whether you find Socrates intriguing or merely annoying. But there is one frequent complaint about Socrates that is worth a closer look. Some of Plato's characters (and some of his readers) are irritated by Socrates' refusal to put forward views of his own, while being quite ready to criticise the views of others. Socrates responds by saying that he genuinely does not know the answers to the questions that he is investigating. Yet he *does* seem to make some philosophical assumptions. These assumptions help to determine the questions that he asks and the lines of argument that he develops. As a result, conversations with Socrates often take certain recognisable turns, returning to the same points again and again. It looks as if Socrates is being irritatingly deceitful when he claims not to know the answers to his own questions.

However, I would suggest that we should find this situation puzzling rather than irritating. It seems unlikely that Plato intended to portray Socrates as guilty of deliberate deceit. So why does Plato present him as denying that he knows the answers to his questions while, at the same time, favouring some answers over others? I will return to this puzzle once we have investigated the arguments of the *Laches*.

1.4 SOCRATES' QUESTION

Nicias (470–413 BCE): Nicias was an Athenian soldier and statesman, known for his extreme caution. He helped to broker the short 'Peace of Nicias' which ended the first decade of the war between Athens and Sparta. In 415 BCE, he was appointed as one of the leaders of an ill-fated expedition to Sicily, which ended in a disastrous defeat for the Athenian forces and Nicias' own death.

Laches (*c.* 475–418 BCE): Laches was a prominent conservative politician and general. He died at the battle of Mantinea, at which the Athenians were routed by the Spartans.

The conversation that Plato presents in the *Laches* is set in Athens at some point around 420 BCE, during a lull in the war with Sparta. Two Athenian gentlemen, Lysimachus and Melesias, are discussing how to educate their sons. They wonder whether a course of 'fighting in armour' – equivalent, perhaps, to martial arts training today – would foster courage and self-discipline in the young men. They turn for advice to Nicias and Laches, both generals in the Athenian army. Unfortunately, Nicias and Laches do not agree about the value of this kind of training. So Laches calls on Socrates to help them to resolve the issue. Socrates suggests that the issue cannot be decided until another, more general question has been addressed.

We are now going to look at a short section of the *Laches*, in which Socrates introduces his question.

Reading a philosophical text can be a time-consuming exercise: in order to understand what is going on, it is usually necessary to pay very close attention to detail. It is often helpful to begin by reading a whole section, in order to get the gist, and then focus on the sentences or paragraphs where the key points are made. You may also find it useful to underline or highlight key words or phrases. But do not stop there: a good way to ensure that you have understood the key points is to put them into your own words. There is no need to rephrase everything. In particular, you are likely to find that some words or phrases cannot be changed without affecting the meaning of what is said: for example, if Plato is talking about 'courage', changing that to 'daring' or 'grit' is likely to distort his meaning. But your aim should be to express the key points as simply and as directly as you can. This usually requires some thought, and a lot of fine-tuning, so it is a good idea to write things down.

Activity

Work through Reading 1.1, studying it carefully (you'll find all the readings at the end of this chapter). I've numbered each paragraph of the dialogue, in order to make it easier to refer to particular claims. Read through the extract once, then focus on the paragraphs identified in the questions below. Note down your answers to these questions:

1. In paragraph 3, what reason does Socrates give for changing the topic of discussion?
2. In paragraph 11, what question does Socrates propose that they should address?

Discussion

Don't worry if you have not phrased your answers exactly as I have here. What matters is the meaning, not the precise wording. (This also applies to all the other activities below.)

1. Socrates suggests that in order to find out how to become virtuous, they must first decide what virtue is.
2. He suggests that they should address the question 'What is courage?'

You might have noticed that Laches is confident that he will be able to answer Socrates' question. However, as we shall see, Socrates rejects Laches' first attempt at an answer. By looking closely at Laches' answer, and the reasons that Socrates gives for rejecting it, we can better understand the nature of the question that Socrates is trying to ask.

Activity Now work through Reading 1.2 and note down answers to the following questions:

1 In paragraph 13, how does Laches answer Socrates' question?

2 Why does Socrates reject Laches' answer? (Look especially at paragraph 22.)

3 Why does Socrates introduce his definition of quickness in paragraph 28?

As background to the extract, note that Socrates mentions the Scythians, a nomadic people who inhabited a large area in what is now central Ukraine and southern Russia, and who were known for their skill at cavalry warfare (see Figure 1.3). He also mentions the Greek poet Homer (date unknown) who composed the *Iliad*, a poem about the legendary war between the Greeks and the Trojans; Aeneas was a Trojan hero.

Discussion

1 Laches answers Socrates' question by describing how a courageous infantryman might behave.

2 Laches has answered Socrates' question by presenting a specific example of courage. As a result, his answer leaves out many other examples of courageous behaviour both on and off the field of battle. What Socrates wants Laches to do is to turn his attention away from the details of a specific example, and instead to identify the characteristic that all examples of courage have in common.

3 Socrates introduces his definition of quickness in order to demonstrate the kind of answer he wants: his definition aims to identify what all examples of quickness have in common.

This exchange between Socrates and Laches illustrates what is involved in asking a philosophical question. In particular, it brings out the point that philosophy is typically concerned with questions of a very general kind. In contrast, the question that Lysimachus and Melesias ask about the education of their sons concerns a specific practical problem involving a specific group of people. Specific problems can often draw our attention to philosophical questions. For example, the situation of Lysimachus and Melesias might prompt questions not only about the nature of courage, but also about the purpose of education and about the duties that parents have towards their children. But answering these very general questions would take us well beyond the particular circumstances of two Athenian gentlemen trying to do the best for their sons.

Much of the time, people deal with the practical problems that they encounter without reflecting on general questions of this kind. They

Figure 1.3 Paseas (attrib.), Attic red figure plate, with a picture of a mounted archer in Scythian or Persian dress, sixth century BCE. Ashmolean Museum, Oxford. Photo: © Ashmolean Museum, University of Oxford/The Bridgeman Art Library.

rely on background assumptions – for example, assumptions about what courage is, or about the purpose of education. Nevertheless, it is possible to take a step back and focus on these assumptions – to reflect on them, perhaps even to change them. To do this is to do philosophy.

1.5 LACHES AND GREEK TRADITION

The answer that Laches gives to Socrates' question reflects traditional Greek views about the nature of courage. In this traditional conception, courage was associated in the first instance with the qualities required of citizen soldiers fighting in defence of their city – in particular, citizen soldiers fighting as hoplites. Hoplites were heavily armed soldiers who would fight in rows, in which each man's shield protected not only his own left side but also the right side of the soldier standing next to him (see Figure 1.4). In this formation, each soldier depended on his neighbour to stand his ground through what must have been a frightening and gruelling struggle with the opposing side. In this context, it is perhaps not surprising that standing in the ranks and not running away came to be regarded as a paradigm of courage,

Tyrtaeus (seventh century BCE): Tyrtaeus was a Spartan poet who wrote patriotic poems intended to encourage his fellow citizens to fight courageously in battle. Little is known about his life.

celebrated in speeches and poetry. For example, you might compare Laches' definition with the words of the Spartan poet Tyrtaeus, writing some two centuries earlier:

> Here is courage ...
> when a man plants his feet and stands in the foremost spears,
> relentlessly, all thought of foul flight completely forgotten,
> and has well-trained his heart to be steadfast and to endure,
> and with words encourages the man who is stationed beside him.
>
> (Lattimore, 1960, p. 14: Tyrtaeus, fragment 12.13–19)

In asking Laches to take a step back from this particular example of courageous behaviour, Socrates is asking him to move beyond what was then the traditional conception of courage (Schmid, 1992, p. 100ff.; Rabbås, 2004, pp. 157–8).

Figure 1.4 Detail of the Chigi Vase, an oinochoe (wine jug) from Corinth showing hoplites in ranks, third quarter of the seventh century BCE. Museo di Villa Giulia, Rome. Photo: Scala, Florence. Courtesy of the Ministero Beni e Att. Culturali.

1.6 IS COURAGE ENDURANCE? SOCRATES' ARGUMENT

Before going on, work through Reading 1.3, trying to get the gist of what happens in this passage. We will look at the extract in more detail in a moment.

In this passage Laches produces a second definition of courage. He suggests that courage is endurance. Socrates confirms that Laches has produced the right kind of answer to his question. He then begins to examine Laches' proposal. By asking Laches a series of questions, he gets Laches to agree that there is a kind of endurance – foolish endurance – that does not amount to courage. Although Socrates does not spell this out, the implication is that Laches' second answer is *too* general: it includes some cases that are not cases of courage.

As Socrates asks his questions, he gets Laches to assent to the different steps of an **argument**. In this section we will begin by finding Socrates' argument in the text. In sections 1.7 and 1.8 we will investigate how the argument works and how we might decide whether or not it is a good argument. As we go on, I shall introduce you to some technical terms that can be used in analysing and evaluating arguments.

The aim of an argument is to support or prove a particular **conclusion**. It does this by presenting one or more claims – called **premises** – that, taken together, suggest or imply that the conclusion is true. The premises of an argument provide reasons to believe the conclusion.

The argument that Socrates gives in Reading 1.3 can be set out like this:

> Premise 1: Courage is an admirable thing.
>
> Premise 2: Foolish endurance is not an admirable thing.
>
> Conclusion: So, foolish endurance is not a kind of courage.

In setting out Socrates' argument, I have tried to present it as briefly and precisely as possible. Although this has involved some rephrasing, I have kept key words ('courage', 'endurance', 'admirable') and I have used these in a consistent way throughout. I have numbered the premises to make it easy to refer to them later.

Activity Turn back to Reading 1.3, studying it slowly and carefully. Find the different points in the text at which Socrates introduces his two premises and then draws his conclusion. Bear in mind that Socrates introduces the steps of his argument as suggestions or questions to Laches, rather than simply stating them himself.

Discussion Socrates introduces Premise 1 in paragraph 32 ('I'm pretty sure, Laches, that you take courage to be an admirable thing'). He introduces Premise 2 in paragraph 36 ('But what if endurance is coupled with foolishness? Would you say that it's an admirable thing then?'). He introduces the conclusion at paragraph 38 ('So you wouldn't agree that this kind of endurance is courage').

You may have noticed that Socrates introduces his conclusion with the word 'so'. When analysing an argument, it helps to look out for words or phrases such as 'so', 'therefore' or 'as a result', which are often used to mark the conclusion of an argument. Conversely, words or phrases such as 'because', 'since' or 'after all' sometimes mark the premises of an argument.

1.7 IS COURAGE ENDURANCE? INTRODUCING DEDUCTIVE ARGUMENTS

Now that we have located Socrates' argument in the text, we can investigate how it fits together. Socrates' argument is a **deductive argument**. The mark of a deductive argument is that it is supposed to be **valid**. When the term 'valid' is applied to a deductive argument it is used in a technical sense, which can be defined as follows.

Definition of validity

If an argument is valid, then, *if* the premises are true, we can be *certain* that the conclusion is true.

One thing to note about this definition of validity is that it includes the word 'if'. To say that an argument is valid is *not* to say that its conclusion is true: it is to say only that *if* the premises are true, the conclusion is true. For example, consider the following (silly) argument:

Premise 1: Metal is good to eat.
Premise 2: Gold is not good to eat.
Conclusion: So, gold is not a kind of metal.

The argument is silly because Premise 1 is obviously false. As a result, the argument has generated a false conclusion. But the argument is valid, none the less: *if* metal is good to eat, but gold is not, gold cannot be a kind of metal.

So, to describe an argument as valid is only half a compliment. It implies that there is nothing wrong with the logic of the argument. But if one or more of the premises are false, the conclusion may still be wrong. To praise the argument unreservedly, you would need to say that it is **sound**. A sound argument is one that is both valid *and* has true premises. When we evaluate a deductive argument, there are two different jobs to do: to consider whether it is valid and to consider whether its premises are true.

A second point to note about the definition of validity is the word 'certain'. If the premises of a valid deductive argument are true, then

we can be absolutely sure that its conclusion is true. In other words, a sound deductive argument *proves* that its conclusion is true. This is a special feature of deductive arguments. Most of the arguments that we encounter in everyday life – and, indeed, many philosophical arguments – are not intended to be proofs. They are intended only to support or to favour a certain conclusion. Socrates, however, does present his arguments as deductive arguments. And so we can demand that his arguments are valid.

Activity Is Socrates' argument valid? Look back at the argument as I set it out in Section 1.6, and try to decide. Remember that I'm asking only about validity, not soundness.

Discussion The argument is valid. If courage is an admirable thing, but foolish endurance is not an admirable thing, we can be certain that foolish endurance is not a kind of courage.

1.8 IS COURAGE ENDURANCE? THE CASE OF THE FOOLISH FIRE-FIGHTER

The argument that Socrates presents in Reading 1.3 is valid. But are the premises of the argument true? Until we have decided this, we cannot know whether or not the argument is sound.

On the face of it, they do seem plausible. But it is always worth thinking carefully about the premises of an argument. One way to do this is to consider how well the premises apply to a particular case. For example, consider the case of a fire-fighter who stays inside a blazing building, at considerable personal risk, in order to retrieve a minor piece of equipment. How should we describe this case?

Activity Here are three different ways in which we might describe the fire-fighter's behaviour. Take a moment to consider whether you agree with any of them.

- Verdict A: The fire-fighter is not being courageous, just foolish, and there is nothing admirable in that.
- Verdict B: The fire-fighter is being courageous. But there is nothing admirable about his or her courage, because it is not being used to good effect.
- Verdict C: The fire-fighter is being courageous, and his or her courage is admirable, even though it is foolish.

Discussion

- Did you agree with Verdict A? If so, that suggests that you do agree with the premises of Socrates' argument.
- Did you agree with Verdict B? If so, that suggests that you disagree with Socrates' first premise – the claim that courage is always admirable. Verdict B implies that there can be cases of courage that are not worthy of admiration.

- Did you agree with Verdict C? If so, that suggests that you disagree with the second premise of Socrates' argument – the claim that foolish endurance is not admirable. Verdict C suggests that foolish endurance can be worthy of admiration.
- Perhaps you don't feel strongly one way or another. If so, that's nothing to worry about. Whether or not the premises of an argument are true is not always easy to decide. Sometimes all we can do is to keep an open mind until we find some further consideration that settles the issue.

You may have noticed that in formulating this example, I made a particular assumption about value: I assumed that it is not worth risking one's life in order to rescue a minor piece of equipment. It is impossible to use examples in moral philosophy without making some assumptions about value. But, of course, it is never possible to be certain that the people who are sharing the discussion (in this case, anyone who is reading this chapter) all share the same values. That is one reason why philosophers often use rather extreme examples: those are examples on which people are most likely to agree. Sometimes you may come across an example where you find yourself disagreeing with values that the writer or speaker is assuming. If so, it may help to consider whether or not that affects the point that the example is being used to support. Could he or she have made just the same point using a different example, one that does not clash with your values? If so, it may be that, although you disagree with the writer's values, you do accept the philosophical point that he or she is trying to make.

1.9 NICIAS DEFINES COURAGE

Socrates and Laches have agreed that foolish endurance is not courage. But if there are cases of endurance that are not cases of courage, endurance and courage cannot be the same thing. So, Laches' second attempt to define courage has failed. After some further fruitless discussion with Laches, Socrates asks if Nicias can help.

Activity Work through Reading 1.4. How does Nicias define courage in paragraph 51?

Discussion Nicias says that courage is knowledge of what is fearful and what is encouraging.

Laches' definition characterised courage as the ability to behave in a certain way – to stand firm in the face of danger or hardship. Nicias, in contrast, focuses on the quality that he takes to underlie courageous behaviour – that is, a kind of wisdom or knowledge. This definition of courage may strike you as surprising. Laches certainly thinks that it is strange, and in the passage that follows this extract he accuses Nicias of talking nonsense.

Pressed by Laches, however, Nicias says a little more about the kind of knowledge he takes courage to be. What Nicias has in mind is not the ability to predict what is about to happen, but rather the ability to evaluate different outcomes as good or bad. So, his point is that courage is a matter of knowing the value of things. A courageous person will know whether or not it is worth sacrificing his or her life for the sake of a military victory, or whether it is worth risking wealth and reputation in order to defend a moral principle. In contrast, a cowardly person will be someone who overestimates the value of his or her own life and comfort in relation to other important goals; while a foolhardy person will be someone who ignorantly puts too little value on personal safety. Unlike Laches, then, Nicias is able to distinguish cases of courage from cases of mere foolhardiness.

You might notice, though, that Nicias does not try to explain what kinds of things a courageous person will value. So his definition of courage will not tell us on its own whether a particular case (that of the foolish fire-fighter, for example) is an example of courage or of foolhardiness. To decide that, we would have to know whether or not personal safety really is more valuable than a minor piece of equipment. That would involve asking all sorts of further questions about what is valuable in life. Plato was acutely aware of the way in which one philosophical claim often leads on to further questions. But he also insisted that, in order to make progress with philosophical problems, we need to concentrate on one question at a time. So Nicias' definition might be regarded as a first step towards a complete account. It is this first step that Socrates is going to interrogate in what follows.

Could Nicias be right to suggest that knowledge is *all* that is needed for courage? One objection that might be made to this is that people sometimes know the best thing to do but lack the willpower to do it. Imagine the situation of a woman who sees a child trapped inside a burning house, and suppose that the woman knows that the best thing she could do is to try to rescue the child. Will she necessarily run into the flames? Nicias seems to be assuming that when people really know the best thing to do, they will necessarily act on that knowledge. If the woman does not try to rescue the child, Nicias will have to insist that, deep down, she does not really accept that this is the best thing to do. It is not obvious that he is right about this. Indeed, this is still a very controversial issue among philosophers. You might wish to think about this issue for yourself.

The implications of Nicias' definition of courage are further explored in the next section of the dialogue (Reading 1.5), which we will examine through the interactive material on the DVD ROM. This material also includes a section on deductive arguments and some activities designed to help you to spot valid and invalid arguments. Ideally, you should work through this material now, before reading the rest of this chapter. You will find more detailed instructions for using the material when you open the DVD ROM. Note that on the DVD ROM, you will also find an interview with Tim Chappell: do not listen to this yet (you will be prompted to listen to this when you reach the end of the chapter).

Figure 1.5 Relief depicting the mythical Calydonian Hunt: a band of heroic hunters and their dogs surround a monstrous boar, Roman, late second century CE, marble, 85 cm x 188 cm. Ashmolean Museum, Oxford. Photo: © The Ashmolean Museum, University of Oxford. In Reading 1.5, Socrates, Nicias and Laches debate whether animals can be courageous. Does a lion or boar show courage when it resists a group of hunters and their dogs?

1.10 IS COURAGE THE WHOLE OF VIRTUE?

In the final part of the *Laches* (Readings 1.6 and 1.7), Socrates develops a second objection to Nicias' definition of courage. He begins by making some preliminary steps. Before continuing here, work through Reading 1.6 and try to get the gist of it.

In this passage, Socrates does two things. First, in paragraphs 61, 63 and 65, he asks Nicias whether he agrees that courage is not the whole of virtue, but just a part of it. In other words, he is asking whether there are good qualities that we need in life – such as temperance and justice – that differ from courage. This was something that Socrates and Laches took for granted at the beginning of their conversation (paragraph 7 in Reading 1.1). Nicias now says that he agrees with Socrates. This is important, because Socrates is about to argue that if courage is just a part of virtue, Nicias' definition of courage must be false.

Second, Socrates persuades Nicias to reword his definition of courage. He does this in two stages. If you remember (see paragraph 51 in Reading 1.4), Nicias' original definition of courage can be expressed like this:

> Courage is knowledge of what is fearful and what is encouraging.

Now, in paragraphs 67 to 72, Socrates persuades Nicias to agree that this is equivalent to the claim that:

> Courage is knowledge of what will be evil and what will be good in future.

Then, in paragraphs 73 to 80, Socrates argues (with Nicias' agreement) that knowing what will be evil and good in the future is no different from knowing what is evil and good in the present or the past. So, consider the case of a wise fire-fighter, who is able to judge correctly what kinds of risks are worth taking in order to save a life. It seems plausible that he or she would be just as good evaluating these risks in any situation, regardless of whether it is in the future, the present or the past. Nicias accepts Socrates' point, and agrees to accept a revised definition of courage, which might be expressed as follows:

> Courage is knowledge of what is evil and what is good.

But Socrates now argues that if courage is just a part of virtue, this reworded definition must be false.

Activity Work through Reading 1.7, studying it slowly and carefully. Note down answers to the following questions:

1. What are the two premises of Socrates' argument? (You'll find them in paragraphs 83 and 85.) Try to express them in your own words, as simply and as directly as you can.
2. What conclusion about courage can be drawn from these premises?
3. Is Socrates' argument valid?

Discussion

1. The premises of Socrates' argument can be expressed as follows:

    Premise 1: Knowledge of what is evil and what is good is not just a part of virtue, but the whole of it.

    Premise 2: Courage is just a part of virtue.
2. Conclusion: So, courage is not knowledge of evil and good.
3. Yes, the argument is valid. If knowledge of evil and good is the whole of virtue, but courage is just a part of virtue, we can be certain that courage is not the same thing as knowledge of evil and good.

At the beginning of this argument, Nicias agreed to two claims:

- Courage is knowledge of what is evil and what is good (his reworded definition).
- Courage is just a part of virtue.

Nicias has now agreed that these two claims cannot both be true. So he must choose which of them to give up. This time, he chooses not to **bite the bullet**: he gives up his definition of courage.

1.11 THE PUZZLE OF THE *LACHES*

There is something very puzzling about the argument that we explored in the last section. You may have noticed that when Nicias first introduces his definition of courage in paragraphs 40 and 42, he says that it is the kind of thing that he has often heard Socrates say. And, indeed, in other dialogues Socrates seems to favour the view that all good qualities, including courage, justice, piety and temperance, can be defined as knowledge of what is evil and what is good. Moreover, he recognises that this implies that all these qualities are fundamentally the same thing. And he seems to regard this not as an objection, but as an interesting and important discovery. So why, in the *Laches*, does Socrates appear to suggest as an objection to Nicias' definition that it implies that courage, justice and temperance are fundamentally the same thing?

In what follows, I shall suggest that this puzzle can be resolved if we pay attention to Plato's views on a rather different issue: the difference between knowledge and opinion.

1.12 KNOWLEDGE, OPINION AND THE STATUES OF DAEDALUS

One of the philosophical questions that interested Plato was the nature of knowledge. He discusses this question in a number of dialogues. In this section we shall explore Plato's views on knowledge by investigating an extract from another of his dialogues: the *Meno*. The *Meno* was probably written after the *Laches*. It portrays Socrates in conversation with Meno, a rather idle and vain young aristocrat from Thessaly in the north of Greece. They spend much of the dialogue exploring the idea that virtue is knowledge. In the extract, Socrates and Meno are discussing the difference between knowing that something is the case, and merely having a true opinion about it.

Activity Work through Reading 1.8, and note down answers to the following questions:

1. In paragraphs 91 to 97 (with Meno's agreement), what does Socrates suggest about the relative merits of knowledge and true opinion as guides to action?
2. In paragraph 105, how does Socrates suggest that it is possible to turn true opinions into knowledge?
3. In paragraph 105, why does Socrates suggest that knowledge is more valuable than true opinion?

In the extract, Socrates mentions the mythical inventor and artist Daedalus. Perhaps the best known story involving Daedalus concerns his son, Icarus, who was said to have drowned after flying too close to the sun. In the *Meno*, Socrates refers to the legend that Daedalus created statues that were so lifelike that they could move by themselves. One later writer tried to explain this legend by speculating that Daedalus was the first Greek sculptor to produce statues which

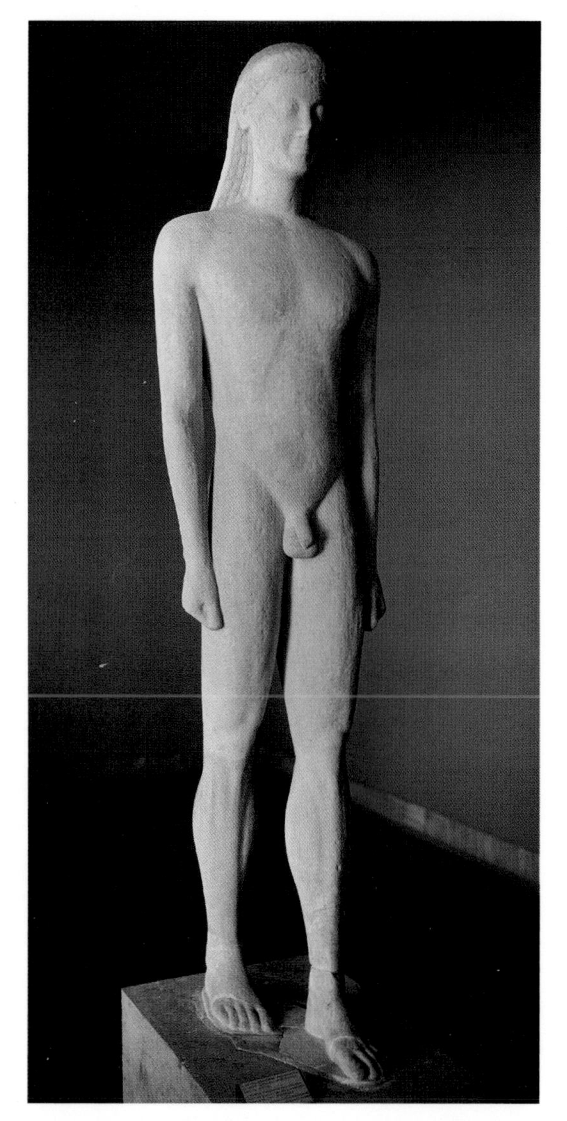

Figure 1.6. Statue of a young man, Milos, sixth century BCE, marble, height 214cm. National Archaeological Museum, Athens. Photo: © National Archaeological Museum, Athens/Lauros/Giraudon/The Bridgeman Art Library. Like other statues made in Greece around the same time, he stands with one foot in front of the other, as if ready to walk.

stood with one foot in front of the other, instead of standing with both feet together (Palaiphatos (1996), section 21) (see Figure 1.6).

Discussion

1. Socrates suggests that, in any particular situation, knowledge and true opinion will be equally reliable as guides to action.
2. Socrates suggests that it is possible to turn true opinions into knowledge 'by figuring out what makes them true'. In other words, knowing something involves not just believing (correctly) *that* it is true, but also understanding *why* it is true.

3 Socrates suggests that knowledge is more valuable than true opinion because, like the statues of Daedalus, opinions tend to stray. For example, suppose that I tell you that a particular argument is valid, and you just take my word for it, without really understanding why. In this situation, you could easily be persuaded by someone else that the argument is invalid. But once you understand *why* the argument is valid, you will be much less likely to be persuaded otherwise. The knowledge has become your own. So, Socrates suggests, knowledge is more valuable than true opinion in the long run, because it stays with us.

Socrates does not seem to think the suggestion that knowledge requires understanding applies to all kinds of knowledge. For example, he does not suggest that the man who knows the way to Larisa needs to understand why the route is a good one, only that he has tested it for himself. The suggestion that knowledge requires understanding makes most sense if we apply it only to certain kinds of knowledge – for example, knowledge of philosophy and mathematics – where it is reasonable to suppose that we can come to know things through reason and reflection.

However, there is a common thread running through all these cases. This is the idea that knowledge requires experiencing something for yourself (Burnyeat, 1980). For example, Plato thinks that in order to know the way to Larisa it is necessary to have travelled the route yourself. Similarly, he thinks, in order to know a philosophical truth you must have worked through the issue yourself, so that you can grasp how this truth connects with other things that you believe.

This notion has an important implication: it implies that knowledge is not something that we can absorb, unthinkingly, from people around us. In Plato's *Symposium*, Socrates puts the point a little ruefully when he says:

> I only wish wisdom *were* the kind of thing one could share by sitting next to someone – if it flowed, for instance, from the one that was full to the one that was empty, like the water in two cups ...
>
> (Plato, 1989, p. 530: *Symposium*, 175d)

According to Socrates, then, you cannot come to know something by parroting someone else's words, even if that person is an acknowledged expert. Nor can you simply soak up knowledge from books – or, for that matter, from Open University course materials – no matter how well qualified the author. Parroting someone else will supply you, at best, with a correct opinion. Knowing something involves experiencing the truth of it for yourself – whether that means testing out a route, or working through an argument in order to understand why a certain philosophical claim is true.

The claim that knowledge cannot be picked up second-hand crops up in a number of dialogues, so it is likely that Plato believed it to be true. If he were right, it would mean quite a radical departure from the way in which many people talk and think about knowledge. Many people would regard the testimony of other people – friends, teachers, experts, eyewitnesses – as an important source of knowledge. But Plato seems to hold that the testimony of other people is a source only of fleeting opinion.

This is a striking suggestion, and it is certainly open to challenge. Here, however, my primary concern is to investigate how Plato's views on this issue might shed light on the puzzle posed by the ending of the *Laches*. I will suggest that once we understand what Plato takes knowledge to be, it is possible to read the ending of the *Laches* in a way that resolves this puzzle. In this interpretation, Plato's point is not about the nature of courage, but about Nicias' attitude to philosophical discussion. This is not the only possible interpretation of the dialogue: some commentators have suggested that Socrates' argument at the end of the *Laches* is intended to be a real disproof of the thesis that courage is knowledge (Devereaux, 1992; Vlastos, 1994, pp. 109–26). However, I think that the interpretation that I am going to present here is an interesting and plausible one.

As we have seen, when Nicias first proposes his definition, he explicitly says that he is repeating something that he has heard Socrates say (in paragraphs 40 and 42). This seems to be a crucial point: it suggests that Nicias has simply parroted Socrates' opinion, without really grasping what it means or why it might be true. In particular, he does not understand that his definition of courage implies that courage, justice and temperance are fundamentally the same thing. As a result Nicias' definition collapses – not because it is false, but because Nicias does not understand it (Irwin, 1995; Penner, 1992). On this reading, Plato's point is that doing philosophy is not a matter of finding out what the experts think. It requires reflection and understanding.

1.13 WHY SOCRATES DOES NOT KNOW THE ANSWERS (AND WHY PLATO WILL NOT TELL US WHAT THEY ARE)

Earlier, I mentioned that there is something very puzzling about Plato's portrayal of Socrates: Socrates claims that he does not know how to answer his own questions, while at the same time appearing to favour particular answers. This is puzzling, because it looks as if Plato is portraying Socrates as behaving in a deceitful way. However, Plato's distinction between true opinion and knowledge suggests another way to understand what is going on. Suppose that Socrates does have some opinions about the questions that he poses. He may even be fairly confident that these opinions are true. Nevertheless, he may be aware that he cannot explain *why* they are true. If so, then in Plato's view, Socrates is right to deny that he knows the answers to his questions. We might still wonder why Socrates does not explain this to

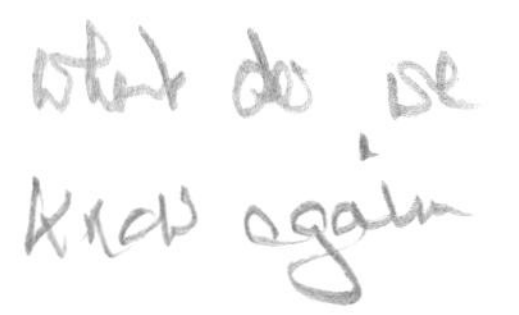

the other characters. However, it is possible that his aim is not to deceive them, but rather to entice them (and us) to puzzle out what he means (Vlastos, 1994, pp. 39–66).

Plato's views on knowledge may also explain why he gives such a prominent role to Socrates' method of question and answer. Socrates does not try to impart his opinions to the other characters by delivering a lecture. Instead, his questions encourage them to think about the issues for themselves. Even if Socrates' questions often lead the other characters towards certain conclusions, the discussion cannot proceed unless they have understood and agreed to each step in the argument. Socrates' method, then, can be used to help people achieve the kind of understanding that Plato believed was required for philosophical knowledge.

A mosaic found in the Roman city of Pompeii is thought to represent Plato in discussion with his students at the Academy (Figure 1.7). The mosaic was made many centuries after Plato's death, so it cannot be treated as direct evidence for his practice at the Academy. I have included it here because it might be seen as presenting an image of philosophical discussion of the sort that we find in the dialogues. You might note in particular that Plato (presumed to be the figure sitting under the tree) is represented as surrounded by his students, not as lecturing them from the front of the class.

Finally, Plato's views on knowledge might explain why he chose to write dialogues rather than essays. By writing a dialogue, Plato, no less than Socrates, avoids simply presenting us with his opinions, but instead encourages us to reflect on the questions raised by his characters. As we read, we can imagine ourselves joining in the conversation, giving our own answers to Socrates' questions and our own reactions to his arguments. Indeed, most of Plato's early dialogues end without a clear answer, inviting us to continue the investigation for ourselves.

1.14 WHY DOES PLATO REJECT TRADITION?

We can now return to the question that I raised at the beginning of the chapter. Why does Plato think that our moral beliefs should be grounded on reason, rather than tradition? Why does he reject moral traditionalism in favour of moral rationalism?

Activity Can you see a connection between the claim that knowledge involves understanding something for yourself and the claim that reason, rather than tradition, is the proper source of moral beliefs?

Discussion Traditional beliefs, as I defined them in section 1.1, are beliefs that we take on trust, without reflecting on them. For Plato, beliefs of this kind are merely opinions. It is only by reflecting on and reasoning about our moral beliefs that we can turn them into knowledge. You might notice that Plato's concern is not that traditional beliefs might be *false*. His concern is that traditional beliefs, even if true, are merely second-hand opinions, which do not amount to knowledge.

Figure 1.7 Roman mosaic showing Plato's Academy, from the House of T. Siminius in Pompeii, copied from a Greek original, first century BCE, marble and glass paste tesserae (tiles), 86 x 85 cm. Museo Archeologico Nazionale, Naples. Photo: The Bridgeman Art Library.

Plato's point does not apply only to commonsense beliefs. It would apply just as well to a philosophical tradition: that is, a set of beliefs passed down from one generation to another by the followers of a particular philosopher. In parroting Socrates' opinions, Nicias treats him as if he were the founder of a philosophical tradition, propounding a set of doctrines that his followers can take on trust. But Socrates does not see his role in this way: his aim is to stimulate people to acquire knowledge for themselves by reflecting on their own beliefs.

1.15 THE SOCRATIC METHOD, TEACHING AND LEARNING

As I mentioned earlier, the historical Socrates does not seem to have presented himself as a teacher. In his dialogues, Plato contrasts Socrates with other intellectuals who did present themselves as teachers, and tried to pass on their wisdom through lectures and books (see Figure 1.8). However, this might prompt us to question what it is to be a teacher or a student. Is teaching just a matter of imparting information or expertise, or is Socrates' method itself a form of teaching? Conversely, is studying just a matter of taking in new information, or does it sometimes require active inquiry? It is perhaps not surprising that Socrates' method has had a profound influence on the theory and practice of education. His name is associated with a model of education in which the process of learning begins from the students' own beliefs and experience, and the role of the teacher is not to impart information, but to engage students in critical discussion, encouraging them to inquire into the issues for themselves.

There is room, then, for different ways of understanding the roles of teacher and student. More practically, there is room for different approaches, even within a single piece of teaching material. The author's approach is likely to depend both on the nature of the subject and on what he or she is trying to achieve at that stage. In order to get the most out of a piece of teaching material, it is worth being conscious of how the author expects you to engage with the material at each point. Is the author's intention to deliver information, to practise a skill, or to prompt you to reflect on the issues for yourself?

Activity As a final exercise, take some time to reflect on your own experience of working through this chapter. Were there any types of information that you felt that you needed to take on trust? Were there certain types of question that you felt able to investigate for yourself?

Discussion I shall give two examples of information that I was conscious of simply providing, and indicate two ways in which I aimed to encourage you to think for yourself. But everyone experiences a piece of teaching material in their own way, so it is likely that you will have come up with different examples.

1 I provided definitions of certain technical terms, such as 'validity' and 'soundness'. This is information of a kind that you could check – for example, by consulting a philosophical dictionary. But it is not something that you could work out by reflecting on the matter for yourself.
2 I provided an interpretation of the ending of the *Laches*. I signalled that this is not the only possible interpretation of the dialogue, but I did not give you an opportunity to question the reading that I presented. This is

Figure 1.8 Unknown artist, miniature painting of a philosophy lesson from a manuscript of the *Ovide Moralisé*, fourteenth century CE, vellum. Bibliothèque Municipale, Rouen, France. Photo: © Bibliothèque Municipale, Rouen, France/Lauros/Giraudon/The Bridgeman Art Library. You might contrast this image with the image of philosophical discussion presented in Figure 1.7.

because my aim on this occasion was not to work on the skills needed to interpret a text, but to provide you with some ideas that might help you to think about the value of tradition as a source of knowledge.

3 I invited you to decide for yourself whether certain arguments are valid. In doing this, my aim was to help you understand the concept of validity for yourself, giving you a tool that you can take away from this chapter and put to use elsewhere.

4 I raised some philosophical issues about courage, knowledge and tradition, but I did not tell you what to think about those issues. Instead my aim was to point up some approaches and questions that might help you to reflect on them for yourself, in the hope of drawing you into the debate which Socrates begins in the *Laches*.

Many of the philosophical issues raised in this chapter are explored further in an interview with Professor Tim Chappell, which you will find on the Audio CD (alternatively, you can find this interview on the DVD ROM). You should complete your work on this chapter by listening to the interview. The interview is about fifteen minutes long, but the material is quite challenging, and you may wish to listen to it twice, perhaps in two or three short sessions. I have included some notes on the interview at the end of the resources section; you should read those first.

REFERENCES

Burnyeat, M. (1980) 'Socrates and the jury', *Proceedings of the Aristotelian Society*, supp. vol. 54, pp. 173–92.

Devereaux (1992) 'The unity of the virtues in Plato's *Protagoras* and *Laches*', *Philosophical Review*, vol. 101, no. 4, pp. 765–89.

Irwin, T. (1995) *Plato's Ethics*, Oxford, Oxford University Press.

Lattimore, R. (trans.) (1960) *Greek Lyrics* (2nd edn), Chicago, University of Chicago Press.

Palaephatus (1996) *On Unbelievable Tales*, translated by Jacob Stern. Bolchazy Carducci Publishers.

Penner, T. (1992) 'What Laches and Nicias miss – and whether Socrates thinks courage merely a part of virtue', *Ancient Philosophy*, vol. 12, no. 1, pp. 1–28.

Plato (1989) 'Symposium' (trans. M. Joyce) in Hamilton, E. and Cairns, H. (eds) *The Collected Dialogues of Plato*, Princeton, NJ, Princeton University Press.

Rabbås, Ø. (2004) 'Definitions and paradigms: Laches' first definition', *Phronesis*, vol. 69, no. 2, pp. 143–68.

Schmid, W. (1992) *On Manly Courage: A Study of Plato's* Laches, Carbondale and Edwardsville, IL, Southern Illinois University Press.

Vlastos, G. (1994) *Socratic Studies*, Cambridge, Cambridge University Press.

FURTHER READING

For a full text of the *Laches*, see Iain Lane's translation in Saunders, T.J. (ed.) (2005) *Plato: Early Socratic Dialogues*, London, Penguin.

For an excellent brief introduction to ancient Greek and Roman philosophy, see Irwin, T. (1989) *Classical Thought*, Oxford, Oxford University Press.

Two short and accessible introductions to the philosophy of Socrates and Plato are: Taylor C. (2000) *Socrates: A Very Short Introduction*, Oxford, Oxford University Press; and Annas, J. (2003) *Plato: A Very Short Introduction*, Oxford, Oxford University Press.

More challenging discussions of Socrates' philosophy can be found in: Brickhouse, T. and Smith, N. (2000) *The Philosophy of Socrates*, Boulder, CO, Westview (History of Ancient and Medieval Philosophy Series); and Vlastos, G. (1991) *Socrates: Ironist and Moral Philosopher*, Cambridge, Cambridge University Press.

For an accessible introduction to moral philosophy, see Blackburn, S. (2002) *Being Good*, Oxford, Oxford University Press.

RESOURCES

Readings 1.1 to 1.4 and 1.6 to 1.7 are edited excerpts from Plato's *Laches*, translated by Carolyn Price.

Reading 1.5 is adapted from a translation of the *Laches* by Iain Lane (in *Plato: Early Socratic Dialogues*, edited by T.J. Saunders, London, Penguin, 2005).

Reading 1.8 is from a translation of the *Meno* by Adam Beresford (in *Plato: Protagoras and Meno*, translated and edited by Adam Beresford, London, Penguin, 2005).

You will notice that each reading is identified using a mix of numbers and letters: for example, the first reading is *Laches* 190b–d. This refers to an important Renaissance edition of Plato's works published by Stephanus (he was a French printer whose real name was Henri Estienne) in 1578: the number gives the page in the Stephanus edition; each page is divided into four sections, labelled a, b, c and d. This is now the standard way to identify a passage in Plato's writings, and you will find these numbers in almost all translations of his works.

Reading 1.1 *Laches* 190b–d

1 SOCRATES: So Laches, our two friends are calling us to advise them on how their sons can acquire virtue and be made into better people. Isn't that right?

2 LACHES: Yes, it is.

3 SOCRATES: In that case, don't we need to know what virtue is? After all, if we had no idea what virtue is, how could we possibly advise anyone on the best way to acquire it?

4 LACHES: I think it would be impossible, Socrates.

5 SOCRATES: So, Laches, we're claiming that we do know what it is.

6 LACHES: We are, indeed.

7 SOCRATES: In that case, my friend, let's not examine the whole of virtue straight off – that might be too big a task. Instead, let's start by looking at a part of it, to see if we know enough about that. That will make our investigation easier, I expect.

8 LACHES: Let's do that, Socrates, as you suggest.

9 SOCRATES: So which part of virtue shall we pick? Obviously, it should be the part that lessons in 'fighting in armour' are supposed to foster. Most people think that's courage. Yes?

10 LACHES: It certainly seems so.

11 SOCRATES: So, Laches, let's start by trying to state what courage is. Then, after that, we'll investigate how young men can acquire it through exercises and training – supposing that's possible.

Reading 1.2 *Laches* 190d–192e

12 SOCRATES: So, as I say, try to state what courage is.

13 LACHES: Really, Socrates! That's not hard to do. If someone's ready to stand in the ranks, to fend off the enemy, and not to retreat, there's no doubt he's courageous.

14 SOCRATES: Well said, Laches! Still, the question you've answered isn't the one I had in mind, but a different one. Perhaps I'm to blame, because I didn't explain it clearly.

15 LACHES: What are you talking about, Socrates?

16 SOCRATES: I'll explain, if I can. This man you describe, the man who stands in the ranks and fights the enemy – he is courageous, I grant you.

17 LACHES: I'd certainly say so.

18 SOCRATES: And I agree. But what about another example – someone who fights the enemy by retreating and giving ground?

19 LACHES: What do you mean, 'by retreating'?

20 SOCRATES: I suppose as people say the Scythians fight – as much in retreat as in pursuit; and perhaps as Homer says when he's praising Aeneas' horses: 'Dashing now here and now there, experts in chase and in flight'.

21 LACHES: And that's fine, Socrates, because he was describing chariots. And you were talking about Scythian cavalry. Cavalry do fight like that, but infantry fight in the way that I described.

22 SOCRATES: Well, that's what I meant just now, when I said that I was to blame when you didn't give a good answer, because I didn't put my question very well. I didn't want you to tell me only about people who are courageous in an infantry action, but also about people who are courageous in a cavalry action, and in every kind of warfare; and not just about people who are courageous in war, but also people who are courageous amid dangers at sea; and all those who are courageous in illness or poverty, and in political life. Because I take it, Laches, that all these people are courageous.

23 LACHES: Yes, very much so, Socrates.

24 SOCRATES: So try again to tell me what courage is. First and foremost, tell me what all these people have in common. Or do you still not understand what I mean?

25 LACHES: Not completely.

26 SOCRATES: Well, this is what I'm getting at. Suppose that I were to ask what quickness is. That's something that can be found in running, and in playing the lyre, and in speaking, and in learning, and in lots of other activities. We can be quick in doing just about anything worth mentioning, whether it's something we do with

our hands, or our legs, or our mouth and voice, or our mind. Would you agree with that?

27 LACHES: Yes, I would.

28 SOCRATES: So now suppose that someone were to ask me: 'What do you say that it is – this quality that, in all these activities, you call "quickness"?' I'd answer that, in my view, what I call quickness is the ability to do much in a little time – whether it's to do with speaking, or running, or any other activity.

29 LACHES: You'd be giving the right answer, too.

30 SOCRATES: Well then, Laches, it's your turn: try to state what courage is in the same way. What is it that's common to all the examples of courage we've just mentioned?

Reading 1.3 *Laches* 192b–192d

31 LACHES: Well now, it seems to me that courage is a sort of endurance in one's character – if I have to say what it is in every case.

32 SOCRATES: But of course you must, if we are going to have an answer to our question! Now, this is how things look to me: you don't think, I suspect, that absolutely every case of endurance is a case of courage. I'm guessing that's so, because I'm pretty sure, Laches, that you take courage to be an admirable thing.

33 LACHES: One of the most admirable things there is, you need have no doubt of that.

34 SOCRATES: When it's coupled with good sense, endurance is admirable and good, isn't it?

35 LACHES: Yes, it is.

36 SOCRATES: But what if endurance is coupled with foolishness? Would you say that it's an admirable thing then?

37 LACHES: That wouldn't be right, Socrates.

38 SOCRATES: So you wouldn't agree that this kind of endurance is courage, because it's not admirable – but courage is admirable.

39 LACHES: That's true.

Reading 1.4 *Laches* 194c–195a

40 NICIAS: Well now, Socrates, I've been thinking for a while that the two of you haven't been defining courage very well. There's a very good suggestion that I've heard you make in the past, which you're not using.

41 SOCRATES: Which suggestion is that, Nicias?

42 NICIAS: I've often heard you say that we're each good in matters on which we're wise; but in matters on which we're ignorant, we're bad.

43 SOCRATES: That's perfectly true, Nicias.

44 NICIAS: So, if a courageous man is good, it's clear that he's wise.

45 SOCRATES: Did you hear that, Laches?

46 LACHES: I did, and I don't have a clue what he's saying.

47 SOCRATES: I think I do. He seems to be saying that courage is some kind of wisdom.

48 LACHES: What kind of wisdom, Socrates?

49 SOCRATES: Are you asking him?

50 LACHES: Yes, I am.

51 NICIAS: What I mean is this, Laches: courage is knowledge of what's fearful and what's encouraging, whether it's in war or in any other situation.

Reading 1.5

Laches 196c–197c

This passage is explored through interactive material on the DVD ROM 'Plato'.

52 SOCRATES: Now, Nicias, tell me – or rather tell us, since Laches and I are sharing the discussion between us – your argument is that courage is knowledge of what is fearful and what is encouraging, isn't it?

53 NICIAS: Yes.

54 SOCRATES: And this isn't something that everyone has. Isn't that what you said?

55 NICIAS: Yes, it was.

56 SOCRATES: So, it's not something any pig would know, as the saying goes, so a pig couldn't be courageous.

57 NICIAS: No, I think not.

58 SOCRATES: Indeed, I think that if one puts forward this theory, one is forced either to deny that any animal whatsoever is courageous, or else to allow that an animal like a lion, or a leopard, or even a wild boar, is clever enough to know things which all but a few human beings find too difficult to understand. And if one has the same concept of courage as you, one is bound to admit that as far as being courageous is concerned, lions, stags, bulls and apes are all in this same position.

59 LACHES: That's a very good point, Socrates! Now let's have an honest answer to this, Nicias: are they wiser than us, these animals we agree are courageous? Is this what you're saying? Or have you the nerve to contradict everyone else and not call them courageous at all?

60 NICIAS: Yes, I have Laches. 'Courageous' is not a word I would use to describe animals, or anything else that's not afraid of danger because of its own lack of understanding: I prefer 'fearless' and 'foolish'. Or do you suppose I call every little child courageous because it doesn't understand, and so is not afraid of

anything? No, to be unafraid and to be courageous are two quite different things. Courage and foresight are, in my opinion, things a very small number of people possess; whereas being reckless, daring, fearless and blind to consequences is the norm for the vast majority of men, women, children and animals. So you see, what you and most people call courageous, I call reckless: courageous actions are wise actions, as I said.

Reading 1.6 *Laches* 197e–199d

61 SOCRATES: Now, Nicias, could you explain it to us again from the start? You remember, don't you, that we began our inquiry into courage by looking at it as a part of virtue?

62 NICIAS: Yes, indeed.

63 SOCRATES: So, do you agree with us that it's a part, and that there are other parts, which, when they're all put together, are called virtue?

64 NICIAS: Yes, obviously.

65 SOCRATES: And by 'parts' we mean the same things, don't we – you and I? Apart from courage, what I call 'parts' includes temperance, justice and other things like that. Are they what you mean too?

66 NICIAS: Yes, they are.

67 SOCRATES: Hold on, then. We agree about these things. But now let's investigate what's fearful and what's encouraging, to check that you don't take them to be one thing, while Laches and I take them to be another. So let me tell you what we take them to be. And if you don't agree, you can put us right. We take it that what's fearful is simply what inspires fear; and that what's encouraging is what doesn't inspire fear. And we take it that what inspires fear are not evils in the past or in the present, but evils that are expected in the future. In other words, fear is the expectation of future evil. That's what you think too, isn't it, Laches?

68 LACHES: Yes, I do, Socrates. Absolutely.

69 SOCRATES: So, Nicias, you've heard our views. We're claiming that what's fearful are the evils that will happen in the future; and that what's encouraging are the good or neutral things that lie ahead. Would you say the same, or something else?

70 NICIAS: I'd say the same.

71 SOCRATES: And it's the knowledge of these things that you say is courage?

72 NICIAS: Precisely.

73 SOCRATES: Then let's look into a third question, to see if you agree with us about that as well.

74 NICIAS: What is it?

75 SOCRATES: I'll tell you. Laches and I are of the view that, with any branch of knowledge, there's no difference between knowing what's happened in the past, knowing what's happening now, and knowing what's going to happen and how things might turn out for the best. It's all the same thing. So, for any subject matter, there's just one body of knowledge, which concerns the future, the present and the past. Do you agree with us, Nicias?

76 NICIAS: Yes, Socrates, that's what I think.

77 SOCRATES: Then, courage can't be knowledge of what's fearful and what's encouraging alone. Like any other kind of knowledge, it will be concerned not only with the future, but also with the past and the present, all in one.

78 NICIAS: I guess so.

79 SOCRATES: So now you're no longer saying that courage is knowledge only of what's fearful and what's encouraging. You're saying that it's effectively knowledge of what's evil and what's good – at any time. Is this your new position, Nicias? Or do you want to say something else?

80 NICIAS: That's what I think, Socrates.

Reading 1.7 *Laches* 199d–199e

81 SOCRATES: Suppose, then, that there's someone who knows about every kind of good thing, whether they are in the present, the future or the past; and suppose that his knowledge of evil things is just as extensive. Do you think that this man would be short of virtue in any way? And, what's more, do you suppose that he'd be lacking in temperance, or justice, or piety? After all, this is the man who's able to guard against what's fearful and to secure what's good, and who knows how he ought to behave, both towards the gods and towards other people.

82 NICIAS: I think you have a point, Socrates.

83 SOCRATES: So surely, Nicias, knowledge of what is evil and what is good won't be a part of virtue, but the whole of virtue.

84 NICIAS: I guess so.

85 SOCRATES: But we did say that courage is just a part of virtue.

86 NICIAS: We did say that.

87 SOCRATES: But what we're talking about now doesn't appear to be just a part of virtue.

88 NICIAS: No, I guess not.

89 SOCRATES: So we haven't discovered what courage is, Nicias.

90 NICIAS: No, it seems we haven't.

Reading 1.8 *Meno* 97a–98b

91 SOCRATES: ... Suppose someone knew the road to Larisa (or wherever) and was on his way there, and showing other people how to get there; obviously, he'd be good at showing them the right way?

92 MENO: Of course.

93 SOCRATES: And what about someone who had an opinion on how to get there – a correct opinion – but who'd never actually been there, and didn't know how to get there; would he be able to show them the way as well?

94 MENO: Of course

95 SOCRATES: And presumably as long as he has his correct opinion ... he'll be every bit as good at showing people the way? With his true belief, but without knowledge, he'll be just as good a guide as the man with ... knowledge?

96 MENO: Yes, he'll be just as good.

97 SOCRATES: In other words, correct opinion is just as good a guide to right action as knowledge. ...

98 MENO: ... It seems that must be right; which leaves me wondering, Socrates: If that's the case, why on earth is knowledge so much more valuable than correct opinion, and why are they treated as two different things?

99 SOCRATES: Well, you know why it is you're wondering about it. Shall I tell you?

100 MENO: Go ahead.

101 SOCRATES: It's because you haven't pondered Daedalus's statues. Maybe you haven't got any up there in Thessaly.

102 MENO: What have they got to do with it?

103 SOCRATES: Well, they're the same: if they aren't shackled, they escape – they scamper away. But if they're shackled, they stay put.

104 MENO: What are you getting at?

105 SOCRATES: If you own an original Daedalus, unshackled, it's not worth all that much ... because it doesn't stay put. But if you've got one that's shackled, it's very valuable. Because they're really lovely pieces of work. It's the same with true opinions. True opinions, as long as they stay put, are a fine thing and do us a whole lot of good. Only, they tend not to stay put for very long. They're always scampering away from a person's soul. So they are not very valuable until you shackle them by figuring out what makes them true. And then, once they're shackled, they turn into

knowledge, and become stable and fixed. So that's why knowledge is a more valuable thing than correct opinion, and that's how knowledge differs from a correct opinion: by a shackle.

Media notes

Notes on the interview with Tim Chappell

In this short interview, I talk to Professor Tim Chappell about some issues raised in the *Laches*. As you listen to the interview, you will notice that Tim Chappell is broadly sympathetic to many of the views that Plato seems to favour in the *Laches*. Hearing a sympathetic account of a philosopher's work can help to get a more rounded view of what he or she was trying to say. Still, you should bear in mind that Chappell's role in this interview is not to be a neutral commentator, but to express his own opinions. I hope that you will listen to what he says in the same analytical and critical spirit in which you approached the *Laches*, and that this material will spur you to further thought and discussion.

Track 1: Chappell mentions two Athenian playwrights, Aeschylus (525–456 BCE) and Sophocles (495–406 BCE). You will be able to read a translation of Sophocles' tragedy *Antigone* later in the course.

Track 2: The early work that Chappell refers to at the beginning of his reply is Plato's *Apology*. He goes on to mention 'Neurath's ship'. Otto Neurath (1882–1945) argued that rationalist philosophers are wrong to think that we can put aside everything we believe and start again from the beginning; we can only examine one belief at a time, in the light of everything else we believe. He illustrates this idea with the image of a ship which is repaired, one plank at a time, while afloat at sea. (Neurath, Otto (1983) *Philosophical Papers 1913–1946* (ed. R.S. Cohen and M. Neurath), Dordrecht, Reidel.)

Tracks 3 and 4: Chappell explains that Plato was impressed by the precision of mathematical thinking, and thought that philosophers should use similar methods. You might notice that Chappell does not say that Plato was right about this: he mentions that 'deductive reasoning is not the only game in town', and that philosophers often make use of analogies and other kinds of creative thinking. You will find an example of the way in which philosophers use analogies in Jon Pike's discussion of 'Cultural Encounters and Cultural Exemptions' in Book 3.

Tracks 5 to 7: In track 6, Chappell mentions two of Plato's works: the *Meno* and the *Protagoras*; and in track 7, he refers to the *Protagoras* and the *Republic*. In track 6, I mention the film *Pan's Labyrinth* (2006, Picturehouse).

As you listen to tracks 5 to 7, try to find one or two points to think further about or to discuss in a tutorial. Are there any points on which you disagree with the views that Chappell is presenting here? If so, try to get as clear as you can *what* you are disagreeing with and *why*.

Here are some specific questions that you might think about:

- Does courage always require thinking things out in advance?
- Is it possible to be courageous in an unjust cause?
- Can someone choose to do something that they really (deep down) know to be wrong?

2 READING POETRY: *THE FABER BOOK OF BEASTS*

Richard Danson Brown

INTRODUCTION		41
1	TRADITION AND DISSENT IN POETRY	41
2	AM NOT I A FLY LIKE THEE? TRADITIONS IN ANIMAL POETRY	42
	William Blake, 'The Fly'	43
	John Donne, 'The Flea'	48
	Miroslav Holub, 'The Fly'	51
3	USING *THE FABER BOOK OF BEASTS*	54
4	D.H. LAWRENCE: POETIC DISSIDENT?	58
REFERENCES		66
FURTHER READING		66
RESOURCES		67
	Reading 2.1	67
	Reading 2.2	68

MATERIALS YOU WILL NEED

- Audio CD: What am I? Beasts and Tradition
- *The Faber Book of Beasts* (Muldoon, 1997)
- Illustration Book

AIMS

This chapter will:

- introduce you to the critical reading and understanding of poetry
- develop your understanding of tradition and dissent through an exploration of the meaning of these terms in relation to poetry
- help you begin to think about the ways in which we read and study poetry through anthologies such as *The Faber Book of Beasts*.

INTRODUCTION

In this chapter you'll find many technical terms which I explain as they're used. This would be a good moment to start using the Oxford English Dictionary (OED) *online to learn more about these words (this is available through the course website). The* OED *is an invaluable tool for all Arts subjects, as it is informative about the history and usage of words. The online version has the huge advantage of being instantly searchable; it also gives you the chance to print out search results. You might start by looking up the word anthropomorphic and making a note of its various meanings. (This term is discussed in the second section of this chapter.)*

This chapter introduces you to *The Faber Book of Beasts*. You should read it in conjunction with the Audio CD 'What am I? Beasts and Tradition', which amplifies the arguments made in the chapter by using different examples. It includes interviews with Paul Muldoon, the editor of *The Faber Book of Beasts*, the poet Carol Ann Duffy and classicist Paula James, alongside readings of poems including John Donne's 'The Flea' and D.H. Lawrence's 'Snake'. The Audio CD has been designed so that it can be listened to independently of the chapter, but you'll get most benefit from it if you can listen to it at least once. I recommend having a first listen after you've read sections 1 and 2 of the chapter. This will give you an opportunity to consolidate the work you've done on poetic tradition. Then listen again when you've worked your way through the whole chapter. With poetry, the more you read, the more you'll understand. These pieces of course material are designed to expand your reading in what I hope will be an exciting as well as a pleasurable way.

1 TRADITION AND DISSENT IN POETRY

Having worked through Carolyn Price's chapter on the *Laches*, you should have a sense of Plato's attitude towards tradition. For Plato, traditional beliefs about courage are open to question: it is not enough to take them on trust. By the end of the *Laches*, it looks as though Plato is sceptical about the value of tradition, and it seems that analytical thinking – the work which philosophers do – allows the interrogation and reassessment of tradition.

This chapter focuses on poetry, where concepts such as tradition and dissent have different connotations. As we shall see, poets don't automatically dissent from tradition. New poems are often generated out of a dialogue with older poems. This is called **imitation** – the process whereby a poet imitates the work of someone else that he or she admires. It's similar to the way that rock musicians begin by playing cover versions of their favourite songs before writing their own material. Bands as diverse as the Beatles, the Sex Pistols and Nirvana started by trying to copy the work of, respectively, Motown artists, the Who and Led Zeppelin. Indeed, it could be argued that traces of those influences remain even in their mature work, like footprints, showing the listener where they started from. (These weren't the *only* influences on these bands: the Beatles responded to among others rock 'n' roll and Bob Dylan; Nirvana drew on the blues of Leadbelly and on 1980s American punk.)

Similarly, D.H. Lawrence's poetry, which you will encounter in this chapter, shows the influence of William Blake and Walt Whitman. Artistic traditions can be platforms for new work through which innovative writers learn their trade and adapt their influences for their own purposes. In this chapter, you'll notice that I discuss a range of traditions – from styles of writing (including rhyme schemes and verse forms) to significant ideas which are conveyed by poems. In other words, we have moved from considering traditional beliefs to traditional poetic practices.

Yet no art form can exist solely to repeat or recycle traditional formulae – there has to be some innovation, some friction between the new and the old in order to stimulate interest and to keep the form alive. To continue the analogy with popular music: tribute bands such as the Bootleg Beatles and Björn Again simulate the experience of seeing, respectively, the Beatles and Abba by replicating the sound and look of the originals. These acts are not changing artistic forms or challenging their audiences. Rather, they purvey nostalgia for the music (and the times) that their audiences already know and love. This represents a conservative attitude towards tradition, where the purpose of the performance is one of accurate reproduction. Conversely, although Lawrence learned from the work of Blake and Whitman, he dissented from many of their ideas. He did not receive the tradition of poetry passively, but worked to transform it into a vehicle for his own distinctive ideas.

The Irish poet Louis MacNeice gets to the heart of the tension in literary ideas about tradition when he writes: 'A poem, to be recognizable, must be traditional; but to be worth recognizing, it must be something new' (MacNeice, 1987, p. 12). This is a useful shorthand to bear in mind when reading poetry for the first time, because it makes the point that tradition is ingrained in poetry, yet that poetry cannot survive – any more than music or philosophy can – through traditional forms and motifs alone. I like what MacNeice says because he captures something of the challenge of reading poetry. Of all literary forms, poetry is the one which is most widely perceived as 'difficult', or 'intellectual', or just 'not for me'. My job in this chapter is not so much to persuade you that poetry isn't difficult or intellectual (it can be both), or that it is for you – this is something you must decide on the basis of your study. Rather, I want to enable you to recognise poetry both through its traditional features and in terms of what makes a text 'something new' – something that might have a claim on your time and your attention.

2 AM NOT I A FLY LIKE THEE? TRADITIONS IN ANIMAL POETRY

We begin with three poems about insects: 'The Fly' by William Blake (1757–1827),'The Flea' by John Donne (1572–1631) and 'The Fly' by Miroslav Holub (1923–1998) (Muldoon, 1997, pp. 93–6).

William Blake, 'The Fly'

Your first task is to read Blake's poem. Although this is a short, seemingly simple poem, you should read it at least twice. More than any other kind of writing, poetry demands to be *re*read: it's seldom that you'll find a poem which you can understand completely on a single reading. Try reading it out loud: this will both slow you down (a good thing, with poetry) and make you conscious of the sounds of the poem. As you will see, sound is an important component of the meaning of poetry.

Activity

Turn to William Blake's 'The Fly' (Muldoon, 1997, pp. 94-5). When you've read the poem a couple of times, I'd like you to:

- list the rhyming words
- find an **image** or figurative use of language.

'The Fly' is made up of short lines – some as brief as three syllables – so his rhymes are unavoidable, especially at the ends of lines. Each verse, or stanza, is composed of lines with alternate rhymes, where the second line rhymes with the fourth, while the first and third lines are usually unrhymed. ('Stanza' is the technical word for a grouping of lines of verse. It derives from the Italian word which means both a stopping place and a room; in the case of 'The Fly', you might say that these poetic 'rooms' are deliberately small, perhaps mimicking the size of the 'Little Fly'.)

Little Fly (A)
Thy summers play, (B)
My thoughtless hand (C)
Has brush'd away. (B)

(Muldoon, 1997, p. 94)

This is an ABCB rhyme scheme: the repeated letters denote the rhyming words. It's one of the simplest and oldest of all rhyming patterns, common in nursery rhymes such as 'Baa Baa Black Sheep' and 'To the Ladybug' (Muldoon, 1997, pp. 17, 252). Blake wanted to evoke the simplicity of nursery rhymes in 'The Fly' because, as we will see, his poem is partly concerned with childhood experience, and it attempts to sound simple and reassuring (see Blake, 1985, p. 220). (Nursery rhymes go back hundreds of years. Blake would have known various versions of these same texts. See Opie and Opie, 1951, pp. 3–4, 88, 263–4.)

My list of rhyming words would include the main rhymes in each stanza: 'play'/ 'away', 'thee'/'me', 'sing'/'wing', 'breath'/'death', 'fly'/'die'. But, as you may have noticed, the last stanza also rhymes the first two lines: 'Then am I/A happy fly'. This stanza is a variant of the ABCB scheme, where the pattern mutates to AABA. And this deviation from the rules observed in the rest of the poem tells us something important: that the ‘I’/‘fly’ rhyme is more significant than simply being an accident of sound. In effect, the final stanza brings ‘I’ and ‘fly’ – which have flitted around one another for the whole of the poem – into direct juxtaposition. The form of the poem insists that there is a connection between ‘I’ and the ‘fly’.

So, for the second part of this activity, I would choose the comparison of the man to the fly: ‘Am not I/A fly like thee?’ But you may have noticed other images. For example, the phrases ‘My thoughtless hand’ and ‘some blind hand’ use the device of **personification**. A personification is a metaphor which establishes a connection between things and people, or which represents an object in terms of human attributes. Blake takes adjectives which usually describe the processes of thinking and seeing and applies these to the hand in order to convey a sense of the automatic reflex of ‘brushing’ a fly away. By describing hands in these terms, Blake gives a more vivid sense of an ordinary action. This is one of the main purposes of poetic **imagery**: to make the thing described vivid to the reader.

Personification is also used in the second stanza:

> Am not I
> A fly like thee?
> Or art not thou
> A man like me?

(Muldoon, 1997, p. 94)

In this case, Blake uses the device of **simile** to compare flies with men. A simile is a formal comparison which uses words such as ‘like’ or ‘as’ to connect one thing with another. By asking these complementary questions, Blake personifies the fly after, as it were, ‘flyifying’ the man: as the speaker can be seen as ‘A fly’, so the fly can be seen as ‘A man’. This enables Blake in the third stanza to make the telling analogy between the fly’s fragility and the man’s:

> For I dance
> And drink & sing:
> Till some blind hand
> Shall brush my wing.

(Muldoon, 1997, p. 94)

In this reckoning, the life of a man is as tenuous, as liable to be arbitrarily ended by ‘some blind hand’, as the fly’s. Earlier, I suggested that Blake wanted ‘The Fly’ to sound familiar, like a nursery rhyme; now we can make the further point that this analogy is a traditional way of writing about animals as a metaphor for humans.

As you read *The Faber Book of Beasts*, you will find numerous examples of the thinking Blake makes explicit. This sort of comparison is properly called **anthropomorphism,** where human attributes are ascribed to something inhuman. Ordinary conversation is littered with anthropomorphic images. If I say that the weather looks threatening, I am personalising it, making it sound like a gangster to convey that bad weather is imminent. Louis MacNeice claimed that 'The poet is a specialist in something which every one practises'(MacNeice, 1938, p. 31). We all use imagery and metaphor in everyday speech; we all personalise the impersonal to make it vivid and tangible.

Anthropomorphic thinking underpins an important tradition in poetry about animals. This practice derives from Aesop's fables, which are now seen as a form of children's literature. These fables originate from ancient Greece. Aesop is a legendary figure with an elusive, almost invisible biography. Fables were attributed to him by later writers, so that the term 'Aesop's fables' has the status of a venerable literary brand. Typically, these fables take the form of miniature moral lessons, in which animals represent people in order to convey almost proverbial wisdom. For instance, the hungry fox who can't reach a bunch of grapes and then persuades himself that they weren't ripe in any case illustrates the moral that 'some men, when they fail through their own incapacity, blame circumstances' (Handford, 1964, p. 5). However, the French poet Jean de La Fontaine dissents from Aesop's moral by praising the fox for looking on the bright side; his version ends 'Fit-il pas mieux que de se plaindre?' – 'Didn't he do better than whining?' (La Fontaine, 1995, pp. 68–9). You'll encounter a version of an Aesopic fable on the Audio CD, which discusses Alexander Pope's 'Imitation ... of Horace' (Muldoon, 1997, pp. 128–9), where an eighteenth-century English poet imitates a classical Roman poet, who in turn has adapted work from ancient Greece.

In writing anthropomorphically, poets aren't doing anything unusual: most of us unconsciously ascribe emotions and thoughts to animals. This is what Blake does in 'The Fly', as the insect apparently feels the human emotion of happiness: 'Then am I/A happy fly'. Of course, you might reasonably say that we know Blake is speaking metaphorically – we don't read the poem literally, and the second stanza explains that the fly represents the speaker. But this is the point I'm making: anthropomorphic poems aren't quite what they say they are. 'The Fly' is as much about the emotions of the 'man' who speaks it, and it certainly isn't a scientific disquisition about **entomology** (the scientific study of insects)! Entomology will become relevant as we go on.

Activity Before we leave 'The Fly', we need to ask the question implicit in the last paragraph: what is this poem about? Reread the poem, and then write a paragraph of no more than a hundred words explaining what you make of it. Think particularly about the overall tone of the poem: what sort of mood does it conjure up?

Writing about poems can be as challenging as writing about music or paintings. There isn't just one valid approach to 'The Fly' – indeed, you

could reasonably suggest that what makes poems valuable is their capacity to be reinterpreted by different readers. Nevertheless, as with Cézanne's paintings or the arguments in the *Laches*, there are points of detail that you should have noticed. Poems are not totally open texts which can mean anything we want them to mean. Your explanation should have considered the comparison between the man and the fly; in other words the fact that Blake connects the two through the sense of their shared fragility. In terms of tone, I would say that something surprising happens within the poem. At first the comparison seems to be a fearful indication of human weakness, but by the end there is a joyful acquiescence in the limitations of existence:

> Then am I
> A happy fly,
> If I live,
> Or if I die.

(Muldoon, 1997, p. 95)

This gives the poem a spiritual inflection – as though Blake is drawing comfort from the very chanciness of existence which the comparison between man and fly makes explicit.

You may have come up with different kinds of explanation. The main point to grasp is that Blake uses insects to make a poetic analogy. When I say that the poem has a spiritual inflection, I'm partly drawing on other sources of knowledge, not just my reading of the poem. As we shall see, contextual information is useful in helping to locate poems. Knowledge of Blake's life and work substantially enriches our understanding even of a poem as brief as 'The Fly'.

Blake epitomises the popular conception of the **Romantic** poet as a lonely outsider, dedicated to his own artistic vision. He wasn't just a poet: as Plates 2.2.1–4 show, he was also a painter and illustrator, who produced elaborate, colourful images which are often integral parts of his poems. 'The Fly' is from his collection *Songs of Experience* (1794). This volume follows the earlier *Songs of Innocence* (1789) and offers a darker representation of experience. As you can see from the title page to the dual volume, *Songs of Innocence and of Experience* (Plate 2.2.1), Blake saw the combined text as 'Shewing [an old-fashioned spelling of 'showing'] the Two Contrary States of the Human Soul'. You will get a sense of this by reading his poem 'The Lamb' (from *Songs of Innocence*; see Muldoon, 1997, pp. 140–1) alongside 'The Tyger' (from *Songs of Experience*; see Muldoon, 1997, p. 271). 'The Lamb' celebrates the miracle of creation by explaining that this creature was 'made' by the 'meek' and 'mild' Jesus, whereas 'The Tyger' probes that animal's 'fearful symmetry' to reveal a more ominous creator: 'what shoulder, & what art,/Could twist the sinews of thy heart?' The link between the

Figure 2.1 Thomas Phillips, *William Blake*, 1807, oil on canvas, 92.1 x 72 cm. National Portrait Gallery, London. Photo: © National Portrait Gallery.

two poems is made explicit when Blake asks: 'Did he smile his work to see?/Did he who made the Lamb make thee?' It's a terrific question from a literally terrific poem, which aims to terrify its readers by using the animal as a vehicle to consider the unimaginable dimensions – the hand, shoulder and smile – of the deity which made the tiger.

As I've said, Blake designed the *Songs* as an artistic totality, in which the words of the poems are matched by the lines of each engraving. It's worth noting that Blake was virtually unknown during his lifetime and sold only a handful of his works. His books were the antithesis of mass production: each one had to be coloured by hand, by the hand of 'The Author & Printer W Blake'.

Activity I'd like you to finish your work on Blake by rereading his poem as you look at Plate 2.2.2, the engraved version of 'The Fly'. Does seeing the engraving change your reading of the poem?

Discussion I'm always struck by the fact that Blake didn't directly represent the fly in the engraving. In contrast with 'The Tyger' (where a rather unconvincing tiger stalks along the bottom of the page; see Plate 2.2.3), 'The Fly' shows a small child playing with a nurse or mother, while a second, older child plays badminton, batting a shuttlecock in the direction of the third stanza. On the right-hand side of the engraving, near a tree which frames that side of the composition, there is a small, indistinct bird-like creature near the word 'die'. I'm not sure that the engraving changes my reading of the poem, but it does enrich it and help to focus elements of the poem. The engraving's depiction of children at play picks up the nursery rhyme element in the form of the poem. The graceful image suggests (although it doesn't explicitly say) that the poem is concerned with childhood experience. This helps to account for the tone of what I earlier called joyful acquiescence: this is a poem which uses the analogy between the man and the fly in order to suggest a way of living – without anxiety, with an accepting consciousness of the limits placed on life.

John Donne, 'The Flea'

Now we're going to turn to John Donne's poem 'The Flea'. Donne was a contemporary of Christopher Marlowe, so you may find his language slightly unusual at first.

Activity Turn to 'The Flea' by John Donne (Muldoon, 1997, pp. 93–4). You may find it useful to listen to the reading of the poem on track 15 of the Audio CD. Again, read the poem several times before continuing with this activity. Then think about these questions:

- How do Donne's rhymes differ from Blake's?
- Do you think Donne uses the flea in the same way as Blake uses the fly?
- How do you react to the poem?

I hope that in your initial reaction to 'The Flea' you registered how different it is from 'The Fly'. In place of Blake's simple idiom, short lines and stanzas, Donne's form and **syntax** (sentence construction) are much knottier and more involved. The rhyme scheme is an elaborate AABBCCDDD, so that each stanza ends with a rhyming triplet. These triplets give an impression of emphaticness, as though the speaker is vigorously underlining his point, stressing to the reader – or listener – what he's driving at.

Consider the final triplet:

> 'Tis true, then learn how false, fears be;
> Just so much honor, when thou yield'st to me,
> Will waste, as this flea's death took life from thee.

(Muldoon, 1997, p. 94)

Figure 2.2 Unknown artist, *John Donne*, *c.* 1595, oil on canvas. Private collection. Photo: The Bridgeman Art Library.

The speaker is attempting to cajole his listener in an almost hectoring manner. Each rhyme stresses his argument: the listener must 'learn how false, fears be', must persuade herself that when she yields 'to me' she will lose as 'much honor' as 'this flea's death took life from thee' – that final line, indeed, rams the point home by the internal rhyme of 'flea' with 'thee'. The poem concludes with a flurry of rhymes which attempt to bind the listener to the speaker's will. Rather than just being verbal ornamentation, Donne's rhymes are more like poetic weaponry through which his speaker bullies himself a hearing.

The way I've described the rhymes implies that 'The Flea' is a poem of persuasion. Unlike 'The Fly', which centres on the analogy between the man and the beast, Donne uses the flea as an elaborate, flexible metaphor through which his speaker attempts to persuade a female listener to sleep with him on the basis of a dubious analogy between being bitten by fleas and having sex. In the course of the poem, the speaker shifts from using the flea as a metaphor for sexual consummation – 'this/Our marriage bed, and marriage temple is' – to construing its death as a further argument in favour of sex: the woman will lose only as much 'honor' as they each lost 'life' when she killed the flea which contained their mingled bloods. The flea is the poetic peg on which he hangs a plea for sex. I would say that although its focus is almost entirely dissimilar from that of 'The Fly', both poems use their insects metaphorically.

Donne uses the flea as a **conceit**; that is, a deliberately far-fetched and ingenious comparison. Conceits were fashionable during Donne's lifetime; they are often called metaphysical conceits to convey the amalgam of the intellectual with the sensuous which underpins poems of this kind. Conceits are also at work in poems such as Robert Herrick's 'The Captiv'd Bee' and Andrew Marvell's 'The Mower to the Glowworms' (Muldoon, 1997, pp. 49, 159). Donne is one of the first English poets to deploy comparisons of this kind. Where Blake responds to the tradition of nursery rhymes, Donne inaugurates a tradition of extravagant poetic conceits.

Your response to Donne's poem will depend on a number of factors. It is, I think, knowingly sleazy, with its numerous *double entendres*, as when the flea 'pamper'd swells with one blood made of two'. Yet the poem's tone is not wholly serious, which makes it difficult to read without smiling. Think about the conversational directness of the poem's opening: 'Mark but this flea, and mark in this,/How little that which thou deny'st me is'. The tone is immediate, veering from the pseudo-educational ('Mark ... mark') to the self-consciously preposterous. And though the speaker is insistent to the point of desperation, the fact that his plea to spare the flea is ignored means that the poem is more than just an elaborate chat-up line. The woman's implied involvement in the conversation means that Donne presents the reader with a condensed comedy of manners: 'The Flea' shows us a flirtation in action, which doesn't endorse the speaker in any unqualified way. You don't have to like the poem, but we should acknowledge that it is more than just a piece of Elizabethan smut. Donne provides an original twist on the old theme of seduction which brings something of the smack of real life into love poetry.

In this context, it's worth knowing that Donne's society held strict views about sex outside of marriage. In the poem, the speaker tries to circumvent both religious objections (which viewed extramarital sex as 'A sin') and social conventions. It's something that 'parents grudge', because a daughter's 'maidenhead' (virginity) was a valuable commodity, not something to be thrown away on the first chancer with a good line in fleas. This raises the broader question of the relationship between the poem and literary convention. 'The Flea' is a witty variant on traditional love poetry, in which usually male speakers idolise and idealise unobtainable women. Instead of these clichés, Donne audaciously shows a man in the process of trying to seduce a woman. Oddly enough, poems about fleas weren't that unusual: 'many poets had already pined to be fleas, hoping to be laid on the bosoms of their beloved and even ... slapped to death' (Patrides in Donne, 1985, p. 23). Donne varies this tradition: his speaker doesn't want to be a flea, but he deploys the insect as a vehicle for seduction. Remember MacNeice's argument that in order to be worth recognising, a poem must be something new. In its vivid combination of sexual innuendo, conversational English and what feels like a genuine exchange between plausible figures, 'The Flea' does indeed still sound like 'something new'.

Before we leave 'The Flea', I want to think a little further about the extent to which it is an anthropomorphic poem. I have argued that what connects it with 'The Fly' is its metaphorical use of its subject. Yet Donne is much more concerned with the realities of animal behaviour than Blake. He provides accurate information about the behaviour of fleas ('It suck'd me first, and now sucks thee'), alongside a strikingly visual description of the insect: the characters' blood is 'cloister'd in these living walls of jet'. Jet is a form of brown coal or lignite often used for jewellery. Donne's poem 'A Jeat Ring sent' centres on a jet ring as a cheap love token which metaphorically expresses the fragility of a failed love affair. Donne throws his despairing voice into the ring: 'I am cheap, and nought but fashion, throw me away' (Donne, 1985, p. 116). In 'The Flea', jet economically conveys the insect's colouring . Though we're perhaps reluctant to see fleas as being in any way beautiful, this phrase shows that Donne had looked carefully at these tiny creatures. During the sixteenth and seventeenth centuries, intellectuals began to take a scientific interest in the natural world. Plate 2.2.5 reflects this trend. It shows a hugely magnified engraving of a flea, taken from Robert Hooke's *Micrographia* (1665). Roughly contemporaneous with this, Donne's flea is simultaneously both a conceited metaphor and a living creature accurately described.

Miroslav Holub, 'The Fly'

We turn now to Miroslav Holub's 'The Fly'. Holub was a Czech poet and immunologist, whose poetry was partly censored by the pro-Soviet regime which ruled Czechoslovakia until the 'Velvet Revolution' of 1989. Bear in mind that this is a translation and not a poem first written in English (we'll consider the implications of this shortly).

Activity Turn to 'The Fly' by Miroslav Holub (Muldoon, 1997, pp. 95–6). Then try to find two or three ways in which this poem differs from those of Blake and Donne. Think particularly about the form of the poem, and the use Holub makes of his fly.

Figure 2.3 Miroslav Holub, 1992. Photographed by Dostál Dušan. Photo: Czech News Agency, Prague, Fotobanka CTK.

Discussion Here are the things I came up with. This isn't an exhaustive list – you may well have chosen different points of contrast. The most important thing is to register that this poem is very different from Blake's 'The Fly' and Donne's 'The Flea'.

1 Holub's poem lacks any rhyme scheme or recurring pattern to the verse. Lines are of radically different lengths; there doesn't seem to be any traditional design which Holub is following.

2 This poem seems much more scientific in its description of insects: 'she mated/with a brown-eyed male fly'; 'she began to lay her eggs/on the single eye/of Johann Uhr'; 'she was eaten by a swift/fleeing/from the fires of Estrées'. Holub's purpose seems to be more descriptive than analytical: the poem describes the behaviour of a fly in the middle of a battle.

3 At the same time, 'The Fly' is very much concerned with the evocation of the battle of Crécy (which took place in 1346 during the Hundred Years War between the English and the French). It provides a graphic, horrifying account of the realities of war: 'the shouts,/the gasps,/the groans', 'a disembowelled horse', 'a few arms and legs/still twitched jerkily'. In effect, the poem is a litany of carnage, strewn with body parts and the misery of men and animals. Its focus on the battlefield points to a further contrast: this text has no speaker – there is no first-person voice with whom the reader can identify or (in the case of 'The Flea') argue. Instead, Holub couches his poem in the language of objective description. It almost has the feel of a grotesque natural history film, in which the camera objectively registers a sequence of violent events.

'The Fly' is a modern poem in both form and content. Holub writes in **free verse**; that is, verse which deliberately eschews traditional devices such as rhyme schemes and conventional metres. It avoids the traditional poetic forms you have previously encountered in the works of Blake, Donne and Marlowe. It's important to distinguish free verse from the blank verse used by Marlowe in *Dr Faustus*; where blank verse is unrhymed verse in which each line has roughly the same number of stresses and syllables, free verse can have virtually any pattern which the poet chooses (see the section on 'Reading a Renaissance play' in Book 1, Chapter 2).

You might, then, think that lines such as 'She sat on a willow-trunk/watching/part of the battle of Crécy' are more prosaic than the rhymed verse of Blake or Donne. Indeed, modern poetry is often attacked for having the appearance of being prose which has been randomly cut into verse. With 'The Fly', there's the further complication that it's a translated text – unless we can read Czech, we view Holub's poem through the filter of George Theiner's translation. To give a point of comparison, the resource material for this chapter reprints a different translation, by Stuart Friebert and Dana Hábová. Although there are some slight differences of detail – for example, Theiner has 'With relief she alighted', where Friebert and Hábová have 'Relieved she alighted' – both versions are similar. Compare Theiner's 'the shouts,/the gasps' with Friebert and Hábová's 'the shrieks,/the moans'. Although the vocabulary is different, the line breaks are identically positioned. This is a good sign that the two translations give accurate reports of the original poem.

But even in translation we can see that there is artistry and intelligence in the way that the lines are organised. Consider the way Holub uses breaks in his lines to emphasise dramatic moments in the syntax. New verbs often signal new lines: 'watching', 'she mated', 'She rubbed', 'she began' and, most dramatically of all, 'a swift/fleeing'. I would say that the power of 'The Fly' is connected with its poetic timing: it repeatedly juxtaposes natural processes with the horrors of war, as in the lines 'With relief she alighted/on the blue tongue/of the Duke of Clervaux'. The 'relief' of the first line here is brutally undermined by the horror of the next two – although this is very much a human perspective on what to the fly is natural behaviour. Free verse, then, is not verse without artifice, but a form which avoids the constraints of traditional rhyming verse.

The content of the poem also shows dissent from traditional ways of writing about warfare. By describing the effects of battle neutrally, Holub eschews any sense of the glory of war. The poem insistently emphasises the fragility of human and animal life, while implying that war is a pointless and almost incomprehensible activity from the quizzical perspective of the fly 'meditating/on the immortality of flies'. Yet it would be a mistake to read 'The Fly' as a wholesale rejection of tradition: we can see vestiges of anthropomorphic thinking in these lines. Although for the bulk of the poem Holub describes the fly scientifically, these lines invest her with almost human thought processes. I suspect that Holub, as a scientist, was aware of what he was doing – 'meditating/on the immortality of flies' suggests that the fly contrasts the aimless slaughter of men and horses with the different life cycles of insects, in which the life of any individual creature is less significant than the survival of the species. In this sense, the fly fulfils her biological function by reproducing. And unlike the casualties of the battle, her death is an unremarkable natural event. Nevertheless, Holub's meditative fly participates, however fleetingly, in the same tradition as Blake's 'happy fly'.

3 USING *THE FABER BOOK OF BEASTS*

The previous section suggests that there is a tradition deriving from Aesop which uses animals metaphorically. We've moved from the strong equation between man and fly in Blake's poem through to the more scientific adaptation of insects to a poetic function in Holub's 'The Fly', via Donne's shifting use of the flea both as a metaphor and as an object of interest in itself. I chose these poems partly because they are printed on consecutive pages in Muldoon's anthology: the book invites us to consider similarities and differences between them. On track 4 of the Audio CD, you can hear Muldoon's rationale for the anthology's format. In this section, we consider anthologies and the role they play in the understanding of poetic traditions.

What is an anthology? According to the *OED*, the word literally means 'a collection of the flowers of verse' and derives from the ancient Greek practice of collecting favourite poems. For almost as long as people have been writing poems, readers have culled special favourites – the choicest 'flowers' – into personal collections. The construction of an anthology of poems is much the same as the compiling of a music playlist for an iPod. There's a widespread impulse to gather favourites into a convenient place, whether this takes the form of a book or a computer file.

But there are significant differences between a personal selection and a collection such as *The Faber Book of Beasts*. A published book is a more powerful document than a private collection because it has the capacity to influence a wider range of people. Similarly, a 'Greatest Hits' collection chosen by a record company will reach more people than the playlist you might devise on the basis of your knowledge of an artist's recordings. A commercial anthology defines how a given kind of poetry is understood, in the same way that a 'Greatest Hits' CD asserts what that artist's best work is. Anthologies construct readers' understanding of poetic traditions – through the act of selection, the anthologist defines and delimits the scope of a tradition.

This means that anthologies are implicitly provocative. If my anthology of the world's best poems excludes the work of your favourite poet, you will feel aggrieved by my choices and will argue that my anthology isn't quite what it purports to be – it's not the world's best poems so much as the world's best poems according to *me*. I often feel the same disquiet about 'Greatest Hits' CDs: why have they chosen this track instead of one of my favourites? From this subjective objection, we can articulate more analytical questions. What are the grounds for selection? What authority does the anthologist have for making these choices? These are useful questions to have in mind when studying *The Faber Book of Beasts*. Its editor, Paul Muldoon, is a distinguished poet, the author of several prize-winning collections. He has edited other anthologies, including *The Faber Book of Contemporary Irish Poetry* (1986). This suggests that, as a poet himself with previous experience of producing anthologies, Muldoon has some authority for the job. So we might expect that *The Faber Book of Beasts* would be more than just a subjective gathering of his favourite animal poems. Note, too, that these are *Faber* books. Although Faber and Faber is a small company, it is hugely prestigious and has published famous poets such as T.S. Eliot, Sylvia Plath, Ted Hughes, W.H. Auden, Seamus Heaney, as well as Muldoon himself. The Faber brand is a guarantor of poetic quality, or at least ambition.

Activity

Now read the introduction to *The Faber Book of Beasts* (Muldoon, 1997, pp. xv–xvii) and think about these questions:

1. How does Muldoon characterise the anthologist?
2. How is his anthology organised?

Discussion

1. In the second paragraph Muldoon says that 'Anthologists tend to be extremely arrogant, perhaps even despotic', and that his introduction will live up to these expectations. It seems as though anthologists are bossy know-it alls, and that Muldoon at least partly conforms to type – although you might suspect that by acknowledging the pretensions of other anthologists, he aims to avoid their worst excesses.
2. About halfway through the introduction Muldoon discusses 'The alphabetical method of the anthology'. Although he doesn't explain why he has chosen to organise the contents in this way, he stresses its advantages: the 'provocative propinquity' of texts 'allows for a great number of ... felicitous fusions', in which the juxtaposition of poems enhances the reader's enjoyment and creates fertile comparisons as different poets write about the same creatures. We've been engaged in this sort of work by reading the fly poems of Blake and Holub alongside Donne's 'Flea'.

Muldoon doesn't disguise the partiality of the anthologist. One of the strengths of his anthology is that the introduction doesn't shy away from its limitations, contradictions, or the many wonderful poems which it has had to exclude. As Muldoon puts it with a refreshing candour, 'To have made this book as doorstoppingly expansive as I'd have liked would have been to make it much more expensive than you'd have liked' (Muldoon, 1997, pp. xv–xvi). It's worth underlining this point: anthologies, like course chapters and assignments, have to have limits. It's the condition of the anthologist, as much as that of the student and of the reader, to have to make choices – to print or discuss one poem instead of another.

Yet Muldoon might have said more about why he chose alphabetical ordering. Most anthologies organise their material either historically, or through the writers whose work they contain. Muldoon's *Faber Book of Contemporary Irish Poetry* organises its contents in both these ways, by selecting ten twentieth-century Irish poets and printing substantial extracts from their work, in the order of the writers' births. Certainly, an alphabetical structure is unusual, and it allows Muldoon to craft creative juxtapositions. But it's also – and this is something he doesn't explicitly say – a less hierarchical (less despotic, you might say) approach than a chronological structure might be. Consider the poems we've been studying. If Muldoon had adopted an orthodox chronology, Donne would have appeared in the first fifty pages of the book, Blake somewhere in the next fifty and Holub in the last fifty. The alphabetical structure doesn't allow the reader to read only older or only more modern poems: rather, it shuffles them together and refuses to privilege distinctions between ancient and modern, between past and present. We read poems from different traditions, written in different styles, on a level playing field.

So the organisation of the anthology tells us something important about Muldoon's attitude towards poetic tradition. The introduction faces up to contradictions in the selection. On the one hand, Muldoon states that his purpose 'is to present a selection of the best animal poems in the English-speaking tradition' (Muldoon, 1997, p. xv); on the other, he admits this plan is undermined by the translations he has included. What are we to make of this? We're back to what Muldoon calls 'exigencies of space': he would have liked to include Welsh, Scottish, Irish, Native American and Inuit poetry, but settles for a limited amount of translated verse which has 'been taken over, to a greater or lesser extent, into the English tradition' (Muldoon, 1997, p. xv). As with the alphabetical ordering, Muldoon's selections are guided by a non-hierarchical, inclusive outlook which wants to extend our awareness of a range of traditions of animal poetry rather than privileging one tradition. We can see the same impulse at work in the admission that he has rationed the number of poems by individual writers – 'the very brilliance' of writers like Seamus Heaney and D.H. Lawrence 'began to weigh against them' (Muldoon, 1997, p. xvi). You can hear more about Muldoon's making of the anthology on track 4 of the Audio CD.

Finally, it's worth noting that *The Faber Book of Beasts* recalls the form of a medieval genre: the bestiary. Bestiaries were gatherings of pseudo-scientific data about animals and things, often accompanied by moralising commentaries and beautiful manuscript illustrations. Plate 2.2.7 shows a page from *The Aberdeen Bestiary* (written and illuminated in England in about 1200 CE) which features a rather grumpy looking red kite, alongside a commentary which fuses accurate ornithological observation (kites do feed on carrion) with an allegorical application of the bird's behaviour: 'The kite signifies those who are tempted by effete pleasures. It feeds on corpses, as pleasure-seekers take delight in carnal desires' (you can find this translation, by Colin McLaren, online at http://www.abdn.ac.uk/bestiary/translat/46v.hti). Muldoon's anthology recalls the medieval tradition of bestiaries, but with the significant difference that he makes no attempt to provide a unified moral commentary: the 'significations' of the beasts included are ultimately as varied as the poetic contents of the volume.

This section has suggested that anthologies are provocative texts which shape our understanding of poetry. You may well feel resistant to some of Muldoon's ideas and some of his choices. When studying an anthology, it's important not to read it passively, or to take its choices on trust. It's also worthwhile reading beyond the even narrower selection of poems which I have space to discuss in this chapter. Indeed, you might have misgivings about the poems I've chosen to discuss here.

Activity So I'd like you to take this opportunity to browse through *The Faber Book of Beasts*. Spend about an hour looking through the book (don't try to read everything!), making a note of poems you find interesting or attractive, or which you don't like at all. Then assemble your own miniature anthology of about five poems, with notes explaining your choices. My choices can be found in the resource material; this should give you an idea of how to structure your thoughts. Try to avoid being too anecdotal: your focus should be on the text of your chosen poems. So include a short quotation from each one you select, and try to explain what is it about these texts which engages your attention. You may include this work as part of the material for your electronic notebook.

4 D.H. LAWRENCE: POETIC DISSIDENT?

In his introduction to *The Faber Book of Beasts*, Muldoon suggests that there's a connection between animal poems and broader questions of human identity. Quoting from Ted Hughes's 'Wodwo', he argues that 'This ongoing question of "What am I?" is ... central not only to animal poetry but to all forms of poetry' (Muldoon, 1997, p. xvii). In this final section, we explore the work of one of the poets who threatened to figure 'too strongly in the book' (Muldoon, 1997, p. xvi): D.H. Lawrence (1885–1930). We'll read the Lawrence poems in *The Faber Book of Beasts* to explore how far he dissents from poetic tradition and to consider his answers to the question: 'What am I?'

Activity Now use the index (Muldoon, 1997, pp. 294–5) to find the five Lawrence poems in the anthology. (As you do this, reflect on the fact that you're partly going against Muldoon's ordering of his work: by singling Lawrence out, we're resisting the alphabetical pull of the book as a whole.) Then read these poems through relatively quickly, making some notes with the following questions in mind:

- What kinds of poem do you think these are? What sorts of formal structure do they have – for instance, do they rhyme? Do they show any traces of anthropomorphic thinking?
- How would you characterise Lawrence as a writer? What attitudes does he show? What impression, if any, does he give you of himself?

These five poems should have reminded you of Holub's 'The Fly'. They are written in free verse and there are virtually no rhymes. Like Holub, Lawrence manipulates line endings for emphasis:

> It is a mountain lion,
> A long, long slim cat, yellow like a lioness.
> Dead.

(Muldoon, 1997, p. 157)

Lawrence bleakly registers the pathos of the animal's death. Note the contrast between the sinewy, repetitious description of 'A long, long slim cat, yellow like a lioness' and the baldness of the single-word line, 'Dead'. The devices and registers of traditional poetry, which deploy imagery and repetition, are juxtaposed with the brute fact of the lion's lifelessness.

My sense is that these poems show relatively little of the kind of anthropomorphic thinking we've seen in Blake and Donne. Although Lawrence often addresses these creatures – 'You know what it is to be born alone,/Baby tortoise!' (Muldoon, 1997, p. 17) – the poems focus on how animals differ from the people who look at them. When Lawrence quizzically probes the thought processes of the tortoise, his words imply that they don't 'wonder' at all:

> Are you able to wonder?
> Or is it just your indomitable will and pride of the first life
> Looking round
> And slowly pitching itself against the inertia
> Which had seemed invincible?

(Muldoon, 1997, pp. 18–19)

A passage like this, with its insistent, questioning tone, leads to the issue of Lawrence's characteristics as a writer. I've already mentioned his repetitions. Although these poems lack the formal props of rhymes and lines of similar lengths, Lawrence typically gets stuck on the same patterns of words and images; new lines are chiselled out of phrases which have themselves just been minted. In this case, the question about the tortoise rephrases in a simpler form the earlier lines: 'Do you wonder at the world, as slowly you turn your head in its wimple/And look with laconic, black eyes?' (Muldoon, 1997, p. 18).

'Bat' shows this technique of what we might call notebook repetition at its most exhilarating:

> Bats!
> Creatures that hang themselves up like an old rag, to sleep;
> And disgustingly upside down.
> Hanging upside down like rows of disgusting old rags
> And grinning in their sleep.
> Bats!

(Muldoon, 1997, p. 23)

Lawrence captures the emotions of disgust by elaborating the simile of bats sleeping 'like an old rag'; the images take on an emotional coloration which exactly conveys the mixture of bewilderment and revulsion that the bats stimulate. As the bats are inverted 'disgustingly upside down', so the verse restlessly transfers the disgust from the description of the bats' sleeping habits to their resemblance to 'disgusting old rags'. I would say that Lawrence is a deliberately repetitious writer: his free verse is shaped by the use of strategic repetitions, which have the effect of dramatising his viewpoint. Another way of putting this is to say that Lawrence's repetitions are **rhetorical**: they have a design on us as readers, they attempt to persuade us of something – even if this is little more than the passion of the poem's speaking voice – through the force of verbal resonance.

On track 8 of the Audio CD, Paul Muldoon makes the related point that the apparent clumsiness of Lawrence's repetitions, along with his insistent use of correctives and modifications, captures his radical sense as a poet that it might take a couple of stabs to get the poem, and the description of the animal, right.

As these examples demonstrate, Lawrence is also an excitable writer. In each poem, the protagonist shows himself to be intrigued, curious, disgusted or fascinated by the creature he encounters. There's nothing neutral about Lawrence's poems or their speaking voice. Each text has a vigorous verbal energy, as though we're being spoken to by someone supercharged by the thrill of what he has seen. The poet W.H. Auden argued that 'it is doubtful if a writer ever existed who ever had less of an artistic *persona* than Lawrence; from his letters and the reminiscences of his friends, it would seem that he wrote for publication in exactly the same way as he spoke in private' (Auden, 1963, p. 288). (A 'persona' is an assumed character, especially of the kind that poets use, like the speaker in Donne's 'The Flea'.) Although it's exciting to have the illusion that we are being directly addressed by the writer, we shouldn't let ourselves be seduced by the Lawrentian voice. The Lawrence revealed by these poems has determined ideas, especially about the relative values of animals and human beings. The most challenging passage comes at the end of 'Mountain Lion':

> I think in the world beyond, how easily we might spare a
> million or two of humans
> And never miss them.
> Yet what a gap in the world, the missing white frost-face of that
> slim yellow mountain lion!

(Muldoon, 1997, p. 158)

When we were reading 'The Flea', I made the point that the poem's sleaziness can be explained by the fact that the verse is a comedy of manners: we don't have to believe that the speaker of the poem was the real John Donne, or that Donne himself used fleas as a way of getting women to sleep with him. We can't do the same with 'Mountain Lion' – partly for the reasons Auden gives, but also because the speaker in each of Lawrence's poems exhibits the same characteristics and attitudes: fascination with the animal world alongside a pervasive disgust at human culture. As 'Snake' puts it: 'I despised myself and the voices of my accursed human education' (Muldoon, 1997, p. 234). In these poems, Lawrence elevates and magnifies the instinctual life of animals at the expense of 'accursed human education'. In this view, 'a million or two of humans' are more expendable than a single mountain lion.

These are difficult, disturbing ideas which we'll need to explore in more detail. Before we do that, it's worth making the caveat that these lines are of a piece with the broader character of Lawrence's work.

Although the sentiments are sociopathic, they are also **hyperbolic** – that is, deliberately exaggerated. 'Mountain Lion' claims we could 'spare a million or two of humans' not so much out of a compulsion towards mass murder, but in order to dramatise for the reader the acute sense of loss which the speaker feels at the death of 'this missing white frost-face'.

How, then, should we approach Lawrence's dissenting take on human life? Auden's essay is helpful. He distinguishes 'The artist, the man who makes' from 'the apostle, the man with a message' (Auden, 1963, p. 277). For Auden, Lawrence typifies the apostle: he was a writer with a dogmatic message particularly in relation to sexuality, who 'detested nearly all human beings if he had to be in close contact with them' and could only direct his feelings of 'affection and charity ... towards nonhuman life' (Auden, 1963, pp. 288–9). Lawrence's biographer, John Worthern (2005), has characterised him as an 'outsider', someone whose ideas were at variance with almost every social milieu he inhabited.

Lawrence was born in the mining village of Eastwood near Nottingham. He was shaped by the conflict between his working-class father and his more middle-class mother. His literary career was controversial from the outset: novels such as *Sons and Lovers* (1913) and *The Rainbow* (1915) were felt by critics to be dangerously sexually explicit. After his marriage to a German, Frieda von Richthofen, Lawrence became disenchanted with Britain and what he saw as the barbarism of the First World War. In his later years he led a peripatetic lifestyle, living in places as diverse as Sicily, Australia and Mexico. The poems we've been reading are taken from the collection *Birds, Beasts and Flowers*, published in 1923, the contents of which were written during these years. As well as his poetry, he wrote numerous novels and stories, most famously *Lady Chatterley's Lover*, which appeared in 1928. During Lawrence's lifetime this novel was banned for being pornographic; it was only in 1960, after a famous obscenity trial, that it was published in full in Britain. *Lady Chatterley* embodies the credo that people should embrace their physicality – for Lawrence, everything which diminished instinctive, natural responses, such as Christian ideas of guilt and sin, was repellent. In Lawrence's view, modern industrial civilisation was a sick delusion, which abstracted people from a consciousness of their bodies and their innermost desires. Lawrence's ideas about sexuality remain controversial. For some, he is a prophet of liberation from Victorian repression; for others, he privileges men over women and reinscribes many of the taboos he was seeking to break.

We can get another angle on these ideas by looking at Lawrence's paintings. Although he was at best an enthusiastic amateur artist, his paintings from the later stages of his life vividly embody his polemical thinking. Like *Lady Chatterley*, these paintings were banned when an

Figure 2.4 D.H. Lawrence, *Self portrait*, 1929, red crayon. Photo: © Keith Sagar.

attempt was made to exhibit them in London in 1929 (Worthern, 2005, pp. 398–400). Plate 2.2.8 is a reproduction of his watercolour 'The Lizard' (1928), which almost directly illustrates his poem 'Lizard'. The poem concludes: 'If men were as much men as lizards are lizards/they'd be worth looking at'. The painting juxtaposes a dreary couple of naked figures (looking at odds with each other emotionally and sexually) with a bright green lizard in the foreground. The painting mirrors the sentiments of the poem: the lizard is 'a dandy fellow', but the people in the painting scarcely seem 'worth looking at' (Lawrence, 1993, p. 524).

Similarly, 'Snake' juxtaposes the snake's majestic beauty with the blinkered voices of conventional morality:

> The voice of my education said to me
> He must be killed,
> For in Sicily the black, black snakes are innocent, the gold are venomous.
>
> ...
>
> For he seemed to me again like a king,
> Like a king in exile, uncrowned in the underworld,
> Now due to be crowned again.
>
> And so, I missed my chance with one of the lords
> Of life.
> And I have something to expiate;
> A pettiness.
>
> (Muldoon, 1997, pp. 233, 235)

I hope you can see that 'Snake' is a different poetic proposition from 'Lizard'. Where the latter baldly asserts the superiority of lizards to men, 'Snake' dramatises the conflicted feelings the snake arouses in Lawrence. Instead of being a polemic, the poem records an event which transforms the speaker's perceptions and, by implication, offers to reshape the thinking of its readers. Although I've warned that we shouldn't be seduced by Lawrence, we do need to be prepared to go along with him in the sense of being prepared to follow through a train of thought with critical attention. In poems like 'Snake', Lawrence's empathetic descriptions of animals and his meticulous recording of his emotional responses to them enable us to do just that. 'Snake' is convincing because it shows that 'the voices of my accursed education' are extrinsic to the individual's delighted response to the animal, 'one of the lords/Of life'. Moreover, by showing that the individual allows himself to be dictated to by these voices, Lawrence enables us to feel the full force of his rejection of conventional ideas: 'I thought how paltry, how vulgar, what a mean act!' (Muldoon, 1997, p. 234).

So far, our reading of Lawrence has suggested that he was an outsider and a poetic dissident. I'm going to close this chapter by querying this argument. Although it's certainly true that Lawrence was an 'apostle' with an idiosyncratic agenda, is it the case that his work is wholly untraditional? As I noted at the start of this chapter, new forms of poetry, however radical they appear, almost always show traces of tradition. You'll also remember that Paul Muldoon wanted to represent 'the best animal poems in the English-speaking tradition'. Does Lawrence stand altogether outside of this?

Lawrence's essay 'Poetry of the present' (1918) helps to answer this question. It shows him defining his work in relation to tradition. He contrasts the poetry of the past with what he calls 'the poetry of the instant present': whereas the poetry of the past demanded formal perfection, the poetry of the present resists such restraints. While the 'treasured gem-like lyrics of Shelley and Keats' must be 'conveyed in exquisite form', current poetry 'can never submit to the same conditions. It is never finished.' (Lawrence, 1993, pp. 182, 184). We can get a sense of the contrast by reading Percy Bysshe Shelley's poem 'To a Sky-Lark' (Muldoon, 1997, pp. 256–9).

Activity

I'd like you to assess the difference between 'To a Sky-Lark' and 'Snake' (Muldoon, 1997, pp. 256–9 and 232–5). How would you differentiate these poems formally?

Discussion

'To a Sky-Lark' is a stanzaic poem with an ABABB rhyme scheme. Each stanza interweaves short lines of three main stresses and a predominantly trochaic beat (a stressed syllable followed by an unstressed syllable) with long, closing lines of six stresses and a predominantly iambic beat (the most widespread English metre, in which unstressed syllables precede stressed ones). Compare the short line '**With** some **pain** is **fraught**' with the next: 'Our **sweet**est **songs** are **those** that **tell** of **sadd**est **thought**' (Muldoon, 1997, p. 258). The poem's formal complexity is enhanced by Shelley's frequent juxtaposition of weak or di-syllabic rhymes in the A position with strong or single syllable rhymes in the B position.

In the following quotation, I've italicised the weak A rhymes and emboldened the strong B rhymes:

> We look before and *after*,
> And pine for what is **not** –
> Our sincerest *laughter*
> With some pain is **fraught**.

(Muldoon, 1997, p. 258)

Each stanza is an intricate unit of formal patterning which responds well to Lawrence's remarks about the 'exquisite form' of Shelley's lyrics. By now it should be fairly clear that the formal structure of Lawrence's 'Snake' is almost wholly dissimilar from that of Shelley's 'To a Sky-Lark'. In place of an 'exquisite form', 'Snake' has a deliberately unfinished or provisional feel which nevertheless has its own verbal majesty. The lines 'And flickered his tongue like a forked night on the air, so black,/Seeming to lick his lips' may lack the formal regularity of Shelley's stanzas, but its lingering alliterations in the repeated 'l' sounds show that Lawrence was every bit as aware of poetic technique as Shelley (Muldoon, 1997, p.234).

While at one level Lawrence is right to distinguish his work from Shelley's, 'Poetry of the Present' is by no means a wholesale rejection of these poets of the Romantic period. Indeed, 'Snake' directly alludes to the work of another Romantic poet, Samuel Taylor Coleridge, in the line ‘And I thought of the albatross’. Coleridge’s poem ‘The Rime of the Ancient Mariner’ tells the fantastic tale of a sailor who kills and is then haunted by an albatross (see Muldoon, 1997, pp. 214–16, and track 19 of the Audio CD). By alluding to Coleridge’s famous tale about the supernatural power of these birds, Lawrence implies that his snake has the same, or a similar, force.

Yet the distinction remains between the formal poetry of the past and the ‘unfinished’ poetry of the present: ‘in free verse we look for the insurgent naked throb of the instant moment’ (Lawrence, 1993, p. 185). But even though Lawrence conceptualises free verse in typically Lawrentian terms, his essay admits that this style of writing was not his own invention: ‘[Walt] Whitman’s is the best poetry of this kind’ (Lawrence, 1993, p. 183). In a later essay Lawrence is even more direct: ‘Whitman put us on the track years ago. Why has no one gone on from him?’ (Lawrence, 1998, p. 88). The implication is that it is Lawrence, rather than any of Whitman’s American compatriots, who has ‘gone on from him’.

Muldoon prints several poems by Whitman. I would recommend starting with the short ‘A Noiseless Patient Spider’ (Muldoon, 1997, p. 171), which neatly shows the stylistic similarities between Whitman and Lawrence. Compare the repetitions of Whitman’s ‘It launch’d forth filament, filament, filament, out of itself/Ever unreeling them, ever tirelessly speeding them’ with Lawrence’s ‘He lifted his head from his drinking, as cattle do,/And looked at me vaguely, as drinking cattle do’.

This suggests that I have overestimated Lawrence’s dissidence. Whitman’s free verse anticipates Lawrence’s method. And yet ‘A Noiseless Patient Spider’ can be seen as a wholly traditional anthropomorphic poem. The poet uses the spider’s patient construction of its web as an analogy for the condition of his own soul: ‘And you O my soul where you stand ... Ceaselessly musing, venturing, throwing, seeking the spheres to connect them’ (Muldoon, 1997, p. 171). Whitman, like Blake or even Aesop, looks at the spider as a metaphoric vehicle – a way of saying something about his own state of mind or character. It seems to me that a poem such as ‘Snake’ largely resists the lure of this kind of thinking. When Lawrence looks at the snake he doesn’t see a metaphor of himself. Rather, he sees ‘one of the lords/Of life’ (Muldoon, 1997, p. 235). And in the ‘undignified’ exchange between man and snake he constructs an indictment of humanity while asserting the individuality and dignity of the animal kingdom. Muldoon suggests that in looking at animals we ‘glimpse the possibility of what we might become’ (Muldoon, 1997, p. xvii). This certainly seems to have been the case for Lawrence.

REFERENCES

Auden, W.H. (1963) *The Dyer's Hand*, London, Faber and Faber.

Blake, W. (1985) *The Complete Poems*, ed. W.H. Stevenson and D. Bindman, Harlow, Longman.

Donne, J. (1985) *The Complete English Poems*, ed. C.A. Patrides, London, Dent.

Handford, S.A. (trans.) (1964) *Fables of Aesop*, Harmondsworth, Penguin.

La Fontaine, J. de (1995) *Selected Fables*, trans. C. Wood, Oxford, Oxford University Press.

Lawrence, D.H. (1993) *The Complete Poems*, ed. V. de Sola Pinto and F. Warren Roberts, Harmondsworth, Penguin.

Lawrence, D.H. (1998) *Selected Critical Writings*, ed. M. Herbert, Oxford, Oxford University Press.

MacNeice, L. (1938) *Modern Poetry: A Personal Essay*, Oxford, Oxford University Press.

MacNeice, L. (1987) *Selected Literary Criticism of Louis MacNeice*, ed. A. Heuser, Oxford, Clarendon.

McLaren, Colin, and Aberdeen University Library (trans.) (1995) *The Aberdeen Bestiary,* available at http://www.abdn.ac.uk/bestiary/intro.hti (accessed October 2007).

Muldoon, P. (ed.) (1986) *The Faber Book of Contemporary Irish Poetry*, London, Faber and Faber.

Muldoon, P. (ed.) (1997) *The Faber Book of Beasts*, London, Faber and Faber.

Opie, I. and Opie, P. (eds) (1951) *The Oxford Dictionary of Nursery Rhymes*, Oxford, Clarendon Press.

Worthern, J. (2005) *D.H. Lawrence: The Life of an Outsider*, London, Allen Lane.

FURTHER READING

Blake, W. (2001) *The Complete Illuminated Books*, ed. D. Bindman, London, Thames and Hudson.

Sagar, K. (ed.) (2003) *D.H. Lawrence's Paintings*, London, Chaucer Press.

RESOURCES

Reading 2.1 A second translation of Miroslav Holub's 'The Fly'

The Fly

She sat on the willow bark
watching
part of the battle of Crécy,
the shrieks,
the moans,
the wails,
the trampling and tumbling.

During the fourteenth charge
of the French cavalry
she mated
with a brown-eyed male fly
from Vadincourt.

She rubbed her legs together
sitting on a disemboweled horse
meditating
on the immortality of flies.

Relieved she alighted
on the blue tongue
of the Duke of Clervaux.

When silence settled
and the whisper of decay
softly circled the bodies

and just
a few arms and legs
twitched under the trees,

she began to lay her eggs
on the single eye
of Johann Uhr,
the Royal Armorer.

And so it came to pass –
she was eaten by a swift
fleeing
from the fires of Estrés.

Translated by Stuart Friebert and Dana Hábová

Source: Holub, Miroslav, 'The Fly' (trans. Stuart Friebert and Dana Hábová), available at http://www.pwf.pragonet.cz/1998/holub.htm (accessed October 2007).

Reading 2.2 A miniature anthology

For my choices, I've followed the alphabetical ordering of the anthology. These aren't my ten favourite poems, or even my ten favourites in the book; rather they're ten poems which I hadn't read before I got *The Faber Book of Beasts*.

1. James Wright, 'A Blessing' (pp. 38–9). This is a poem of hallucinatory beauty, in which the encounter between the speaker and the ponies seems to suggest a better way of living as the poem records a moment of ecstatic clarification: 'Suddenly I realize/That if I stepped out of my body I would break/Into blossom'. It's free verse, but completely different in tone and effect from that of Lawrence or Holub.
2. Sylvia Plath, 'Blue Moles (pp. 39–40). Where Wright's poem is almost sentimentally beautiful, Plath's is full of the violence of the lives of the dead moles described at the beginning of the poem. I like the quality of weird empathy with creatures apparently wholly unlike human beings: 'I enter the soft pelt of the mole./Light's death to them: they shrivel in it', though the last three lines suggest that there is a congruity between people and moles: 'What happens between us/Happens in darkness, vanishes/Easy, and often as each breath'.
3. Robert Burns, 'The Book-Worms' (p. 41). This is a neat demonstration of how effective and funny short poems can be, as Burns playfully views books as intellectual capital ('inspired leaves'), food for 'maggots' and as the status symbols of pretentious aristocrats who are only interested in the books' 'golden bindings'.
4. Yehuda Amichai, 'A Dog After Love' (p. 72). Another short, light-hearted poem, but with a sting in the tail: after the apparent tranquillity of the first stanza, the second transforms the dog into an unlikely agent of erotic revenge. Amichai's 'I found an old textbook of animals' (p. 126) is also well worth reading.
5. Louis MacNeice, 'Dogs in the Park' (p. 73). MacNeice is one of my favourite writers, but I'd overlooked this poem until I read it in this anthology. Like many of MacNeice's best poems, 'Dogs in the Park' manages to be simultaneously a poem which is eloquent about the everyday ('The precise yet furtive etiquette of dogs' is a marvellously exact description) yet which locates the everyday in the far past.
6. Jean de La Fontaine, 'The Grasshopper and the Ant' (p. 105). A superb translation of a classic piece of anthropomorphic writing: La Fontaine's Grasshopper and Ant are transparent portraits of a spendthrift and a miser. Wilbur's translation of the last couplet precisely captures the disdainful meanness of the French ant ('Vous chantiez? J'en suis fort aise./Et bien! dansez maintenant.')

7 Philip Larkin, ‘The Mower’ (p. 159). Though Larkin is often thought of as being a pessimistic poet, this poem touchingly records the death of a hedgehog and asserts a simple connection between human and animal in terms of mortality: ‘we should be kind/While there is still time’.
8 William Diaper, from Oppian’s *Halieuticks* (p. 189). I’d never heard of William Diaper (1685–1717) before reading this, but it’s a brilliant, beguiling piece of writing. Diaper translates an ancient Greek poem on sea creatures and how to catch them; this extract describes the mating habits of tortoises as a ‘State of War’, showing an empathetic response to the sexual reluctance of female tortoises: ‘They dread the Tryal, They conscious fly/ Joyless Caresses, and resolv’d deny’.
9 Norman MacCaig, ‘Toad’ (p. 264). ‘Toad’ shows the advantage of beginning with an arresting statement: ‘Stop looking like a purse’. Like ‘A Blessing’ and ‘The Mower’, this is a poem which uses an encounter with an animal as a way of registering a transformation within the speaker as the myth that toads have jewels in their heads illuminates the last stanza: ‘Toad,/you’ve put one in mine,/a tiny radiance in a dark place.’
10 Thom Gunn, ‘Yoko’ (pp. 287–8). This poem tells the story of a dog’s daily walk around New York from the perspective of the dog. As such, it’s a piece of poetic illusionism, as the poet imagines the emotional responses of the dog into words: ‘Joy, joy,/being outside with you, active, investigating it all,/with bowels emptied, feeling your approval’.

Read & Take Notes.

3 TRADITION AND DISSENT IN ENGLISH CHRISTIANITY

John Wolffe

INTRODUCTION 73

3.1 CATHOLIC AND PROTESTANT CHRISTIANITY 74

3.2 ANGLICAN TRADITION AND RELIGIOUS DISSENT 83

3.3 THE NINETEENTH CENTURY: EXPANDING DISSENT AND RENEWING TRADITION 88

CONCLUSION 96

REFERENCES 97

RESOURCES 99

Reading 3.1 99

Reading 3.2 100

Reading 3.3 102

Reading 3.4 104

MATERIALS YOU WILL NEED

- DVD ROM: St Chad's and Religious Art

AIMS

This chapter will enable you to:

- understand different ways of 'being religious'
- acquire a broad overview of the development of Christianity in England between the sixteenth and the nineteenth centuries, in particular examining the differences between Protestants and Catholics
- appreciate mutations in the interplay of tradition and dissent, as a previous generation's 'dissent' itself becomes 'tradition', and a previously dominant 'tradition' becomes 'dissent'.

INTRODUCTION

In Book 1, Chapter 7 you were introduced to the academic study of religion through an examination of the person of Tenzin Gyatso, the fourteenth Dalai Lama. You will recall Helen Waterhouse's initial working definition of religion as 'a system of practices, institutions and beliefs that provides meaning to life and death'. As the chapter proceeded you should have become aware that just as there are many answers to the question 'who is the Dalai Lama?', religion itself has many different meanings and associations. It can be both intensely personal and highly public and political. It can both sustain ancient tradition and engage purposefully with the contemporary world. It can be a basis both for peace and reconciliation and for violent confrontation.

What does it mean to be 'religious'? Think for a moment about your immediate reactions to this question. Do you think of yourself as a 'religious' person? If you do, what beliefs, activities and lifestyle issues follow from your sense of a 'religious' identity? If you would say, 'I'm not religious,' what do you mean by that? Is it that you never (or very rarely) go to any place of worship, except as a tourist or, say, to attend a concert? Is it that you reject all belief in a God, gods, or supernatural forces outside normal everyday human experience? Or is that you do not follow certain kinds of lifestyle – for example lifelong heterosexual marriage, or abstinence from certain foods or alcoholic drink – that you perceive to be required by particular 'religious' groups with which you are familiar? Perhaps, though, when you really think about it, you may not be sure whether you are 'religious' or not. You might think, 'I go through the motions, but I don't really believe it,' or, on the other hand, 'I never go to church, but I am a Christian,' implying that you hold Christian beliefs, and/or that you try to live your life according to Christian standards and teachings, although for whatever reasons you do not take part in organised 'religious' activities. You might say, 'I am a Muslim, but I do not pray five times a day,' implying that you identify with a particular religious group but are aware that you do not fully conform to its official standards. Or you might see yourself as 'religious' in your own way, holding certain supernatural beliefs and lifestyle commitments, but not identifying with any particular organised group or framework of doctrine.

The object of encouraging you to think on these lines at the beginning of this chapter is not to question the particular set of religious and/or non-religious beliefs and practices that you have, but to highlight how there are many different ways of being 'religious'. In order further to develop your thinking about the word, when you have an opportunity look at the entry for 'religion' in the online *Oxford English Dictionary*. There is no need to attempt to remember all the numerous definitions given there; rather, note how the word has, over the centuries, acquired a wide variety of nuances and shades of meaning. These include the very specific lifestyles of monks and nuns, reverence 'for a divine power', the following of 'a particular system of faith and worship', and the much more generalised 'devotion to some principle'.

In this chapter we shall be expanding that understanding by looking at the development of English Christianity over three of the most turbulent centuries in its history. In the process, too, you should gain an awareness of the development of the historically dominant religious tradition in England. (The discussion here is limited to England, because developments in Scotland, Ireland and – to a lesser extent – Wales were very different, and would be impossible to consider adequately without adding substantially to the length and complexity of this chapter.) At the same time we shall be exploring the theme of this book, tracing the interplay of tradition and dissent as older well-established ideas and practices were questioned and eventually superseded by new ones. These in their turn were later subjected to fresh challenges, both from innovators and from those who wanted to restate and reassert past traditions.

3.1 CATHOLIC AND PROTESTANT CHRISTIANITY

The historical label 'Reformation', used with reference to Europe in the era between the fifteenth and seventeenth centuries, signifies numerous complex movements and events, but in this chapter it signifies a period of intense debate and conflict about what it meant to be 'religious' or, more specifically, 'Christian'. In order to understand the issues that arose in this period it is necessary first to summarise the core teachings of Christianity.

The traditional Christian numbering of the years (AD = Anno Domini, the year of the Lord, and BC = Before Christ; secularised as CE = Common Era and BCE = Before Common Era) is based on an error of four years in the calculation of the probable date of Jesus' birth.

The central and defining Christian convictions are beliefs relating to Jesus of Nazareth, the Christ (4 BCE–29 CE). These can be outlined as follows:

- Jesus is both fully divine and fully human.
- Humankind is inherently sinful (the doctrine known as 'original sin'), signifying estrangement from God as well as moral wrongdoing.
- Jesus, the sinless Son of God, is the essential means of reconciliation between God and humankind.
- Jesus' teachings, recorded in the New Testament, have unique spiritual and moral authority.
- Following his death on the cross and subsequent miraculous resurrection, which overcame the power of sin and death, Jesus is still living in heaven.
- All who have true faith in Jesus have the prospect of forgiveness of sins in this world and eternal life in the world to come.
- After Jesus' life on earth, God sent the Holy Spirit to initiate and empower the church in its continuing witness to these central truths.

Mainstream Christianity thus teaches that God exists in three forms, or persons: the Father, who created the world; the Son, Jesus, who redeemed humankind; and the Holy Spirit, the continuing supernatural power in the life of the church.

This central core of belief has inevitably given rise to numerous questions and differences of interpretation that have divided Christians across the centuries. What does it really mean to say Jesus is/was both 'fully divine and fully human'? What do human beings actually have to do to secure the forgiveness and eternal life promised to them through Jesus? Do they need help from other supernatural beings (for example, saints and angels) or from the rituals of the church, or is individual commitment and trust in God sufficient to attain salvation? Is one's eternal fate, destined everlastingly for heaven or hell, irrevocably settled in this life, or is there still hope of changing one's destiny even after death? How do Christians best gain a true knowledge of Jesus' teachings – through the Bible which claims to record his exact original words, or through the church which claims the ongoing divine guidance of the Holy Spirit in interpreting him to each succeeding generation? In worship, is it better to follow tradition, maintaining the same rituals that have been carried on year after year, or should Christian practice be reshaped to reflect changing contexts or even the immediate personal convictions and experience of individual believers?

Questions like these lay at the heart of the conflicts that split the western Christian world during the Reformation. The dominant expression of western Christianity up to the sixteenth century emphasised the importance of tradition, and the authority of the church as the interpreter of Christian teaching. The observance of particular rituals and the reception of sacraments administered by the church were perceived as vital for personal salvation. Saints were venerated as intermediaries with God who would assist the prayers of the faithful and could work miracles of healing. After death even those ultimately destined for salvation were believed to pass into purgatory, a place of trial and cleansing. However it was thought that their sufferings there could be reduced by the prayers of the living and by 'indulgences' (a cut to one's appointed time in purgatory) granted by the church to the deceased in his or her life, as a reward for pious acts.

For a rich evocation of pre-Reformation Christianity turn now to Reading 3.1, an account of Long Melford Church in Suffolk written in the late sixteenth century by Roger Martyn (*c.*1527–1615), a local gentleman, who recalled how it was when he was a child in the 1530s. Martyn's language is very visual, so use it to try to imagine the scenes he describes. Studying Figures 3.1 and 3.2, which present two twentieth-century images of the church, will assist you in this task, but will also help to underline how much has changed. The exterior of the building (originally built in the fifteenth century), with the large Lady Chapel at the east end, is largely as it was when Martyn knew it, apart from the tower which was added in the early twentieth century, but the interior now looks much plainer and less decorated than it would have done in the early sixteenth century.

Figure 3.1 Holy Trinity Church, Long Melford, Suffolk, 1955. Unknown photographer. National Monuments Record, Swindon. Photo: © Crown Copyright. National Monuments Record.

Activity On the basis of this passage, how would you summarise Roger Martyn's conception of what it was to be 'religious'?

Discussion I would identify the following features:

- reverence for material objects, which helped him to visualise and understand Christian teaching, and which were hallowed by long association and presence in the church
- participation in rituals, processions and music highlighting the perceived presence of God in the consecrated bread and wine
- observance of an annual cycle, focused on numerous holy days
- a perception that religion was central to the life of the village community as a whole.

The religious world evoked by Martyn has been analysed in depth by a modern scholar, Eamon Duffy, in his book *The Stripping of the Altars: Traditional Religion in England* c.*1400*–c.*1580* (1992). Duffy uses the term 'traditional' rather than 'Catholic' in relation to pre-Reformation Christianity (the terms 'Catholicism' and 'Protestantism' as we use them today were initially defined by the conflicts of the sixteenth century). Duffy emphasises particularly the richness of the liturgical

Figure 3.2 Interior of Holy Trinity Church, Long Melford, Suffolk, 1955. Unknown photographer. National Monuments Record, Swindon. Photo: © Crown Copyright. National Monuments Record.

calendar that marked out the cycle of the year, and the centrality to worship of the Mass and the consecrated bread believed to become the actual body of Christ. Above all, he portrays late medieval religion as closely bound up with community life, both the actual community present in parish worship or in the brotherhood of trade guilds, and the spiritual communities affirmed by the veneration of saints and by prayers for the dead. Private devotions reinforced the communal ethos of traditional religion, for example, by being focused on artefacts used in public worship, while church buildings provided not only the location for collective observance, but also visual inspiration for the piety of individuals.

As Martyn's nostalgic tone indicates, the religious world he was describing was largely swept away from England during the middle decades of the sixteenth century. In contrast to Catholicism, Protestantism stressed that salvation depended primarily on personal faith rather than participation in the rituals of the church, that believers could legitimately draw direct spiritual inspiration from God rather than being dependent on a hierarchy of priests and bishops, and that ultimate authority lay in the original text of the Bible rather than in church traditions. The concept of purgatory was emphatically rejected: those who had manifested true faith in Christ during their lives went straight to heaven after death; those who had not were condemned to hell. Hence there was no purpose in indulgences or prayers for the dead. It followed, too, that church buildings had to be much plainer; the colourful rituals and images that Martyn loved were seen as distractions from essential spiritual realities and had to be suppressed.

In briefest outline, these changes took place in four phases:

1 **The break with Rome and moderate reform (1529–47).** King Henry VIII's initial conflict with the Papacy was not so much religious as personal and dynastic, because the Pope's refusal to annul his first marriage, to Catherine of Aragon, both prevented him from marrying Anne Boleyn and denied him the opportunity of fathering a male heir. Hence although King and Parliament renounced the authority of the Pope in 1533 and Henry subsequently dissolved (abolished) the monasteries, during his lifetime the English church continued to be essentially traditional in doctrine and religious practice. Protestant influence did grow, however, notably through the work of Thomas Cranmer (1489–1556), archbishop of Canterbury from 1533.

2 **The introduction of Protestantism (1547–53).** Henry's death in 1547 opened the way to much more radical religious change, led by the people who ruled in the name of his son, the boy-king Edward VI. Cranmer compiled a new and distinctively Protestant order of service, which was imposed in 1549 and revised in a more emphatically Protestant direction in 1552. Determined efforts were made to stamp out Catholic practices.

3 **The restoration of Catholicism (1553–58).** Before the reforms of Edward VI's reign could be fully implemented, the young king died. His half-sister Mary I established control, and sought to impose Catholicism. She faced determined opposition from the minority of convinced Protestants, some of whom (including Archbishop Cranmer) were burnt at the stake, while others went into exile. At the grass-roots, on the other hand, the return to older religious traditions was generally welcomed, or at least accepted.

4 **Stabilisation and the establishment of the Church of England (1558–1603).**
When Mary in her turn died she was succeeded by Elizabeth I, the child of Henry VIII and Anne Boleyn, a convinced Protestant but also a shrewd politician who wanted religion as far as possible to unite rather than divide her subjects. The Church of England's position was defined in clearly Protestant terms in the Act of Uniformity of 1559 (which enforced the use of the Protestant forms of worship contained in the Book of Common Prayer) and the Thirty-Nine Articles of 1563 (which specified the doctrine of the church), but it retained some traditional features, such as the hierarchy of bishops. During the ensuing decades the church was attacked from both sides, by a continuing Catholic minority who sought to depose Elizabeth and restore the 'old religion', and by radical Protestants, known as Puritans and separatists, who felt the settlement still did not go far enough.

Figure 3.3 Unknown artist, Edmund Grindal, archbishop of Canterbury, aged 61, 1580. Lambeth Palace Library, London. Photo: © Lambeth Palace Library.

Note how, in this rapid sequence of events, the meanings of 'tradition' and 'dissent' changed. At the outset Catholicism would be characterised as 'traditional' religion and Protestantism as 'dissent', but under Edward VI a determined attempt was made to eliminate former 'tradition' and turn former 'dissent' into standard belief and practice. Then under Mary the government had to recognise that although it might claim to be restoring 'tradition', it could not reverse all the changes of the previous twenty years, nor in fact did it necessarily want to do so. The 'tradition' that was revived was more that of 1547 than of the 1520s. Finally, under Elizabeth, the effective marginalisation of Catholicism meant that the dominant Church of England began to acquire something of the aura of 'tradition'.

In order to get a sense of how the experience of church-goers was changing as Protestantism became secure, turn now to Reading 3.2, and read the injunctions (orders) to churchwardens (the principal lay officers in the church responsible for the upkeep of the building and for making practical arrangements for public worship) in the north of England issued by an energetic reformer, Edmund Grindal, then archbishop of York, in 1571. This kind of document served to make the Protestant agenda fully explicit.

Activity Assuming Grindal's injunctions were implemented, how do you think a Protestant church would have differed from a Catholic one, as described by Martyn? What do these injunctions reveal about the progress of the Reformation by 1571?

Discussion Images, especially roods, were to be removed and destroyed and the books listed 'set up in some convenient place'; all the physical paraphernalia of Catholic worship were to be removed and replaced with a board displaying the Ten Commandments and 'a comely and decent table' for the celebration of Holy Communion; clergy were no longer to wear colourful vestments but merely 'a decent large surplice with sleeves'. The interior of churches became much plainer, and visual representations of Christian teaching gave way to written ones. Grindal also emphasised preaching rather than ritual in his instruction that there should be 'a convenient pulpit well placed'. (Look at Figure 3.4, an image of a surviving post-Reformation church interior in Grindal's own cathedral city, to see how implementation of such instructions meant that the pulpit became a very prominent feature.) In a nutshell, ritual and spectacle were replaced by restrained non-visual worship; Christian teaching was now to be communicated through the study of the biblical text, by participation in the prescribed language of the liturgy of the Book of Common Prayer, and, above all, by preaching.

The very fact that Grindal found it necessary to issue these injunctions implies that, after Elizabeth I had already been on the throne for more than a decade, Catholic practices were still much apparent at a parish level. Indeed the transition to Protestantism at the grass-roots was a slow and patchy one, which has led some scholars to conclude that we should see the Reformation as continuing well into the seventeenth century. It also seems probable that although Grindal himself had a sharp black-and-white sense the Catholic objects and practices he wanted to root out and of the Protestant ones he wanted to encourage, many contemporary laypeople and perhaps parish clergy were combining aspects of both in their religious practice.

Figure 3.4 Nave and box pews in Holy Trinity Church, Goodramgate,York, 1970. Unknown photographer. National Monuments Record, Swindon. Photo: © Crown Copyright. National Monuments Record. The central focus of worship in the late sixteenth century was the pulpit and the reading desk – the desk is shown here immediately below the pulpit on the right hand side of the church.

Before we move on, it is worth highlighting two wider implications. First, it is often necessary, as we did when looking at Grindal's injunctions, to distinguish between the ideas and convictions of religious leaders and the actual experience and beliefs of their nominal followers. Just as the recorded orders of a sixteenth-century archbishop of York could suggest that what was actually happening may have been close to the reverse of what he wanted, we should be wary of treating the pronouncements of other historical or contemporary religious leaders as evidence of generally held attitudes. Leaders may be upholders of tradition faced by rank-and-file dissent, but Grindal's case reminds us that the leaders may well themselves be the dissenters, challenging entrenched tradition. Indeed, at the end of his career, as

archbishop of Canterbury, Grindal found himself suspended from office because of his refusal to carry out Queen Elizabeth's instructions to suppress more radical Protestant tendencies that she thought politically dangerous. It is therefore important not to assume that tradition should automatically be equated with authority.

Second, the distinction between richly ritualistic and visual Catholic religious practice on the one hand, and austere word-based Protestant practice on the other, has its parallels in other religious traditions. For example, Hindu temples are normally filled with images of the gods and provide the centre-piece for processions and colourful rituals. By contrast, in Islam images are excluded from mosques in favour of Qu'ranic texts and Muslim worship is a simple combination of prayer and preaching. The purpose of these parallels is emphatically not to suggest that Catholics believe the same as Hindus, or that Protestant teaching resembles that of Muslims. Rather it is to draw attention to what scholars of religion call 'phenomenological' (external) similarities despite differences in belief and outlook. Such an understanding may well help to illuminate patterns of religiously motivated behaviour. Seen in isolation, the Protestant physical attack on religious images during the Reformation can look like wanton vandalism, destroying as it did much of the rich artistic heritage of the medieval church. If, though, it is considered alongside other examples of intense religious opposition to visual representations of the divine, not only by Muslims but also by the so-called iconoclasts (people who broke images) in the Greek Church of the eighth and ninth centuries, we can appreciate better the force and integrity of the recurrent conviction that mere human beings, whatever their artistic skill, can never adequately portray God.

In religion, as in other matters, something that appears to be disruptive and innovatory to one generation can be accepted by their children as rational and necessary change, by their grandchildren as the natural order of things, and by later generations as something hallowed by long tradition. As the last of those who (like Roger Martyn) could remember the pre-Reformation religious world passed away, the Church of England itself had acquired a past that began to lengthen into history. Its position was strengthened by the stereotyping of Catholicism as authoritarian, persecuting and antagonistic to England, a view stimulated by the widespread circulation of John Foxe's *Book of Martyrs*, first published in 1563, which celebrated the heroism of those who died when Queen Mary attempted to suppress Protestantism. Such attitudes were confirmed (as noted by Anita Pacheco in Book 1, Chapter 2) by the Pope's pronouncements against Elizabeth I, and by the attempted attack on England in 1588 by the Armada of Catholic Spain. These events were reflected in the anti-Catholic sentiments evident in Marlowe's *Doctor Faustus*. Feelings of this kind were further reinforced in the aftermath of the Gunpowder Plot of 1605, when Catholic conspirators attempted to assassinate

Elizabeth's successor, James I (James VI of Scotland), and the assembled Lords and Commons at the opening of Parliament. The conspiracy was thwarted on 5 November, making that day an enduring focus for the celebration of national Protestant identity, a tradition that has sustained itself even when the original ideological impetus behind it has been largely forgotten.

Nevertheless, as the Church of England became more secure it became less inclined to define itself negatively in relation to Roman Catholicism and, at the same time, developed a more positive sense of tradition and a distinctive identity – as reflected in the gradual emergence of the word 'Anglicanism'. A key early Anglican thinker was Richard Hooker (*c.*1554–1600), whose great work, *The Laws of Ecclesiastical Polity*, appeared between 1594 and 1597. Hooker and other writers presented Anglicanism as representing a middle way between Roman Catholicism and more radical Puritan or Calvinist developments of Protestantism. In particular Hooker argued that the Church of England, although reformed and Protestant, was still an authentic continuation of the pre-Reformation medieval church. (In Scotland, on the other hand, the church that emerged after the Reformation adopted a Presbyterian style of organisation (i.e. a church without bishops) and a Calvinist outlook. It therefore represented a more emphatic break with the past.)

3.2 ANGLICAN TRADITION AND RELIGIOUS DISSENT

Not only did religious 'tradition' come to be hotly contested during the Reformation, but such tensions continued in the ensuing centuries. The Church of England itself was now an inescapable point of reference, even though it remained controversial and sometimes unstable. In this section we shall first summarise religious developments between the early seventeenth and early eighteenth centuries, and then look rather more closely at the Evangelical/Methodist movement, which began in the 1730s and gave a significant new direction to the interplay of tradition and dissent. The following section will then take our survey further forward into the nineteenth century, focusing particularly on the revival of Catholicism in that period, a conscious attempt to bring back the 'traditional religion' that had held sway in England before the Reformation.

As in the previous section, it is helpful briefly to identify four successive phases of religious change during the seventeenth century, representing swings of the pendulum between Protestant and Catholic influences. As you read, be assured that it is not essential to remember everything that happened. Rather, you should focus on grasping the essential message that the relationship between religious tradition and dissent continued to be contested and fluctuating.

The four phases can be briefly summarised as follows:

1 **Recovering tradition (1625–42).**
During the early part of the reign of Charles I (who became king in 1625) the leaders of the church, especially William Laud (1573–1646), archbishop of Canterbury from 1633, tried to restore a more elaborate Catholic tradition of worship, expressing what was called 'the beauty of holiness'. They also sought to replace altars, which, as we have seen, Laud's predecessor Grindal had wanted removed from churches in the 1570s. These policies were actively supported by the king, but public hostility to them combined with wider political antagonisms to Charles's rule in giving rise to the civil war of the 1640s.

2 **The triumph of dissent (1642–60).**
Following the military triumph of Parliament over the king and the execution of Charles I in 1649, the temporary outcome was a recasting of the church in a much more Protestant direction, with the abolition of bishops and the banning of the Prayer Book. A variety of more radical Protestant groups flourished in the 1640s and 1650s. These included the Independents (later Congregationalists), who stressed the autonomy of individual congregations, and the Society of Friends (Quakers), founded by George Fox (1624–91), who emphasised the individual's personal experience of God and rejected formal church structures.

3 **Reasserting Anglicanism (1660–85).**
When Charles II (the son of Charles I) was restored to the throne in 1660, the pendulum swung back again: bishops were reinstated and in 1662 a modified version of the Book of Common Prayer was reimposed. About 2,000 clergy who refused to accept this settlement were ejected from their parishes, and for some years religious groups who refused to conform to the Church of England continued to be persecuted. These included Baptists (characterised by baptising adult believers, rather than infants) and Presbyterians as well as Independents and Quakers. Collectively these denominations came to be known as Dissenters. (Note how the word became capitalised to define groups that had now become institutionalised.) Given the confusion of recent decades, however, it was by no means clear whether these groups or the restored Church of England better represented the tradition of the English Reformation.

The 1662 Book of Common Prayer remains (in 2007) the official liturgy of the Church of England, although in practice it has been replaced in most churches by much more recent forms of worship. It is a revealing illustration of how religious tradition develops, that a text that was so controversial and divisive when it was imposed in 1662 appears to a later age to be a bastion of stability and continuity, and one which, according to the current Prince of

Wales, puts 'the essential values of resilience and balance' into English culture (Charles, Prince of Wales, 2006).

4 **Crisis and settlement (1685–1714).**
When Charles II died in 1685 he was succeeded by his brother James II (James VII of Scotland), who was a Roman Catholic. Hostility to James's rule and suspicion that he intended to restore Catholicism led to the revolution of 1688 when he was deposed and replaced by his Protestant daughter, Mary II, and her husband, William III. The religious consequence of these political events was the reaffirmation of the Protestant identity of the Church of England, and additional measures to suppress Roman Catholicism. On the other hand, the situation of Protestant Dissenters was made somewhat easier.

In general, the eighteenth century saw a marked reduction in the intensity of the religious conflicts that had characterised the preceding period. The legacy of earlier disputes remained, in the potential for different interpretations both of the identity and tradition of the Church of England and of its place in the wider fabric of English religion. Nevertheless the general trend was for organised religion to become more of an uncontentious feature of the social fabric and less of a force that destabilised and disrupted society by demanding total commitment from its adherents.

This environment, however, gave rise to a new wave of challenges to the dominant order in the Church of England, as embodied in the Evangelical or Methodist movement, whose most prominent early leaders were John Wesley (1703–91) and George Whitefield (1714–70). Evangelicalism became a wide and diffuse movement supported by many who remained in the Church of England and the older Dissenting churches, whereas Methodism developed an organised institutional structure and eventually became a distinct religious denomination. All Methodists were Evangelicals, but not all Evangelicals were Methodists. The Evangelicals highlighted particular Protestant teachings, especially the supreme authority of the Bible as a guide for the church and for individual believers, and the pivotal significance of Jesus' sacrificial death on the cross in bringing about reconciliation between God and humankind. They also emphasised the importance of individuals having a crisis moment of conversion to true Christian commitment, and were vigorously activist in spreading their teachings. Both Wesley and Whitefield were Anglican clergymen and their initial aspiration was to renew and reform the Church of England itself, rather than to create a new denomination. During the early 1730s both men were active in the so-called Holy Club at Oxford, continuing a tradition of earlier Anglican religious societies that sought to support their members in living spiritually disciplined lives. Both men experienced life-changing conversions, which they were convinced were personal encounters with God – Whitefield in 1735 and Wesley in 1738. As a result they committed the rest of their lives to zealous preaching, initially in churches, but then, when Anglican pulpits were increasingly closed to them, in the open air. Whitefield in particular was a compelling performer, a 'divine dramatist' (Stout, 1991), who drew large crowds to his sermons and endeavoured to communicate a basic framework of Christian teaching to unsophisticated audiences.

Figure 3.5 Robert Pranker after John Griffiths, *Enthusiasm Displayed*, depicting George Whitefield, leader of the Calvinistic Methodists, preaching under a tree in Old Street, London, 1750, engraving on paper, 21 cm. Print Room, Guildhall Library, London. Photo: © Guildhall Library.

In order to get more of a flavour of Evangelical teaching and its relationship to Anglican tradition, turn now to Reading 3.3, part of a sermon that Whitefield preached on Kennington Common, then on the southern outskirts of London, in the spring of 1739. (Note that if you would like to see what the original text of this sermon looked like, you can view it in *Eighteenth Century Collections Online*, accessible through the Open University Library.) In this excerpt Whitefield is expounding a passage from the Gospel of St John which describes Jesus' encounter with Nicodemus, a 'member of the Jewish ruling council' who had come to Jesus secretly and told him that he believed him to be 'a teacher who has come from God'. Whitefield focuses particularly on the subsequent exchange between the two, which, to assist you, I quote from a modern translation of the Bible (Whitefield himself quotes from the Authorized (King James) Version (1611)):

> In reply Jesus declared, 'I tell you the truth, unless a man is born again, he cannot see the kingdom of God.'
>
> 'How can a man be born when he is old?' Nicodemus asked. 'Surely he cannot enter a second time into his mother's womb to be born!'
>
> Jesus answered, 'I tell you the truth, unless a man is born of water and the Spirit, he cannot enter the kingdom of God ...'
>
> (John 3: 3–5, New International Version)

Jesus' concept of spiritual rebirth, reinforced by the symbolic washing in the water used in baptism, was taken up with great enthusiasm by the Evangelicals, who equated it with their concept of conversion. Note first Whitefield's summary of his teaching in the first paragraph: Jesus Christ was sinless in his earthly life, but all other human beings are inherently sinful and incur the wrath of God. God's justice, however, has been satisfied by Jesus' 'Death and Sufferings for our Sins'. But if his hearers are to escape Hell, they must experience conversion ('the New-Birth') and receive the (Holy) Spirit of Christ.

Activity Whitefield then turns to a spirited attack on the Anglican clergy of his day. Read carefully through the rest of the passage and summarise his objections to them. Do you think he considered himself a dissenter or a traditionalist?

Discussion Whitefield advances four main criticisms of the clergy.

First, many of them deny what he maintains is essential Christian doctrine, that in order to enter heaven one must experience a spiritual new birth in conversion, as well as baptism with water. In other words, Whitefield argues that true religion is a matter of inward conviction and experience, whereas he suggests his opponents see it as a matter of outward observance and ritual.

Second, their moral conduct is deficient. They frequent taverns, engage in dubious secular pastimes and are too interested in financial gain.

Third, they neglect their spiritual duties, failing to catechise (i.e. teach) children, to visit their parishioners, or to provide necessary moral and spiritual guidance.

Finally, their deficiencies and hypocrisies mean that Christianity appears a sham – although if they really lived by the standards they profess, it would flourish and transform the whole land.

Given this stringent attack on the religious leaders of his day, one's first reaction is to think that Whitefield saw himself as a dissenter. On a closer reading, however, it is evident that he saw himself as a true traditionalist, upholding what he believed to be the religious values of an earlier age ('They have quite forsaken the good old Way, and brought up a new one which their Fathers knew not'). It is unclear precisely what past period Whitefield is thinking of, but it is likely that he had an idealised view of the Reformation era in mind.

It is a common pattern in religious history for dissenters from what appears to be the dominant tradition in their own day to believe themselves to be the real traditionalists. Such groups are conscious of being in a minority. In the eighteenth century Methodism did not become a mass movement: even in 1770 membership of the branch of the movement led by John Wesley amounted to only 25,400 (Currie et al., 1977, p. 139). The same state of mind was present among the Protestant reformers of the sixteenth century, who saw themselves as restoring the 'purity' of an early Christianity distorted by the perceived corruption of the late medieval church.

In the context of the eighteenth century, the position of Whitefield, Wesley and their followers can also instructively be compared with that of the surviving Roman Catholic minority (known as recusants). They too were relatively few in number, estimated at just 60,000 in around 1700, when the total population of England and Wales was about 5.5 million, and increasing to 80,000 in 1770 (Bossy, 1975, pp. 189, 298). (In Ireland, by contrast, Roman Catholics continued to make up the majority of the population, but under the penal laws of the eighteenth century they were made politically and socially subordinate to Protestants.) Persecution subsided during the eighteenth century, but Catholics suffered from substantial legal disabilities, being unable to take any significant part in public life. The continuity of their religious life had been broken when the great medieval churches and cathedrals were appropriated by the Church of England. Their clergy were overseen by missionary 'vicars-apostolic' rather than by the traditional bishops of fixed geographical dioceses. This Catholic minority nevertheless saw itself as the guardian of the authentic tradition of true Christianity, although in many ways it came to appear to be just one more variety of dissent in a religious world dominated by the Church of England.

3.3 THE NINETEENTH CENTURY: EXPANDING DISSENT AND RENEWING TRADITION

The early nineteenth century was a period of substantial social and political stress in England. The population was growing very rapidly, at a rate that might now be associated with present-day developing countries – from 8.9 million at the first census in 1801, to 12 million in 1820 and 17.9 million in 1851. Moreover, people were becoming increasingly concentrated in towns: in 1801 London was the only city with more than 100,000 people, but by 1851 Birmingham had 233,000 inhabitants, Leeds 172,000, Liverpool 376,000 and Manchester 303,000 (Mitchell, 1962, p. 24). Such urban growth was associated with a fundamental shift in the balance of the economy from agriculture to industry, known as the Industrial Revolution. There was also substantial political unrest, stirred in part by the aftermath of the French Revolution in 1789, when the monarchy was overthrown and a radical republican regime held sway for some years. There were also the pressures of prolonged war with France between 1793 and 1815. Persistent demands for major constitutional change were partly, but not entirely, relieved by the so-called Great Reform Act of 1832, which gave more political influence to the middle classes.

As in other societies undergoing rapid and sometimes stressful change – for example the later Roman Empire and the Middle East in the later twentieth and early twenty-first centuries – this was a period of both innovation and reassertion of tradition in religious life. The most obvious innovation was the massive expansion of organised religious Dissent. Whereas in the eighteenth century the Church of England continued to be numerically dominant, in the first half of the nineteenth century its supremacy was steadily eroded. Its inherited organisational structures proved too inflexible to respond sufficiently to the expanding and shifting population. Broadly speaking, there were more than enough clergy and churches in the countryside, but too few in the new industrial towns. The gaps in provision provided openings for other denominations. The most dramatic growth was that of the Methodists, whose reported membership expanded from 55,705 in 1790 to 135,870 in 1810, to 285,530 in 1830 and to 489,286 in 1850 (Currie et al., 1977, pp. 139–41). While this last figure still amounted to only 2.7 per cent of the population, it must be borne in mind that many non-members also identified with the Methodists and attended their services. Meanwhile the Roman Catholic population, swelled by immigration from Ireland, increased nearly tenfold between 1770 and 1850, when it is estimated to have risen to about three-quarters of a million (Bossy, 1975, p. 298). When the first and only census of religious attendances was taken in 1851, the Church of England had the largest share of any single denomination, at 48.57 per cent, but the combined forces of Protestant Dissent amounted to 47.43 per cent. Roman Catholics accounted for most of the balance (Wolffe, 1994, p. 64).

Behind these statistics lay strong competition between different Christian groups. This environment heightened expressions of tradition and dissent: for some a sense of tradition, stability and continuity seemed essential; for others effective Christian witness seemed rather to require radical change to existing structures. Thus in 1833 John Keble, a prominent Anglican clergyman, could describe a moderate reform of the Church of Ireland as 'national apostasy'

Figure 3.6 St Peter's Parish Church, Leeds, West Yorkshire, *c.*1880. Photographed by G. Barnes. National Monuments Record, Swindon. Photo: © Crown Copyright. National Monuments Record.

(Keble, 1833), while in 1830 John Angell James, a Dissenter, wrote of the Church of England: 'Deeply must it be deplored by every friend of pure and undefiled religion, whatever be his denomination, that so much evil should be allowed to exist under the sanction of the Christian name' (Dale, 1861, pp. 183–4).

The Church of England was experiencing fresh internal tensions. The Oxford Movement (so called because many of its early leaders were associated with the University of Oxford) of the 1830s (in which Keble was a leading figure) sought to recover the more Catholic side of Anglican identity, emphasising the traditions and authority of the church and eventually seeking to restore more ritualistic forms of worship. Some of its members, notably John Henry Newman (1801–90), eventually converted to the Roman Catholic Church. Depending on one's point of view, the Oxford Movement can be characterised as either a reassertion of 'tradition' or as radical 'dissent'. In its own eyes, it was bringing the church back to its true tradition, but in the eyes of its critics it was unwelcome dissent from the moderate Protestant consensus that had dominated the church since the early eighteenth century. In particular, the movement was viewed with alarm and hostility by Evangelicals in the Church of England, who continued to assert a much more Protestant understanding of Anglican identity.

One very visual way in which religious tradition was asserted was in church buildings. For example, in 1841 Walter Hook, the vicar of Leeds, rebuilt his parish church on a grand scale in an imitation medieval style, as a conscious challenge to the Methodists who had a very strong presence in the town (see Figure 3.6). Conversely in York, a short distance from the massive Anglican cathedral (York Minster), the Methodists had in 1838 built a grandiose Centenary Chapel – commemorating the conversion of John Wesley a century before – which replaced their earlier much more modest building (see Figure 3.7). The classical style of the chapel's portico asserted a contrast to nearby Anglican medieval churches by appealing to an even older architectural tradition, just as the Methodists claimed that their worship and preaching restored the spiritual purity of early Christianity. York's Roman Catholics also asserted themselves in stone by building St Wilfrid's church (1864), which when viewed from the west appears to make a very direct visual challenge to York Minster (see Figure 3.8).

In order to illustrate rather more specifically the interaction of such rival religious traditions, take the case of Birmingham, in the late eighteenth century the third largest town in England (after London and Bristol) and described in 1791 as 'the first manufacturing town in the world' (quoted in Ward, 2005, p. 2). Despite its size and importance, however, Birmingham was remote from historic centres of Anglican authority, such as Lichfield and Worcester, and until the early eighteenth century it had been served by only one parish church, St Martin's. Between 1711 and 1719 this situation was rectified by the erection of St Philip's (now the Anglican cathedral), a grandiose baroque building described by the town's first historian as 'the pride of the place' (Hutton, 1835, p. 262). The Church of England further asserted its position in the town with the building of eight more new churches between 1749 and 1833. With two exceptions, all these churches were constructed in classical styles which in Birmingham, in contrast to York, became the characteristic architectural expression of the Church of England (Hutton, 1835, pp. 258–71). Meanwhile, other Christian traditions were also thriving in Birmingham. The Dissenters had had a place of worship there since 1672, although their Old Meeting House was twice destroyed by rioters, in 1715 and 1791 – an indication of the strong antagonisms that could be stirred by religious difference. A New Meeting House was erected in 1732, a Baptist chapel in 1738, an Independent (Congregational) one in 1748 and a Methodist one in 1782. Repeated enlargements and rebuildings of these structures reflected the expansion and growing confidence of their respective communities. There was also a flourishing Quaker

Figure 3.7 Centenary Methodist Chapel, St Saviourgate, York, 2007. Photographed by John Wolffe. Photo: © John Wolffe.

meeting house (Hutton, 1835, pp. 271–4). In 1849 John Angell James, who was a leading Congregationalist minister in the town, published a history of Protestant Nonconformity (Dissent) which left the reader in no doubt that it should be regarded as an entirely legitimate expression of Christian tradition and accorded a prominent role in society alongside the Church of England (James, 1849).

Figure 3.8 St Wilfrid's Roman Catholic Church (left) and York Minster (background right), 2007. Photographed by John Wolffe. Photo: © John Wolffe.

Birmingham was also a notable centre of Roman Catholic resurgence. A first, unpretentious chapel was built there in 1786, but this rapidly became too small to accommodate the Catholic population and a second chapel was opened in 1808. Numbers continued to grow and in 1838 Thomas Walsh, the vicar-apostolic (bishop) of the Midland District, commissioned the leading architect Augustus Welby Pugin to design a new, much larger church. Walsh and Pugin, however, were concerned not only to address the practical need to accommodate all the Catholics in the town, but to make a strong visual statement to symbolise the renewed Catholic presence in England. Thus St Chad's (see Figure 3.9), constructed between 1839 and 1841, was not merely a church but a cathedral, the first to be built in England since the Reformation, a spectacular addition to the Birmingham sky-line that contrasted dramatically with the unassuming Catholic chapels of earlier years. (You will learn more about this building, and about

Figure 3.9 St Chad's Cathedral, Birmingham, 2004. Unknown photographer. National Monuments Record, Swindon. Photo: © Crown Copyright. National Monuments Record.

Pugin himself, in the next chapter and in the accompanying DVD ROM.)

The Catholic revival reached a high point in 1850 when Pope Pius IX created, or restored (depending on one's point of view), a structure of territorial bishoprics in England and Wales. Since the Reformation, Catholics in England had been led by missionary bishops without fixed sees, but Walsh's successor, Bernard Ullathorne, now became bishop of Birmingham while eleven other bishops were also created, headed by Nicholas Wiseman who was created a cardinal and archbishop of Westminster. This measure, perceived by Protestants as an act of 'papal aggression' against England, was very controversial and provoked strong antagonisms between Protestants and Catholics. Protestants perceived the Catholic bishops as being in direct competition with the existing Anglican ones. They objected particularly to what the prime minister, Lord John Russell, called:

> a pretension of supremacy over the realm of England, and a claim to sole and undivided sway, which is inconsistent with the Queen's supremacy, with the rights of our bishops and clergy, and with the spiritual independence of the nation, as asserted even in Roman Catholic times.
>
> (Quoted in Norman, 1968, p. 160)

For the Catholic perspective, turn now to Reading 3.4, which is an eloquent mid-nineteenth century evocation of the decline and subsequent revival of a religious tradition. It comes from a sermon by John Henry Newman, the former Anglican clergyman and future Roman Catholic cardinal, preached at the first formal meeting of the Catholic bishops of England. Although feelings had calmed down somewhat by the time this sermon was preached in July 1852, Newman still felt the need to articulate vigorously his own understanding of the course of history. He used the analogy of the cycle of the seasons to describe the fortunes of Catholicism in England during the preceding three centuries.

Activity Read the passage now, and try to summarise in your own words how Newman saw the relationship between the medieval church and the Catholic Church of his own day. In what ways do you think a Protestant would disagree with his interpretation of English religious history?

Discussion Newman believed the medieval church had represented Catholicism in England, but it had died. A vulnerable minority of Roman Catholics remained, but they were too scattered to form a credible church. (Note that modern scholarship, such as that of Bossy (1975), suggests that Newman here exaggerated the weakness of pre-nineteenth-century Catholicism.) In his own day, however, he saw the church as reviving, in a surprising and, indeed, miraculous manner. It was not identical with the church of the past (for example old bishoprics such as Canterbury, York, Durham and Winchester had been replaced with new ones such as Nottingham, Beverley and Shrewsbury), but it represented the continuity and recovery of the same religious tradition.

A Protestant supporter of the Church of England would disagree with Newman's interpretation of what happened in the sixteenth century by arguing that the medieval church did not die, but was legitimately reformed to produce the Church of England. From this point of view it followed that the Roman Catholic remnant comprised not traditionalists but rather dissenters from the authentic tradition of English Christianity. Newman's claim that the 'second spring' was a revival of earlier English religious tradition would therefore be seen as spurious. Indeed, one of the key complaints of Protestants about nineteenth-century Catholicism was that its growth was a consequence of 'foreign' influence, from Irish immigrants, Italian popes and continental missionaries: it was an 'unEnglish' import.

Thus even three centuries after the Reformation interpretations of what had happened remained hotly contested, and the question of who were the traditionalists and who were the dissenters emerges as being quite as much a matter of opinion and perspective as one of objective fact. The future Conservative prime minister, Benjamin Disraeli, wrote this of the Church of England in 1861:

> Broadly and deeply planted in the land, mixed up with all our manners and customs, one of the main guarantees of our local government, and therefore one of the prime securities of our common liberties, the Church of England is part of our history, part of our life, part of England itself.
>
> (Disraeli, 1865, p. 18)

Such a vision might have seemed plausible in a small Anglican cathedral city such as Canterbury, Worcester or Durham, or in a rural village dominated by its parish church. It was much less credible in the burgeoning industrial towns where Protestant Nonconformity was usually quite as strong as the Church of England, or in places such as Birmingham where the Roman Catholic presence was also becoming very much apparent.

CONCLUSION

As you have worked through this chapter you should have begun to see that matters of tradition and dissent in religious history, which may have initially seemed quite straightforward, become much more complicated as we move through time. I hope you find this complexity stimulating. An essential feature of the academic discipline of Religious Studies is to stand back from positions of explicit commitment and to seek rather to understand why and how people come to believe (or not believe) and to practise religion in the ways that they do. In this task an understanding of the fluid dynamics of tradition and dissent plays a crucial part.

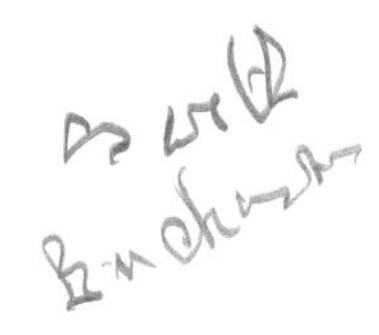

In this chapter we have focused particularly on England between the sixteenth and nineteenth centuries, but comparable issues arise in a wide variety of geographical and chronological contexts. For example, in nineteenth-century India, against the background of British imperial rule and western Christianity, both Hindus and Muslims redefined and reasserted their own traditions, but also at times seemed to be dissenting from accepted interpretations of their respective faiths. In the present-day world, it is a good starting point for an analysis of the numerous varieties of religious fundamentalism to see them as at one and the same time both movements of militant dissent from conventional secular and religious norms, and as assertions of their own deeply held convictions of what constitutes authentic tradition. Thus the appeal to the Qu'ran by contemporary radical Muslims has a good deal in common with the appeal to the Bible by sixteenth-century Protestant reformers and eighteenth-century Evangelicals.

Finally, think again about the question posed at the beginning of this chapter: 'What does it mean to be "religious"?' Before you read on, note down your own ideas on this in your electronic notebook.

As you reflect back on the material you have studied, you should be able to see a wide variety of answers to this question, including Roger Martyn's affectionate reverence for images, ritual and community life, Edmund Grindal's emphasis on the preaching and teaching of the word of God, George Whitefield's stress on personal experience of 'New-birth', and John Henry Newman's excitement at the revival of a seemingly moribund tradition that he believed represented 'the fair form of Truth'. It must, moreover, be emphasised that each of these texts merely expresses the perspective of one individual in a specific historic context, and that each in its different way reveals the ongoing debates and even conflicts about the nature of religion. For example, the Church of England clergy so bitterly criticised by Whitefield had their own contrasting perspective, advocating a religion that emphasised not individual spiritual experience but the good order and harmony of society. In studying religion, it is essential both to recognise and suspend one's own stereotypes, and to appreciate the diversity and integrity of the beliefs and practices of others.

Activity
You should allow about half an hour for this activity.

Now turn to the DVD ROM 'St Chad's and Religious Art'. You should work through the section 'Introducing sacred space' (you will study the rest of the DVD ROM at the end of Chapter 4).

REFERENCES

Bossy, J. (1975) *The English Catholic Community 1570–1850*, London, Darton, Longman & Todd.

Charles, Prince of Wales (2006) 'Charles tribute for Prayer Book', BBC News, 16 September 2006 <http://news.bbc.co.uk/go/pr/fr/-/1/hi/uk/5351250.stm> (Accessed 18 May 2007).

Currie, R., Gilbert, A. and Horsley, L. (1977) *Churches and Churchgoers: Patterns of Church Growth in the British Isles since 1700*, Oxford, Clarendon Press.

Dale, R.W. (1861) *The Life and Letters of John Angell James*, London, James Nisbet.

Disraeli, B. (1865) *'Church and Queen': Five Speeches Delivered by the Rt Hon B. Disraeli, MP 1860–1864*, London, G.J.Palmer.

Duffy, E. (1992) *The Stripping of the Altars: Traditional Religion in England c.1400–c.1580*, New Haven, CT and London, Yale University Press.

Hutton, W. (1835) *The History of Birmingham* (6th edn, with considerable additions by James Guest), Birmingham, James Guest.

James, J.A. (1849) *Protestant Nonconformity*, London, Hamilton Adams & Co.

Keble, J. (1833) *National Apostasy Considered*, London, J.H. Parker.

Mitchell, B.R. (1962) *Abstract of British Historical Statistics*, Cambridge, Cambridge University Press.

Norman, E.R. (1968) *Anti-Catholicism in Victorian England*, London, George Allen and Unwin.

Stout, H.S. (1991) *The Divine Dramatist: George Whitefield and the Rise of Modern Evangelicalism*, Grand Rapids, MI, Eerdmans.

Ward, R. (2005) *City-State and Nation: Birmingham's Political History* c.*1830–1940*, Chichester, Phillimore.

Wolffe, J. (1994) *God and Greater Britain: Religion and National Life in Britain and Ireland 1843–1945*, London, Routledge.

RESOURCES

Reading 3.1

Long Melford church before the Reformation

Roger Martyn (c.1527–1615) describes the church furnishings and annual round of services at Long Melford, Suffolk, as he recalled them from his youth before the Reformation.

At the back of the high altar, in the said church, there was a goodly mount [a carved and gilded sculpture behind the high altar, which depicted the death of Christ at Calvary, with bystanders], made of one great tree, and set up to the foot of the window there, carved very artificially [with great skill (artifice)], with the story of Christ's Passion, representing the horsemen with their speares, and the footmen, etc. as they used Christ on the Mount of Calvary, all being fair gilt, & lively and beautifully set forth. To cover and keep clean all the which, there were very fair painted boards, made to shut too, which were opened upon high and solemn feast dayes, which then was a very beautifull shew; which painted boards were there set up again in Queen Mary's time [1553–58]. And at the north end of the same altar, there was a goodly gilt tabernacle [a carved frame and canopy of stone or timber, used to contain and show off an image], reaching up to the roofe of the chancell, in the which there was one fair large gilt image of the Holy Trinity, being patron of the church, besides other fair images. The like tabernacle was at the south end.

There was also in my ile [aisle], called Jesus Ile, at the back of the altar, a table with a crucifix in it, with the two thieves hanging, on every side one, which is in my house decayed, and the same I hope my heires will repaire, and restore again, one day. And there was two fair gilt tabernacles, from the ground up to the roofe, with a fair image of Jesus, in the tabernacle at the north end of the altar, holding a round bawle [ball] or bowle in his hand, signifying, I think, that he containeth the whole round world. And, in the tabernacle at the south end, there was a fair image of our Blessed Lady [Mary, the mother of Jesus], having the afflicted body of her dear son, as he was taken down, off the Cross, lying along in her lapp, the tears, as it were, running down pittyfully upon her beautiful cheeks, as it seemed, bedewing the said sweet body of her son, and therefore named the image of our Lady of Pitty.

... There was a fair roodloft,with the rood [a screen in the middle of the church surmounted by a loft (roodloft) and a large cross (rood) depicting the crucifixion of Christ], Mary & John [the disciple who, according to tradition, stood with Mary at the foot of the cross], of every side one, with a fair pair of organs standing thereby; which loft extended all the bredth of the church, and on Good Friday a priest, there standing by the rood, sang The Passion. The side thereof, towards the body of the church, in 12 partitions in boards, was fair painted [with] the images of the 12 Apostles.

All the roof of the church was beautified with fair gilt stars.

...

Upon Palm-Sunday, the Blessed Sacrament [the consecrated bread or 'Host', believed to be the body of Christ] was carryed in procession about the church-yard, under a fair canopy, born by 4 yeomen; the procession coming to the church gate, went westward, and they with the Blessed Sacrament, went eastward; and when the procession came against the doore of Mr Clopton's Ile, they, with the Blessed Sacrament, and with a little bell & singing, appeared at the east end of Our Lady's Chappel, at which time a boy, with a thing in his hand, pointed to it, signifying a prophet, as I think, sang, standing upon the tyrret [turret] that is on the said Mr Clopton's Ile, doore, ECCE REX TUUS, VENIT [Latin: 'Behold your king comes'], etc.; and then all did kneel down, and then, rising up, went and met the Sacrament, and so then, went singing together, into the church, and coming near the porch, a boy, or one of the clerks [adult members of the choir], did cast over among the boys flowers, and singing cakes [perhaps a version of Holy Bread, blessed and distributed to the people by the priest after Mass], etc.

On Corpus Christi day, they went likewise with the Blessed Sacrament, in procession about the Church Green, in copes [ornamental symbolic over-garments worn by clergy during services]; and I think also, they went in procession on St Mark's day, about the said green, with handbells ringing before them, as they did about the bounds of the town, in Rogation Week [a time of special prayer for a good harvest, held in early summer], on the Munday, one way, on the Tuesday, another way, and on the Wednesday, another, praying for raine or fair weather, as the time required, having a drinking and a dinner there, upon Munday, being fasting day; and Tuesday, being a fish day, they had a breakfast with butter & cheese, etc. at the Parsonage, & a drinking at Mr Clopton's by Kentwell, at his manur of Lutons, near the pond in the park, where there was a little chapel, I think of St Ann, for that was their longest perambulacion. Upon Wednesday, being fasting day, they had a drinking at Melford Hall. All the quire dined there, 3 times in the year at the least, namely St Stephen's day, Midlent Sunday, & I think, upon Easter Munday.

Source: 'The State of Melford Church and Our Ladie's Chapel at the east end, as I did know it', adapted from D. Dymond and C. Paine (1992) *The Spoil of Melford Church* (2nd edn), Ipswich, Salient, pp. 1–9.

Reading 3.2 Archbishop Grindal enforces the Reformation, 1571

Extracts from instructions by Edmund Grindal (1519–83), then archbishop of York and later archbishop of Canterbury, give an idea of the Protestant agenda for the Church of England.

The Churchwardens in every Parish shall at the costs and charges of the Parish provide ... all things necessary and requisite for common Prayer and Administration of the Holy Sacraments, ... especially the Book of Common Prayer, ...the English Bible ..., the two tomes [volumes] of the Homilies [published sermons for reading by clergy who did not write their own], with the Homilies lately written against Rebellion, the table of the ten Commandments, a convenient Pulpit well placed, a comely and decent table, standing on a frame for the

Holy Communion, with a fair linen cloth to lay upon the same, and some covering of silk, buckram, or other such like, for the clean keeping thereof, a fair and comely Communion cup of silver, and a cover of silver for the same, which may serve also for the ministration of the Communion bread ...And shall also provide ... the Paraphrases of Erasmus [a highly influential early sixteenth-century scholar] in English upon the Gospels, and the same set up in some convenient place within their church or chapel ... all which books must be whole and not torn or imperfect in any wise [way]. And the Churchwardens also shall from time to time, at the charges of the Parish, provide bread and wine for the Communion ...

That the Churchwardens shall see that in their churches and chapels, all Altars be utterly taken down and clear removed even unto the foundation, and the place where they stood paved, and the wall whereunto they joined, whited over and made uniform with the rest, so no breach or rupture appear. And that the Altarstones be broken, defaced, and bestowed [given] to some common use. And that the Rood lofts be taken down, and altered so, that the upper boards and timber thereof both behind and above, where the Rood lately did hang, and also the ... loft be quite taken down unto the cross beam, ... and the said beam have some convenient crest put upon the same. And that all the boards, beams, and other stuff of the Rood lofts, be sold by the churchwardens to the use of the church, so as no part thereof be kept and reserved ...

That the Churchwardens and the Minister shall see, that antiphoners, mass books, grails, portesses, processionals, manuals, legendaries [a list of the various books used in traditional services], and all other books of late belonging to their church or chapel, which served for the superstitious Latin service, be utterly defaced, rent [torn up] and abolished. And that all vestments, albs, tunicles, stoles, phanons, pyxes, paxes, handbells, sacringbells, sensors, crismatories, crosses, candlesticks, holy water stocks or fats, images [a list of clothing and equipment used in traditional services], and all other relics and monuments of superstition and idolatry be utterly defaced, broken and destroyed ...

When any man or woman dwelling near to the church in any city, borough or great town, is ... passing out of this life, the Parish clerk or Sexton shall toll the bell to move the people to pray for the sick person. And after the time of the departing of any Christian body out of this life, the churchwardens shall see, that neither there be any more ringing, but one short peal before the burial, and another short peal after the burial without ringing of any handbells or other superfluous or superstitious ringing, either before or at the time of the burial or at any time after the same, nor any other form of service said or sung, or other ceremonies used at any burial, than are appointed by the Book of Common Prayer. And also that neither on All Saints Day [1 November] after Evening Prayer, nor the day next after, of late called All Souls Day, there be any ringing at all other than to common prayer, when the same shall happen to fall upon the Sunday. And that no month's minds or yearly commemorations of the dead, nor any other superstitious ceremonies be observed or used which tend to the maintenance either of prayer for the dead, or of the Popish Purgatory.

Source: Adapted from *Iniunctions giuen by the most reverende father in Christ, Edmonde ... Archbishop of Yorke,* London, 1571, from *Early English Books Online* (http://eebo.chadwick.com/home, accessible through the Open University Library).

Reading 3.3

George Whitefield's Evangelical preaching, 1739)

Preaching in the open air, George Whitefield (1714–70) expounds the characteristic emphases of the early Evangelical and Methodist movements.

Except a Man be born again, he cannot see the Kingdom of God.

(John 3: 3)

When Jesus Christ came down from Heaven, which was in the Fulness of Time, he came and dwelt upon Earth, and took up his Abode among the Sons of Men; he was like unto us, my Brethren, in all Things, Sin only excepted, and his constant Practice was, going up and down continually doing Good; he went about to do the Will of his Father; his Obedience otherwise would have been imperfect, and then his Satisfaction to the divine Majesty would have been so too, and then his Death and Sufferings for our Sins, would have been of no Signification; but, my dear Brethren, Christ so fully satisfied the Justice of his offended Father, that he will accept of the Sinner, how vile, how sinful, how heinous soever he be, so he does but come unto him, thro' the Lord Jesus Christ; come, and plead what Christ has done and suffered for you, and God will receive you thro' the Merits of his Son; therefore seek unto him, that ye may be born again; for if you are regenerated, if you do not experience the Pangs of the New-Birth, you cannot, indeed, my Brethren, you cannot be saved: You may flatter yourselves by imagining that you are in a safe State, if you do but lead civil honest moral Lives, but you are much mistaken, for you may not only be great Moralists, but have great Gifts from the Spirit of God, for if you were by the Spirit of God enabled to overcome the greatest Difficulty, to remove Mountains, to stop the Sun in its Course, what Service would this be to thee, if thou hadst not the Graces of it? It would, my Brethren, be of no more Service to thee than to hurry thee to Hell with the greatest Solemnity. You must have the Spirit in its sanctifying Influences, working upon your Souls; you must have the Spirit of Christ, or you are none of his.

And is it not amazing, my Brethren, that any one who call themselves Members of the Church of *England*, who are Teachers thereof, should deny this Doctrine of being born again? and indeed, my Brethren, too many of our Clergy do deny this Doctrine, tho' it is the very Words of Christ; for as it is said, *Verily, verily, I say unto you, except a Man be born again, he cannot enter into the Kingdom of Heaven*; and it is repeated twice or thrice in the same Chapter, and yet it is esteemed, by many of our learned Rabbies [Rabbis, the official Jewish religious teachers of Jesus' times, with whom Whitefield equates the Anglican clergy of his own day], as sufficiently done, and as compleated when you are baptiz'd in your Infancy; but, my Brethren, you must be baptized with the Spirit as well as with Water, or your Baptism will be of no Signification: And our learned Rabbies of this Age seem to me to be as ignorant of the true Nature and Effect thereof as *Nicodemus* was, when he came to Christ, and ask'd, how such Things could be; he could not think that being born a second Time was possible; *Can a Man*, says he, *enter again into his Mother's Womb, and be born?* And are not our learned Rabbies of this Day much the same? Do not they deny all inward Feelings, and inward Holiness? They do not in Words directly deny the Operation of the Spirit of God, but they say, they must not feel it; but this, my Brethren, is contrary to all Scripture and Experience, for as Peoples Consciences tell them when they are committing Evil, and running directly opposite to the Word of God, so, my dear Brethren, when the Spirit of God has been at Work upon any of our Souls, we must certainly feel its Operations thereon; for how can I tell I have receiv'd the Holy Ghost, if I cannot feel it?

'Tis true, the Clergy of this Age, these learned Rabbies, charge us with being over-righteous; but let them take Care lest they are not over-remiss; let them examine to find out the Beam in their own Eyes, before they offer to pull the Mote out of others Eyes; let them examine their own Lives before they condemn others for Enthusiasts: It is manifest that their Actions are unbecoming of Christians, and more especially are they unbecoming of Ministers of the Church of *England*. They make no Scruple of frequenting Taverns and publick Houses, they make no Conscience of playing several Hours at Billiards, Bowls, and other unlawful Games, which they esteem as innocent Diversions: Plurality of Livings [the holding of more than one parish by the same clergyman], and not the Salvation of your Souls, is the Aim, the chief Aim of many, very many of our present Clergy.

They have quite forsaken the good old Way, and brought up a new one which their Fathers knew not. They don't catechize, they don't visit from House to House, they don't watch over their Flock, by examining their Lives; they keep up no constant religious Conversation in Families under their Care: No, my Brethren, these Things are neglected, and if they were to be acted by any one, the Person would be esteemed as an Enthusiast, and one who was over-righteous.

But, for my Part, if I had a Parish, I would not, I dare not act in this Manner for the whole World; I would not have so many Souls under my Ministry, and I so unconcern'd for their Welfare, not for Ten Thousand Worlds; no, let the World say what they please, let Men despise me, let Devils rage, and his Agents breathe out Threatnings, yea, my Brethren, if they breath'd out Slaughter too, I would not regard them, I would visit that Flock that was committed to my Charge; I would, I say, visit them, and pray with them, I would advise them that wanted it, I would reprove, exhort and comfort them, and in all their Difficulties, I would beseech them to have Recourse unto Jesus Christ.

Source: *Jesus Christ the only way to salvation: A Sermon Preached on Kennington-Common by George Whitefield* (London, 1739), pp. 3–7 from *Eighteenth Century Collections Online* (http://www.gale.com/EighteenthCentury accessible through the Open University Library).

Reading 3.4

John Henry Newman celebrates the recovery of Catholicism, 1852

J.H. Newman (1801–90) preached this sermon on 13 July 1852 at St Mary's College, Oscott, at the first formal gathering of Cardinal Wiseman and the recently appointed Roman Catholic bishops of England.

> Arise, make haste, my love, my dove, my beautiful one, and come. For the winter is now past, the rain is over and gone. The flowers have appeared in our land.
>
> (Song of Songs, 2: 10–12)

We have familiar experience of the order, the constancy, the perpetual renovation of the material world which surrounds us. Frail and transitory as is every part of it, restless and migratory as are its elements, never-ceasing as are its changes, still it abides. It is bound together by a law of permanence, it is set up in unity; and, though it is ever dying, it is ever coming to life again. Dissolution does but give birth to fresh modes of organization, and one death is the parent of a thousand lives. Each hour, as it comes, is but a testimony, how fleeting, yet how secure, how certain, is the great whole. It is like an image on the waters, which is ever the same, though the waters ever flow. Change upon change, – yet one change cries out to another, like the alternate Seraphim, in praise and in glory of their Maker. The sun sinks to rise again; the day is swallowed up in the gloom of the night, to be born out of it, as fresh as if it had never been quenched. Spring passes into summer, and through summer and autumn into winter, only the more surely, by its own ultimate return, to triumph over that grave, towards which it resolutely hastened from its first hour. We mourn over the blossoms of May, because they are to wither; but we know, withal, that May is one day to have its revenge upon November, by the revolution of that solemn circle which never stops, – which teaches us in our height of hope, ever to be sober, and in our depth of desolation, never to despair. ...

The English Church was, and the English Church was not, and the English Church is once again. This the portent, worthy of a cry. It is the coming of a Second Spring; it is a restoration in the moral world, such as that which yearly takes place in the physical.

Three centuries ago, and the Catholic Church, that great creation of God's power, stood in this land in pride of place. It had the honours of near a thousand years upon it; it was enthroned in some twenty sees up and down the broad country; it was based in the will of a faithful people; it energized through ten thousand instruments of power and influence; and it was ennobled by a host of Saints and Martyrs. ... And then, too its religious orders, its monastic establishments, its universities, its wide relations all over Europe, its high prerogatives in the temporal state, its wealth, its dependencies, its popular honours, – where was there in the whole of Christendom a more glorious hierarchy? Mixed up with the civil institutions, with king and nobles, with the people, found in every village and in every town, – it seemed destined to stand, so long as England stood, and to outlast, it might be, England's greatness.

But it was the high decree of heaven, that the majesty of that presence should be blotted out. It is a long story, my Fathers and Brothers – you know it well. I need not go through it. The vivifying principle of truth, the shadow of St. Peter, the grace of the Redeemer, left it. That old Church in its day became a corpse (a marvellous, an awful change!); and then it did but corrupt the air which once it refreshed, and cumber the ground which once it beautified. So all seemed to be lost; and there was a struggle for a time, and then its priests were cast out or martyred. There were sacrileges innumerable. Its temples were profaned or destroyed; its revenues seized by covetous nobles, or squandered upon the ministers of a new faith. The presence of Catholicism was at length simply removed, – its grace disowned, – its power despised, – its name, except as a matter of history, at length almost unknown. It took a long time to do this thoroughly; much time, much thought, much labour, much expense; but at last it was done. Oh, that miserable day, centuries before we were born! What a martyrdom to live in it and see the fair form of Truth, moral and material, hacked piecemeal, and every limb and organ carried off, and burned in the fire, or cast into the deep! But at last the work was done. Truth was disposed of, and shovelled away, and there was a calm, a silence, a sort of peace; – and such was about the state of things when we were born into this weary world ...

[O]ne and all of us can bear witness to the fact of the utter contempt into which Catholicism had fallen by the time that we were born. You, alas, know it far better than I can know it; but it may not be out of place, if by one or two tokens, as by the strokes of a pencil, I bear witness to you from without, of what you can witness so much more truly from within. No longer, the Catholic Church in the country; nay, no longer I may say a Catholic community; – but a few adherents of the Old Religion, moving silently and sorrowfully about, as memorials of what had been. 'The Roman Catholics;' – not a sect, not even an interest, as men conceived of it, – not a body, however small, representative of the Great Communion abroad, – but a mere handful of individuals, who might be counted, like the pebbles and *detritus* of the great deluge, and who, forsooth, merely happened to retain a creed which, in its day indeed, was the profession of a Church. Here a set of poor Irishmen, coming and going at harvest time, or a colony of them lodged in a miserable quarter of the vast metropolis. There, perhaps an elderly person, seen walking in the streets, grave and solitary, and strange, though noble in bearing, and said to be of good family, and a 'Roman Catholic.' An old-fashioned house of gloomy appearance, closed in with high walls, with an iron gate, and yews, and the report attaching to it that 'Roman Catholics' lived there; but who they were, or what they did, or what was meant by calling them Roman Catholics, no one could tell; – though it had an unpleasant sound, and told of form and superstition. ....

What! those few scattered worshippers, the Roman Catholics, to form a Church! Shall the past be rolled back? Shall the grave open? Shall the Saxons live again to God? Shall the shepherds, watching their poor flocks by night, be visited by a multitude of the heavenly army, and hear how their Lord has been new-born in their own city? Yes; for grace can, where nature cannot. The world grows old, but the Church is ever young. She can, in any time, at her Lord's will, 'inherit the Gentiles, and inhabit the desolate cities.' 'Arise, Jerusalem, for thy light is come, and the glory of the Lord is risen upon thee. Behold, darkness shall cover the earth, and a mist the people; but the Lord shall arise upon thee, and His glory shall be seen upon thee. Lift up thine eyes round about, and see; all these are gathered together, they come to thee; thy sons shall come from afar, and thy daughters shall rise up at thy side.' 'Arise, make haste, my love, my dove, my beautiful one, and come. For the winter is now past, and the rain is over and gone. The flowers have appeared in our land ... the fig-tree hath put forth her green figs; the vines in flower yield their sweet smell. Arise, my love, my beautiful one, and come.'... A second temple rises on the ruins of the old. Canterbury has gone its way, and York is gone, and Durham is gone, and Winchester is gone. It was sore to part with them. We clung to the vision of past greatness, and would not believe it could come to nought; but the Church in England has died, and the Church lives again. Westminster and Nottingham, Beverley and Hexham, Northampton and Shrewsbury, if the world lasts, shall be names as musical to the ear, as stirring to the heart, as the glories we have lost; and Saints shall rise out of them if God so will, and Doctors once again shall give the law to Israel, and Preachers call to penance and to justice, as at the beginning.

Source: 'The Second Spring: a sermon delivered to the First Provincial Council of Westminster' from Newman's *Sermons Preached on Various Occasions* (1857), reproduced in the *Internet Modern History Sourcebook,* http://www.fordham.edu/halsall/mod/newman-secondspring.html

4 PUGIN AND THE REVIVAL OF THE GOTHIC TRADITION

Carol Richardson, Elizabeth McKellar and Kim Woods

INTRODUCTION 109

4.1 THE PALACE OF WESTMINSTER 111
- Rebuilding the Palace of Westminster 111
- The parts and the whole 114

4.2 PUGIN'S WRITINGS 119
- *Contrasts* 120
- *The True Principles of Pointed or Christian Architecture* 128

4.3 PUGIN AND THE FURNISHING OF CATHOLIC CHURCHES 132
- Chancel screens and rood lofts 135
- Images and altarpieces 138
- Reviving the past 141

CONCLUSION 141

REFERENCES 142

FURTHER READING 143

RESOURCES 144
- Reading 4.1 144
- Reading 4.2 146

MATERIALS YOU WILL NEED

- DVD ROM: St Chad's and Religious Art
- Illustration Book

AIMS

This chapter will:

- introduce you to the study of architecture through the work of the architect A.W.N. Pugin
- demonstrate how architectural traditions were reinterpreted in the nineteenth century
- explore the themes of tradition and dissent in relation to the imagery and design of English churches.

INTRODUCTION

In art history, dissent is often understood as radical defiance of an allegedly stultifying tradition or convention, leading to new and, for the time, daring styles. In this chapter we shall be exploring a very different sort of dissent: one which rejects current practices but, instead of devising something new, advocates a return to past traditions of a different kind.

Augustus Welby Northmore Pugin (1812–52) was a nineteenth-century architect and designer who rejected the classical style dominant during his lifetime. Rather, he turned for his inspiration to Gothic styles current in the period before the **Reformation**. However, his emulation of **Gothic architecture**, ecclesiastical furnishings and art was not just about the revival of an old artistic tradition. It was as much about finding a style that could epitomise the national, cultural and religious character of Britain. He argued that the return to the medieval traditions of Gothic architecture represented a return to a much better past. As you discovered at the end of the last chapter, continuity with the past was an essential concept in the re-establishment of the Roman Catholic church in England (and indeed in the other parts of the British Isles, although the details vary). For Pugin, who was a Catholic convert, Gothic architecture epitomised that continuity. The Gothic, he argued, was a Christian style indigenous to northern Europe, while the classical style was derived from ancient Greece and Rome and so it was pagan and alien to northern Europe. Pugin believed passionately that the new Roman Catholic churches built as a result of the Relief Act of 1791 should be designed and furnished in the Gothic style and used as churches had been before the Protestant Reformation.

After the Reformation in the sixteenth century, Roman Catholics were excluded from many aspects of British culture and society. In 1791 they were relieved (hence the term 'Relief Act') from many restrictions and were, for example, allowed to practise their religion, to become lawyers and to have their own schools.

Pugin was far from being the only enthusiast for the Gothic in nineteenth-century Britain, but throughout his prolific, if short, career and through his writings he perhaps did more than anyone to promote and defend its cause. At the same time, although he represented himself as a traditionalist, he was a highly innovative designer whose ideas had a profound effect on subsequent architecture and design.

Each of the three parts of this chapter looks at a different aspect of Pugin's career: his collaboration with Charles Barry to design the Palace of Westminster; his understanding of the Gothic and classical architectural styles; and his attitude towards furnishing his newly built Gothic churches. In this chapter you will explore a range of visual imagery, building on the skills you learned in Book 1, Chapter 3, on Cézanne. In addition, you will learn how primary source material in the form of letters and treatises may be examined in order to deepen our understanding of art and architecture. The DVD ROM material accompanying this and the previous chapter offers you the opportunity to explore one of Pugin's buildings in more depth: St Chad's Roman Catholic cathedral in Birmingham. You will also find footage of Lübeck in northern Germany, one of the many late medieval cities whose Gothic buildings and church furnishings Pugin visited. You should work through the DVD ROM at the end of this chapter.

An eccentric enthusiast for the Gothic, Pugin is one of the great characters in the history of architecture. He was introduced to art and architecture both in Britain and France by his father, a French artist, designer and writer, who had settled in England. At the age of only 15, Pugin designed Gothic furniture for Windsor Castle. Still principally a furniture designer, by 1829 he was working for the Edinburgh architect Gillespie Graham. From 1835 onwards he started to work with the architect Charles Barry. Pugin's career as a writer began in 1832, when he completed his late father's work *Examples of Gothic Architecture*, and in 1836 he went on to publish the first of several books of his own, *Contrasts* (see section 4.2), drawing on his profound experience of European Gothic art and architecture acquired through his extensive travels at home and abroad.

Pugin's work on the Palace of Westminster (in 1836–7, 1844 and 1852) established his reputation as an architect. The 1840s marked the height of his career, when he was recognised as an authority on church building, although he also designed schools, colleges, houses and stately homes. Most of his commissions came from Roman Catholic clients, following his conversion to that religion in 1835, but his outspoken views and uncompromising promotion of the Gothic style made him a controversial figure.

Pugin's writings extended his sphere of influence beyond those involved in the practice of architecture or design. His main publications were:

- *Contrasts: Or, a Parallel between the Noble Edifices of the Fourteenth and Fifteenth Centuries and Similar Buildings of the Present Day; Shewing the Present Decay of Taste* (1836; second edition 1841)
- *The True Principles of Pointed or Christian Architecture Set Forth* (1841)
- *An Apology for the Revival of Christian Architecture in England* (1843)
- *The Glossary of Ecclesiastical Ornament and Costume* (1844)
- *A Treatise on Chancel Screens and Rood Lofts* (1851).

Pugin's architectural career lasted less than 20 years: in 1852 he suffered a breakdown, apparently from overwork, and spent some time in the Bethlehem Hospital for the mentally ill before dying at his home in Ramsgate, Kent, that same year. However, the Pugin firm of architects continued until the early twentieth century under his sons

Edward Welby (1834–75), Cuthbert (1840–1928) and Peter Paul (1851–1904). Together, the Pugin architects were responsible for hundreds of new churches and other buildings in England, Wales, Scotland, Ireland, Belgium, France, the USA and Australia. You can find a list of some of them on the website of the Pugin Society (for details, see the course website).

4.1 THE PALACE OF WESTMINSTER

Carol Richardson

Sir Charles Barry (1795–1860), architect and draftsman, designed churches before moving on to design public buildings in the mid-1820s. He often worked for wealthy patrons. This enabled him to design large and ornate structures.

This section begins not with a church but with one of the largest secular buildings of them all: the Palace of Westminster, which comprises the two Houses of Parliament, the Lords and the Commons. Commissioned in 1836, the rebuilding of the palace took almost 30 years to complete. These same years coincide with the rise and fall of Pugin's grand vision. Pugin made his name on the project, working as assistant to Charles Barry, and he is generally credited with giving the building its very distinctive **Gothic Revival** character: the Clock Tower, for example, commonly known as 'Big Ben' after one of its bells, was designed by Pugin.

The rebuilding of the Palace of Westminster in the Gothic style was a major catalyst for the widespread acceptance of the style in Britain, the United States and Australia right up to the first decades of the twentieth century, but it all came about because of an accident. During the night of 16/17 October 1834 a fire almost completely destroyed the buildings that made up the old palace. Only isolated parts of the original palace survived the fire, at the extreme north and south of the sprawling complex of old buildings – Westminster Hall and its adjoining courtrooms, and the Crypt Chapel (see Figure 4.1). The artist J.M.W. Turner (1775–1851) witnessed the fire and made several paintings of the palace as it burned (Plate 2.4.1). In them he tried to capture both the actual blaze and the apocalyptic calamity that the terrible scene represented. One witness to the fire wrote in the *Gentleman's Magazine* that 'I felt as if a link would be burst asunder in my national existence' (quoted in Cannadine et al., 2000, p. 13).

English kings from Edward the Confessor to Henry VIII used the Palace of Westminster as a royal residence until 1529, when Henry VIII moved to York Place, which he had confiscated from Cardinal Wolsey and renamed Whitehall, but Westminster kept its role as the seat of government. Many people felt that the fire of 1834 offered a unique opportunity to re-create the Palace of Westminster as a distinctive symbol of British government.

Rebuilding the Palace of Westminster

A special committee was established in March 1835 to commission a new Palace of Westminster. An open competition was announced and

Figure 4.1 George F. Robson, *View of the Palace of Westminster from the River*, 1808, watercolour. Palace of Westminster WOA 1654. Photo: Palace of Westminster Collection.

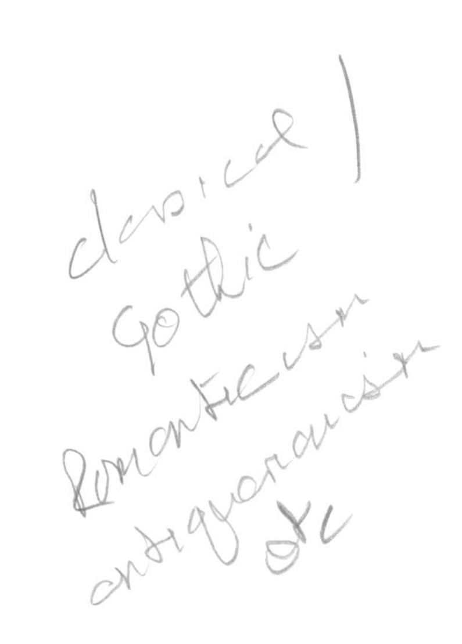

architects were invited to submit their designs. The plans had to be in either the Gothic or the Elizabethan style and to occupy a slightly larger site than the old palace, which was to be extended towards the River Thames by the addition of the Thames Embankment.

Why were the Gothic and Elizabethan styles thought appropriate? They were bold choices, as for almost two centuries **classical architecture** had been the dominant architectural style for official buildings, from town halls to churches – notably St Paul's cathedral in London. The choice of style was a controversial decision that soon had members of the architectural establishment, who were trained in the principles of classical architecture, up in arms. The classical style came with associations with the ancient Greeks, and thus with democratic ideals. But it had also come to be tainted by its connection with the French Revolution and the Napoleonic wars, and so with the overthrow of the French monarchy and the existing order.

The new Palace of Westminster had to represent the British establishment embodied by, at its top, the monarchy, followed by the

House of Lords and then the House of Commons. All three institutions had to be combined both symbolically and practically in the new design. Like the Scottish Parliament and Welsh Assembly buildings, which opened in 2004 and 2006, respectively, the style chosen for the new Palace of Westminster had to be able to communicate more than just the purpose of the building. It had to embody national identity, continuity with the past, stability, innovation and the promise of great things ahead. Although the designs of all these buildings refer to past traditions, none could really be called 'traditional', which shows the extent to which new 'traditions' are deliberately constructed from the old at specific junctures.

The choice of Gothic or Elizabethan styles was both pragmatic and symbolic. The buildings that survived the fire, and Westminster Abbey which stands next to them, were originally built in the Gothic style. At the same time, the Gothic and Elizabethan were believed to be uniquely British – unlike classical architecture. Charles Eastlake, whose history of the Gothic Revival was published in 1872, noted that 'Gothic or Elizabethan' actually left the choice of style for the building very open. He called the Gothic 'pointed architecture' because of its characteristic use of pointed arches, but remarked that it could be very simple, as in Early English examples from the twelfth century, or highly ornate, as in the flamboyant or **perpendicular** forms common in the fifteenth and sixteenth centuries (Eastlake, 1872, p. 169). The Elizabethan 'style' was similarly vague, describing no more than the architecture used during the reign of Elizabeth I. This was a period when great palaces, known as prodigy houses, were built by members of the royal court to impress the queen, like Hardwick Hall in Derbyshire (Plate 2.4.2). The Gothic was essentially an architecture of religious buildings. Buildings in the Elizabethan style were distinctly secular, a variation of the Gothic often combining tall and slender Gothic proportions with classical details (which Pugin hated) and large windows that flooded long galleries and halls with light.

Pugin was much more convinced of the significance of the Gothic rather than the Elizabethan or classical styles because, he argued, it was distinctly English (though this was not strictly correct). In 1835, just before he started working for Barry, he published a tract defending its use for the Palace of Westminster. In the following extract, note how Pugin emphasises continuity with the style of the remains of the old palace (Figures 4.1 and 4.2), excluding the classical, before going on to stress the advantages of using a style (Gothic) that, he argues, suits the native climate:

> their vicinity [the surviving buildings] should not be disgraced by another of those half-English, half-Pagan [classical] erections which have so woefully disfigured the architecture of the last century.... It has been discovered, that, in lieu of borrowing our

> architecture from foreign climes, we possess buildings whose character is much more suited to our country and climate.
>
> (Pugin, 1835, pp. 13–14)

Pugin's strong opinions about the significance of the Gothic style led him to publish *Contrasts* the following year. You will consider this publication in the next section.

There were 97 entries in the competition for the new Palace of Westminster and all but six of them were in the Gothic style. The committee agreed that most of the proposals, however, were either too much like an Elizabethan palace, or too much like a Gothic cathedral or monastery – that is, either too secular or too religious. Charles Barry's designs were presented in attractive drawings by Pugin, and in March 1836 Barry was announced as the winner of the competition (Plate 2.4.3). The second prize went to John Chessel Buckler, whose design was much more overtly Elizabethan, derived from the prodigy houses (Plate 2.4.4). All of the competition designs were exhibited at the National Gallery in April 1836. The adoption of the Gothic style for the Palace of Westminster gave it official recognition, which helped to encourage architects to consider it as a serious contender for their new buildings.

Barry was not known as an architect who worked in the Gothic style. Although he and Pugin managed to find a balance somewhere between palace and cathedral, as we shall see shortly, Barry would probably rather have worked in an Italian style using classical details. The style Barry proposed for the new building was Perpendicular Gothic from the Tudor period of the sixteenth and early seventeenth centuries, distinguished by rich details usually reserved for ecclesiastical buildings: **fan vaulting** and architectural, sculptural and painted decoration. In this way he combined Gothic (the style) and Elizabethan (the period).

The parts and the whole

Although it is not known for certain, it seems most likely that Barry was mainly responsible for the plan of the new Palace of Westminster, while it was Pugin who conceived the details (including Big Ben) which lend it its highly distinctive identity today.

In this section you are asked to consider how much you can learn about a building from its plan. A plan is a horizontal section through a building; that is to say, the 'footprint' of the building on the ground that that would be left if you took away all the walls and roofs and could look down on it from above. It is what architects use to establish how all the different rooms, corridors, staircases and courtyards relate to one another. The following activity asks you to think about both the kind of information you can get from a plan and, more specifically, the relationship between the old Palace of Westminster and Barry's new plans.

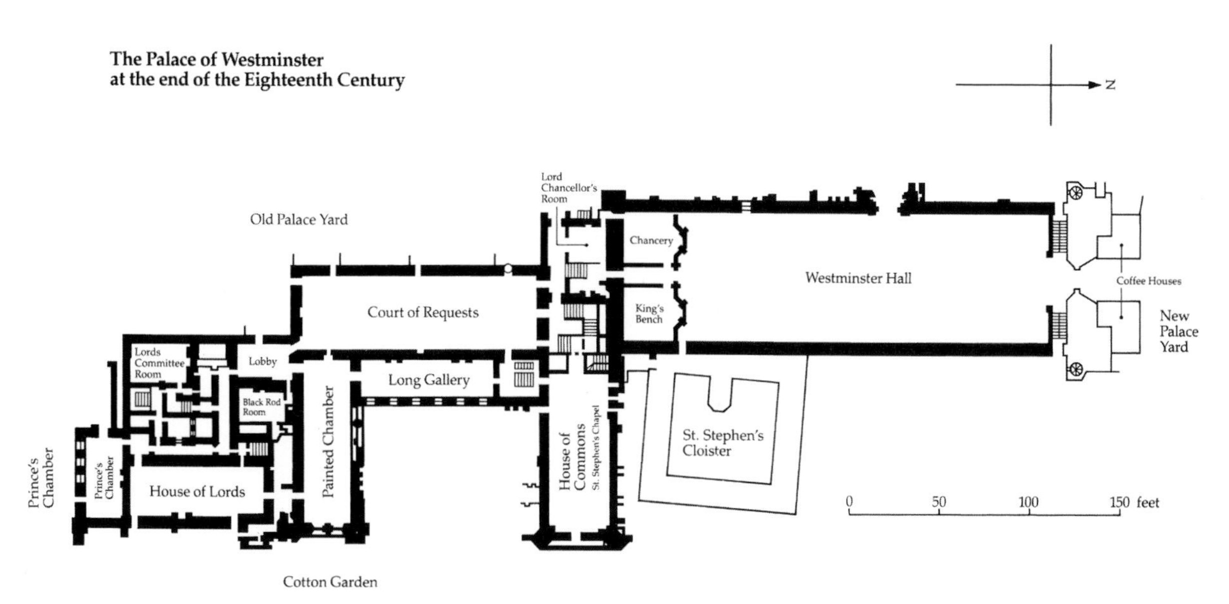

Figure 4.2 Plan of the Palace of Westminster at the end of the eighteenth century, from Fell and Mackenzie, 1994, pp. 90–1. Photo: © Crown copyright material reproduced with the permission of the Controller of HMSO and the Queen's Printer for Scotland.

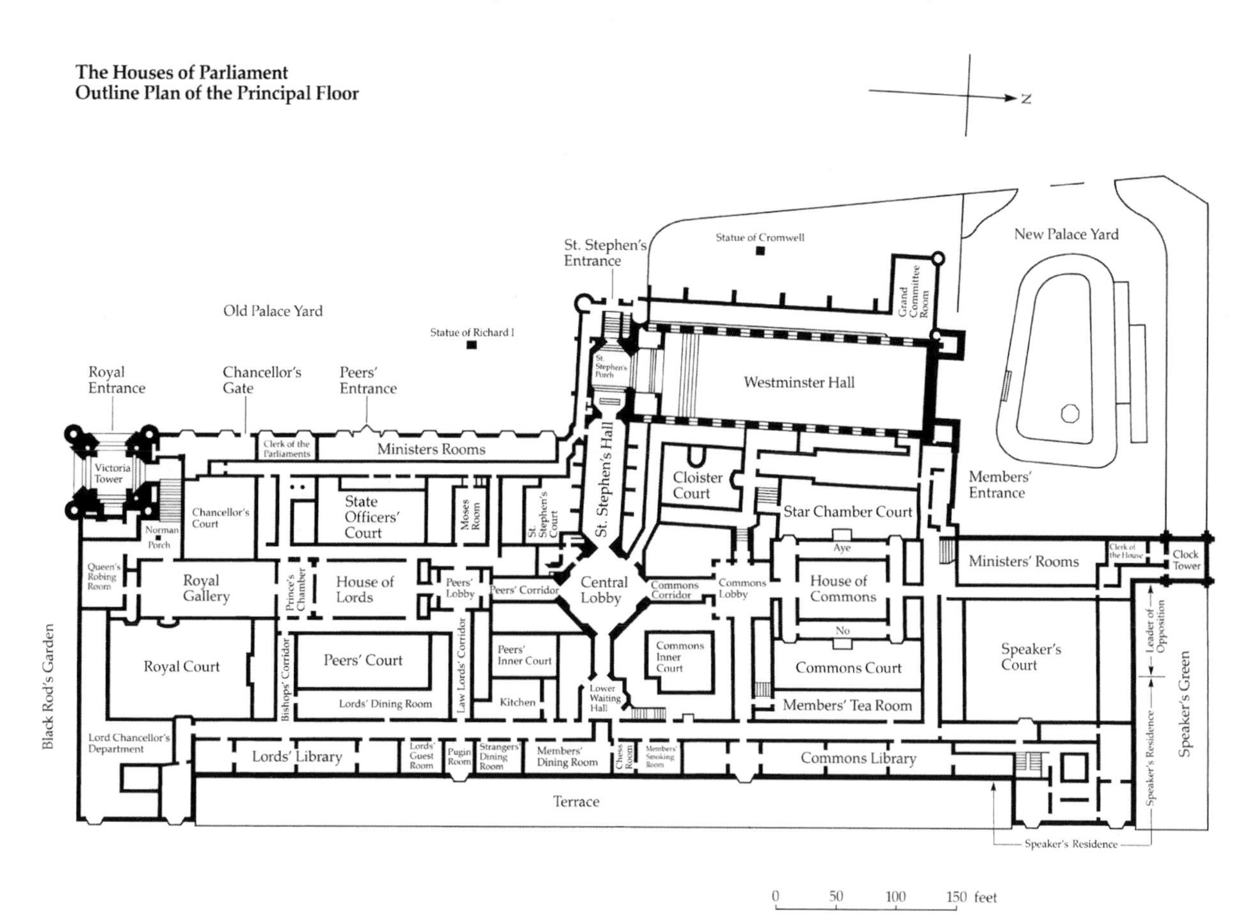

Figure 4.3 The Houses of Parliament: outline plan of the principal floor, from Fell and Mackenzie, 1994, pp. 88–9. Photo: © Crown copyright material reproduced with the permission of the Controller of HMSO and the Queen's Printer for Scotland.

Activity Compare Figures 4.2 and 4.3, the plans of the old Palace of Westminster and Barry's plans for the new palace. Make a list of the differences and similarities between the two. What do you notice about the overall shape and size of each of the buildings these plans represent and the way all the different parts are combined?

Discussion I hope you spotted the parts of the old palace that were integrated into the new. Westminster Hall was the largest building to survive, while the old House of Commons (St Stephen's Chapel) became St Stephen's Hall. You probably also noticed how much bigger the new plan is compared with the old one. The old palace is much more random and each of its quite separate halls and chambers would have been visible from the exterior, while the new one, although it has many more rooms and courtyards, is arranged around an octagonal court – the central lobby. This central lobby is the key to the plan, so that the different parts connect through it like the arms of a cross. Whereas to get from one part of the old palace to another you would probably have had to walk round the outside, the new palace is designed to be completely self-contained. Corridors, staircases, meeting rooms and dining rooms are all included, so that all of the functions of those attending Parliament are accommodated within a single enormous building.

To return to the vexed question of style, Pugin, although he worked closely with Barry, did not altogether approve of the way in which Barry applied his beloved Gothic. Pugin described Barry's designs as 'All Grecian, Sir: Tudor details on a classic body' (Ferrey, 1861, p. 248). What did Pugin mean by this?

Barry could not hide from Pugin the fact that the new Palace of Westminster may have been Gothic in style, but is essentially a classical building. The features that give this away most clearly are, first, the plan, and, second, the side of the building visible from the River Thames (see Figure 4.4). The symmetry of the plan centred on the central lobby means that the building can be divided roughly in half, the northernmost part accommodating the House of Commons and the southernmost the House of Lords. Such symmetry is distinctive of classicism. The view of the new palace from the river also communicates the strict control that makes the building such a success. Although it is a highly ornate building, covered inside in paintings and outside with sculptural decorations in the Gothic style, if you were to take this ornamentation away you would be left with a very regular row of vertical and horizontal lines – like the columns in a classical colonnade. See Book 1, chapter 4, section 4.5 for the classical Corinthian columns Faraday added to the Royal Institution.

But while Barry's building was based on strict control of plan and elevation, the overall character of the new Palace of Westminster was inspired by one of the most remarkable and eccentric buildings in

Britain in its day (which was also renowned for having collapsed shortly after it was built): Fonthill Abbey, designed by James Wyatt, begun in 1796 (see Plate 2.4.5). Like the Palace of Westminster, Fonthill was cruciform (cross-shaped) and centred on a massive octagonal hall which was topped with a soaring tower some 100 metres high. It offered a particularly useful precedent for the new Palace of Westminster because, as you may recall, many of the competing designs for that were deemed by the select committee to be either too secular or too religious in character. Inspired by both religious and secular buildings, Fonthill was compared either to a Gothic cathedral or abbey in terms of its size and design, or to a palace because of its purpose as an ostentatious residence.

At Fonthill the dramatic buildings that comprised a variety of shapes and heights were thought to have a particularly pleasing relationship with its surroundings, the hilly landscape of Wiltshire. Indeed, this was one of the measures of the picturesque, which was not so much an architectural style as a frame of mind shared by architects and garden and landscape designers. By the nineteenth century, designing a building or landscape on picturesque lines meant using features of a building in order to enhance its surroundings, or vice versa. Decoration, asymmetry and variety were all used so that a building could be viewed as a pleasing whole and the composition of its parts appreciated from a distance, like a painting.

Activity

Look at the view of the Palace of Westminster from the River Thames shown in Figure 4.4 and compare it with the view from Parliament Square seen in Figure 4.5. In Figure 4.4, can you identify any features of the palace which reflect or contrast with its natural setting? In Figure 4.5, how do the new buildings relate to the old ones that survived the fire?

What might this suggest to you about the ways in which the palace represents continuity with the past?

Discussion

Figure 4.4, the view of the Palace of Westminster from the Thames, presents a regular façade of vertical and horizontal elements. The long straight lines reflect the horizontal lines of the banks of the river. The only parts of the building that break this ponderous, repetitive façade are the huge towers at both ends, the Central Tower and the smaller turrets just visible in the centre which hint at the complex of buildings behind.

In Figure 4.5, the aerial view, the building (or buildings, as they more obviously are from this side) is much more varied. The palace is divided into two halves, with the left-hand (north) end incorporating most of the buildings that survived the fire, including Westminster Hall (the side of this hall is visible, sticking out alongside the newer parts of the building on the right). The spire over the central lobby (the Central Tower) is visible in the middle. It is a completely different height and of a completely different material from the various other towers and turrets. At the left-hand end is the Clock Tower (Big Ben), and at the opposite end the Victoria Tower. These towers are also on quite different scales and heights. Instead of trying to incorporate all these different parts into a coherent whole by hiding them behind a large screen

Figure 4.4 Palace of Westminster, river front. Photographed by Wolfgang Kaehler. Photo: © Wolfgang Kaehler/CORBIS. The palace frontage here is 265.7 metres long, and decorated with the coats of arms of the kings and queens of England and Britain from William the Conqueror to Victoria.

wall, as in the view from the river, the architect has made a feature of the different heights and degrees of decoration by adding towers and pinnacles which seem almost random. They are not really random but the whole look of the building is very carefully designed to give that effect. Both views could be called picturesque: that from the Thames because of the interaction of the building and the river; that from Parliament Square because of the interesting variations of size and height.

Overall, these regular and irregular features can be interpreted to give the building meaning. The potency of the consistent river façade represents the continuity, power and stability of government. From the other side, the mix of old and new represents the continuity with the past on which government relies for its authority.

It is not known for sure exactly which parts of the Palace of Westminster were Pugin's, although his sons later argued that he had been cheated of the recognition he deserved as he was paid a small proportion of what Barry earned for the job. Pugin died in 1852, before the towers and details that were probably his addition to Barry's more controlled plans were completed. His contribution to the designs for the interiors – from inkwells and tables to wall coverings – is less controversial. Today the interior of the House of Lords survives intact (unlike the plainer House of Commons, which was badly damaged in the Second World War). The effect is like a Gothic Aladdin's cave, from the royal throne and its canopy to the woodwork with its details picked out in gold, blue and red (Plate 2.4.6).

Figure 4.5 Palace of Westminster, aerial view from the north, 2003. Unknown photographer. Photo: London Aerial Photo Library.

The competition and the eventual building of the new Palace of Westminster represented a triumph for the revival of the Gothic style. Here the choice of Gothic rather than the prevailing classical style signified not so much dissent as the conscious use of architectural style to create an emblem of British identity, tradition and legislative authority. This represented continuity with the past, but an improved version of it. The public acclaim the buildings received meant that the Gothic style became a serious contender for most architectural projects during much of the rest of the nineteenth century.

4.2 PUGIN'S WRITINGS

Elizabeth McKellar

At the same time that Pugin was involved in designing the Palace of Westminster, he was also busy formulating architectural theories promoting a return to the Gothic style. In this section we'll look at the important ideas behind his built works through a study of two of his writings, *Contrasts* (1836; second edition 1841) and *True Principles* (1841).

Architects in the west have always used texts as a way to explain and promote their ideas. This is especially true of classicism, which has been written about since Roman times. Pugin took this existing tradition of architectural writing and subverted it by arguing that it was the Gothic rather than the classical which was the true European architectural heritage. He was well aware of the importance of the written word in publicising his ideas; as he wrote in a letter: 'Building without teaching and explaining is almost useless' (Pugin, letter to the *Tablet,* 15 March 1851; reprinted in Belcher, 1987, p. xii). Pugin's writings transformed attitudes to the medieval and helped spark off the mid-nineteenth century Gothic Revival in Britain. They were also highly influential on the subsequent **Arts and Crafts Movement** and the **Modern Movement**, both of which incorporated aspects of his theories. Let us begin by looking at some of these ideas in his first major book, *Contrasts*.

Contrasts

All quotations from Pugin in this section are taken from the second (1841) edition of his book, Contrasts.

When his work *Contrasts* first appeared Pugin had actually completed work on just one house, yet the book made him instantly famous because of its controversial opinions and combative style. It was intended to show that true architecture was Roman Catholic in form and that it had flourished during the Middle Ages. It was the Reformation and **Protestantism**, Pugin argued, that had brought about the decline of architecture. He wrote: 'Men must learn that the period hitherto called dark and ignorant far excelled our age in wisdom, that art ceased when it is said to have been revived, that superstition was piety and bigotry faith' (pp. 16–17).

Pugin illustrated the book himself with polemical and highly provocative plates, and our discussion here will largely concentrate on these. The two frontispieces with which the book opens set out the debate (see Figures 4.6–7).

Pugin's intention was to contrast the architecture of the fourteenth and fifteenth centuries with that of the nineteenth. You should not take this title too literally. During the early nineteenth century knowledge of medieval architecture was very limited and Pugin really intended his reference to earlier centuries to signify the Middle Ages in general. You should also be aware that he does not use the term 'Gothic' in the book, as we would today, but instead he calls it 'pointed' or 'Christian' architecture.

Have a look at the two frontispieces and think about how they compare. The Gothic work in Figure 4.6 is heavily shaded and drawn, emphasising the depth of the design, while the stiff, sketchy style used for the modern one in Figure 4.7 makes the buildings look mean and flat. The graphic style alone, therefore, is making a point about the superiority of what would have been a hand-produced medieval design as opposed to a cheap mass-produced modern alternative. The Gothic plate (Figure 4.6) looks like an **altarpiece** (an artwork forming a backdrop to the **altar**, the table used to celebrate **Holy Communion**).

Most crucially, it includes architects and religious figures within the frame. For example, Bishop William of Wykeham (d.1404), who appears in the centre top, was an important architectural patron of his time. By contrast, people are wholly absent from the drawings of the modern world.

Turning to the nineteenth-century plate (Figure 4.7), you might notice that Pugin calls it 'The new square style', in other words **neo-classicism**, the type of classicism then currently fashionable. The caption tells us that the buildings are taken 'from the works of various celebrated British architects', most of whom were still alive, including well-known figures such as Sir Robert Smirke (mentioned towards the bottom centre of the illustration) and Sir John Soane (referred to above the angels in the middle of the picture). The buildings that are shown are all real and demonstrate the undisputed reign of classicism as the national style up until the Palace of Westminster fire. For instance, William Wilkins's National Gallery (still under construction in 1836) appears across the top, while John Nash's All Souls church in Langham Place (1822–4), with its pointed spire, is on the far left of the upper-middle section. This was a deliberate assault on the existing architectural establishment, lampooning its works and offering a radical alternative. Pugin is setting up a premise here that the dominant classical style is in fact false and shallow and that it should be replaced by a return to the nation's oldest and truest form of architecture. He is therefore portraying the present-day neo-classicists as the real dissenters from the longer-established Gothic architectural tradition.

The church

As was pointed out in the introduction, Pugin converted to Roman Catholicism in 1835, just before *Contrasts* was written. And for him, the revival of Gothic architecture was not just a stylistic matter but a religious and moral one too. Gothic had been the dominant style when Britain was Roman Catholic and, he believed, it was to this style that the nation must return. This was essential if the country was ever to free itself from its current secularism and moral degeneracy, a degeneracy that he felt was fostered by the complacency of the **Anglican church** (the official Protestant church of England and Wales). Pugin's mission therefore was both architectural and spiritual, and the renewal of the church lay at the heart of his ambitions.

Let us have a look at how Pugin compares the modern and medieval church in Plate 2.4.7, 'Contrasted Royal Chapels'. We'll start with the nineteenth-century Chapel Royal, Brighton. It might strike you that this doesn't look much like a holy place. If we disregard the preacher and **pulpit** in the middle, there is nothing to indicate that this is a church at all. It could easily be a theatre, a hall or another such gathering place. By contrast, if we look at the medieval St George's Chapel, Windsor (Pugin calls it 'Winsor'), this probably represents

Figure 4.6 Frontispiece from Pugin, A.W.N. (1836) *Contrasts: Or, a Parallel between the Noble Edifices of the Fourteenth and Fifteenth Centuries and Similar Buildings of the Present Day; Shewing the Present Decay of Taste*, London, etching. British Library, London, 560*.d.32. Photo: © The British Library Board. All rights reserved.

many people's idea of a church. It is richly ornamented, there is an altar at the far end and the architecture dominates the setting.

Activity First, can you describe the differences in the relationship between the people and the architecture shown as contrasting images in Plate 2.4.7? Second, can you identify the central feature of each building?

Figure 4.7 Frontispiece 'Selections from the works of various celebrated British architects' from Pugin, A.W.N. (1836) *Contrasts: Or, a Parallel between the Noble Edifices of the Fourteenth and Fifteenth Centuries and Similar Buildings of the Present Day; Shewing the Present Decay of Taste*, London, etching. British Library, London, 560*. d.32. Photo: © The British Library Board. All rights reserved.

Discussion The most obvious difference is that in the nineteenth-century example (on the left of Plate 2.4.7) the people dominate the architecture, while in the medieval one (on the right of the same plate) it is the other way round. The relative importance of the congregation in each scene is partly created by

Pugin's exaggerated use of scale in both pictures. See how in the medieval one the gathering is drawn overly small, while in the modern one it appears overly large. In the Brighton chapel these people fill up the interior space. If we look at the Brighton congregation, the church seems to be arranged for people's display, so that they can admire each other, just as they might in a theatre at the time. In the medieval chapel, on the other hand, the people seem small and insignificant. They are relegated to particular zones within the building and there is an implication of hierarchy in the use of the space. Look at the tiers of seating at the sides and the way in which only a small number of people are visible in the central space or at the far end.

Could you find the central point in each case? In the Chapel Royal it is the pulpit where the preacher is standing. In St George's, Windsor you might feel the central point is much harder to identify because of the elaborate ornamentation everywhere, but the long, narrow shape of the chapel draws the eye to the end wall and the altar, the most important place in a Roman Catholic service.

With its fashionably dressed congregation and domestic-style decoration, particularly the swagged curtains and the fireplace, Pugin has deliberately made the nineteenth-century Chapel Royal in Brighton look like a secular space. He writes that the churches of his time have 'become but show-places for the people' (p. 41). He particularly detested the **box-pews** (enclosed bench seats), which he calls 'dozing pens' (p. 31). He disliked them because they were rented out and so represented the commercial exploitation of the church. The modern chapel's location in Brighton is also significant. It had strong links with the previous king, George IV, who had created the exuberant Brighton Pavilion. George was known for his loose morals and extravagant spending. Pugin doesn't actually name him in the text, but he writes in a very pointed way of monarchs 'whose lives are a mere routine of fashionable luxury, their greatest achievement a pony drive, their principal occupation – to dine!' (p. 43).

In these two images of chapels Pugin was also reflecting some of the fundamental differences in the Protestant and Roman Catholic churches' beliefs and practices. The Brighton chapel is an example of what was known as a 'preaching box'. In the Protestant tradition the emphasis is on hearing the preacher – hence the dominance of the pulpit and its placement in the middle of the interior. This is known as a **central plan** and is used in some Protestant churches. By contrast, in the Roman Catholic church the main emphasis is on the altar, which is placed at the far end of the building. The Roman Catholic church therefore generally uses a **longitudinal plan**, with the focal point at one end (see the **Latin cross plan** in Figure 4.8). In the Protestant tradition the preacher may be placed among the congregation, but in the Roman Catholic church the altar end, the **chancel** or **choir**, is reserved for the clergy and the main body of the building, the **nave**, for the people. Pugin was keen to reintroduce these hierarchies, as you can see in Reading 4.1, where he discusses the present state of the nation's medieval Gothic cathedrals.

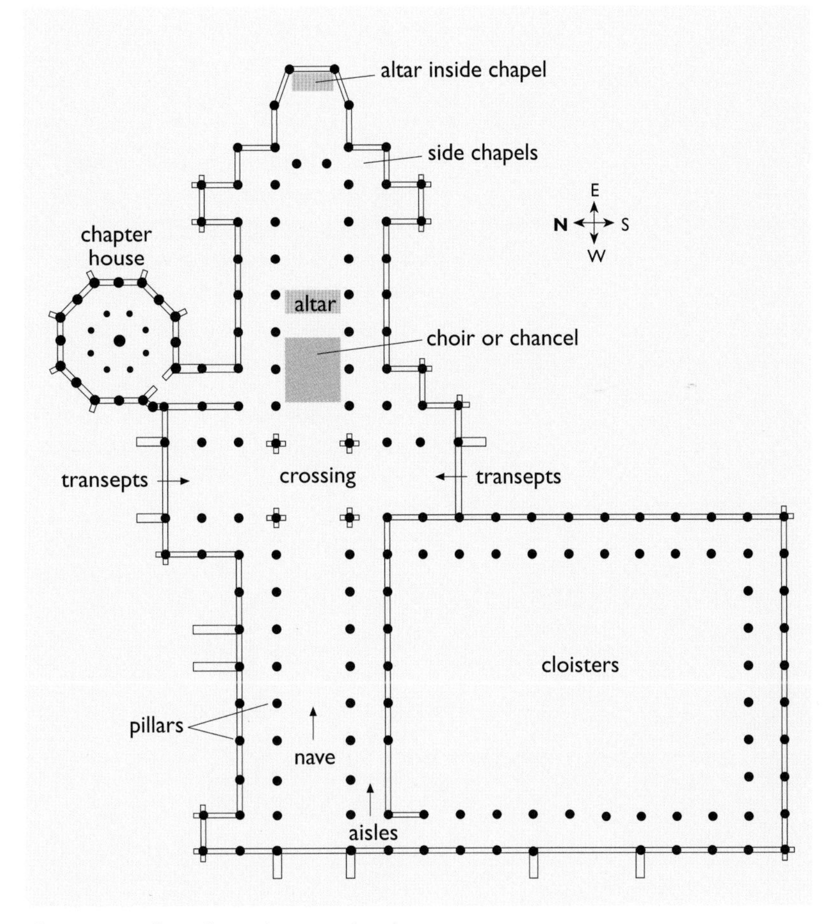

Figure 4.8 Plan of a Latin cross church.

Activity In no more than one paragraph, summarise Pugin's arguments in Reading 4.1, 'On the present degraded state of ecclesiastical buildings', about what he thought was wrong with the contemporary church and why he thought the medieval church was superior.

Discussion The main point to emphasise is the contrast between the position of the medieval church as the spiritual centre of society with the current situation of churches as tourist attractions and places for musical performance. Only on Sundays do they function as places of worship – and even then this is performed perfunctorily, 'by rote'. By moving away from its core function the church has become secularised and debased.

You may feel there are some interesting parallels between Pugin's ideas and twenty-first century debates – over the function of cathedrals, in particular.

Church building was particularly topical in the 1830s, for two reasons. First, legislation from the late eighteenth century onwards, culminating in the Catholic Emancipation Act of 1829, had opened up the possibility of building new Roman Catholic churches in Britain for the first time since the Reformation. This was naturally a matter of great interest to Pugin. Second, Anglicans had been equally exercised by the issue of building new churches, following the Church Building Act of 1818. This act was passed to allow for the building of churches in the suburbs of London in celebration of the British victory against Napoleon's forces at the battle of Waterloo in 1815 and led to an intensive building programme, with nearly 30 new churches completed by 1825. They were built in both the Gothic and the classical styles. In Plate 2.4.8 you can see examples of both a classical church of the period (All Souls, Langham Place, which also featured in Figure 4.7), and a Gothic one (Redcliffe church, Bristol). In Plate 2.4.9, however, Pugin presented a contrast between a contemporary Gothic-style church and a medieval one.

Pugin detested the type of pseudo-modern Gothic illustrated here (and in Plate 2.4.13) almost as much as he disliked the classical example shown. Look at Reading 4.2, where Pugin vents his disgust at the 'Commissioners' churches', so-called because the million pounds voted for by Parliament for their erection was distributed by a commission. He writes that even the building of churches has 'dwindled down into a mere trade'. He rails against their lack of architectural ambition or direction: in his view a symptom of the low esteem in which the church is held in a materialist society. The Commissioners', or Waterloo, churches are also Pugin's target in Plate 2.4.10, an illustration 'advertising' a 'New church open competition' which, echoing the Palace of Westminster competition, could be either Gothic or Elizabethan in style. The billboards in Plate 2.4.10 make mention of a great variety of styles. How many can you count? There must be at least 12, and possibly as many as 15 if you include Pugin's made-up terms, such as the 'plain style'. Here Pugin is satirising the stylistic confusion of his time. He is also attacking 'The Trade', to whom the plate is dedicated 'without permission'. The plate is set out as a series of advertisements and so is a comment on the commercialisation of architecture which he also attacks in Reading 4.2.

Architecture and society

This linking of the architectural and the social was one of the most important and radical themes in *Contrasts*. Pugin introduced the idea that there was a direct relationship between society, its values and its artefacts. This can be seen most clearly in two plates which were added to the 1841 edition of his work: 'Contrasted towns' and 'Contrasted residences for the poor' (Plates 2.4.11–12).

Activity Have a look at Plates 2.4.11 and 2.4.12. How does Pugin present his comparisons here? It is worth looking at the page layout of the 'Contrasted towns', which were originally illustrated together on the same page as you have them here. You can see that the Roman Catholic town is given more than half the page. What impact does this have? You should also consider the building types in the two pictures, as well as their style and arrangement in the town.

You might think about how the 'Contrasted residences for the poor' relates to Pugin's idea that society declined after the Reformation, particularly with the dissolution (closing down) of the monasteries in the 1530s, during the reign of Henry VIII. It may also be helpful to know that the 'Modern poor house' arose as a result of the Poor Law of 1834 which abolished any assistance to the poor outside the confines of the workhouse.

Discussion

Let us begin with the page layout for the 'Contrasted towns'. Did you notice that by giving the 1440 town more space the page design emphasises the spires of the churches and their verticality? – soaring up to heaven, one might say. In comparison, the 1840 town seems cramped and predominantly horizontal, nearer to the earth than to God. The modern skyline is dominated by the chimneys of the factories depicted. In other words, the pursuit of commerce has replaced the pursuit of religion.

Which new building types could you find in the illustration of the modern town in Plate 2.4.11? Warehouses (which you can clearly see, although they are not specifically mentioned in Pugin's key), gas and iron works, a hospital for mentally ill people ('lunatic asylum') and a gaol were on my list. This provides a great contrast with the Roman Catholic town, where the churches are the most noticeable buildings. Did you see what has happened to the original churches by 1840? The one in the foreground has been rebuilt and has a clashing, classical parsonage erected next to it, while others lie derelict or with their spires broken. You might also have seen how the boundaries of the town are clearly defined in the Middle Ages by the city walls and gateways. The modern city has obliterated and spilt over these divisions, so that it now sprawls into the surrounding countryside. Pugin's argument here seems to be that the physical and social unity of the medieval city has been replaced by the chaos and disorder of its modern counterpart.

Now turn to the 'Contrasted residences for the poor' (Plate 2.4.12). The medieval illustration at the bottom depicts a system of charity dispensed by the church in which the poor are well looked after. However, the 'Modern poor house' at the top is based on punishment and a harsh regime. Indeed Pugin suggests that, far from being Christian, the workhouse inflicts the final indignity on its victims by selling its dead for dissection rather than giving them a proper burial.

You may have noticed that the gaol (labelled as no. 3) in the upper part of Plate 2.4.11 is built to the same pattern as the poor house in the upper part of Plate 2.4.12. This design was the idea of the political philosopher Jeremy Bentham (1748–1832) and was used for some mid-nineteenth century gaols such as Pentonville and Holloway prisons in London. It was called a panopticon, which means 'all-seeing', because it included a central control hub from which radiated spokes housing the cells. The guards therefore sat in the centre, able to observe the inmates' activities from every direction. Bentham was the founder of utilitarianism, a secular philosophy which holds that public policy should be decided by calculating what will promote the greatest amount of happiness among the greatest number of people. This philosophy ran counter to the hierarchical society which Pugin favoured, which was based on traditional values and social relationships.

The True Principles of Pointed or Christian Architecture

All quotations from Pugin in this section are taken from his book, True Principles.

In his book *True Principles* Pugin continued with his mission to prove that Gothic was the only true Christian architecture. He argued that this was because classical architecture is derived from the pagan temples of the druids and the Greeks, as you can see in Figure 4.9. This is what is known as **trabeated architecture**, based on combining vertical and horizontal blocks. The figure shows how, in contrast with pagan representations, the Gothic uses the pointed arch to demonstrate a reaching up to heaven and the symbolising of Christ's **resurrection**.

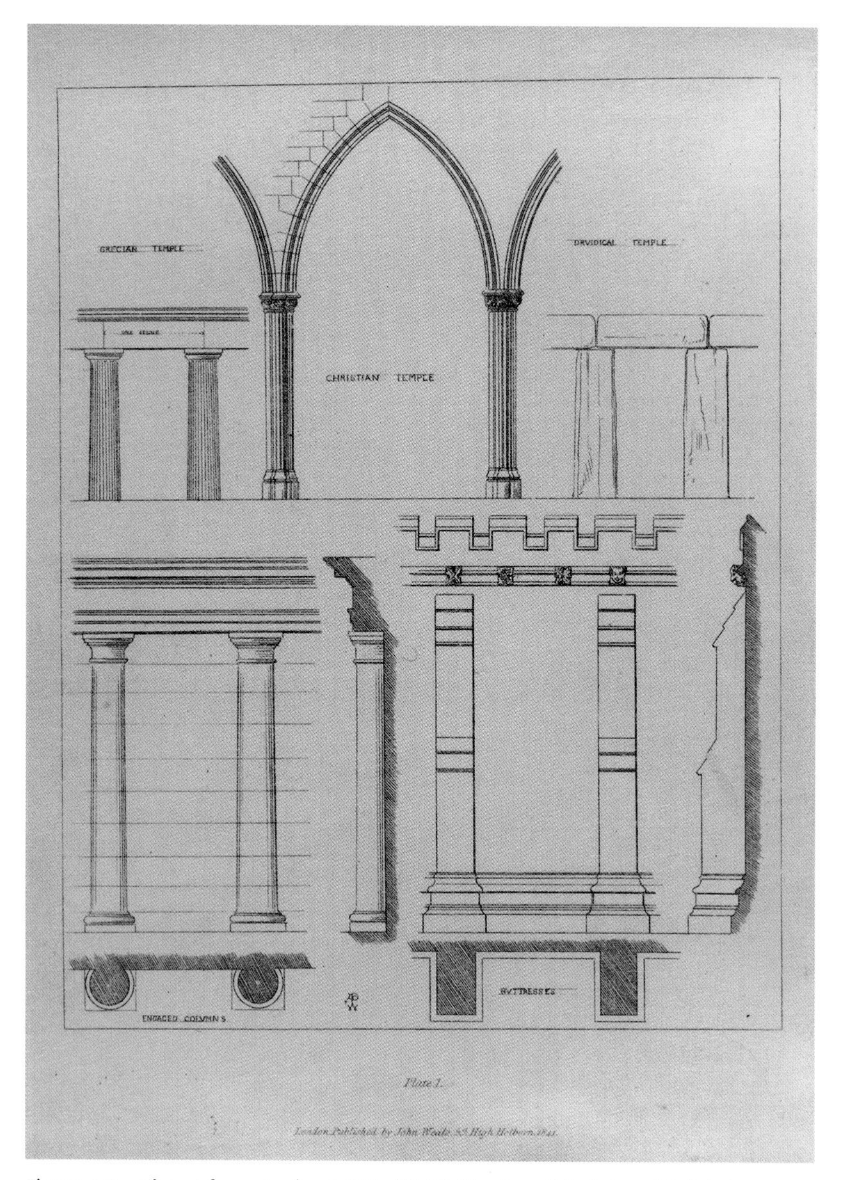

Figure 4.9 Plate I from Pugin, A.W.N. (1841) *The True Principles of Pointed or Christian Architecture*, London, John Weale, steel engraving. British Library, London, 786.k.29. Photo: © The British Library Board. All rights reserved.

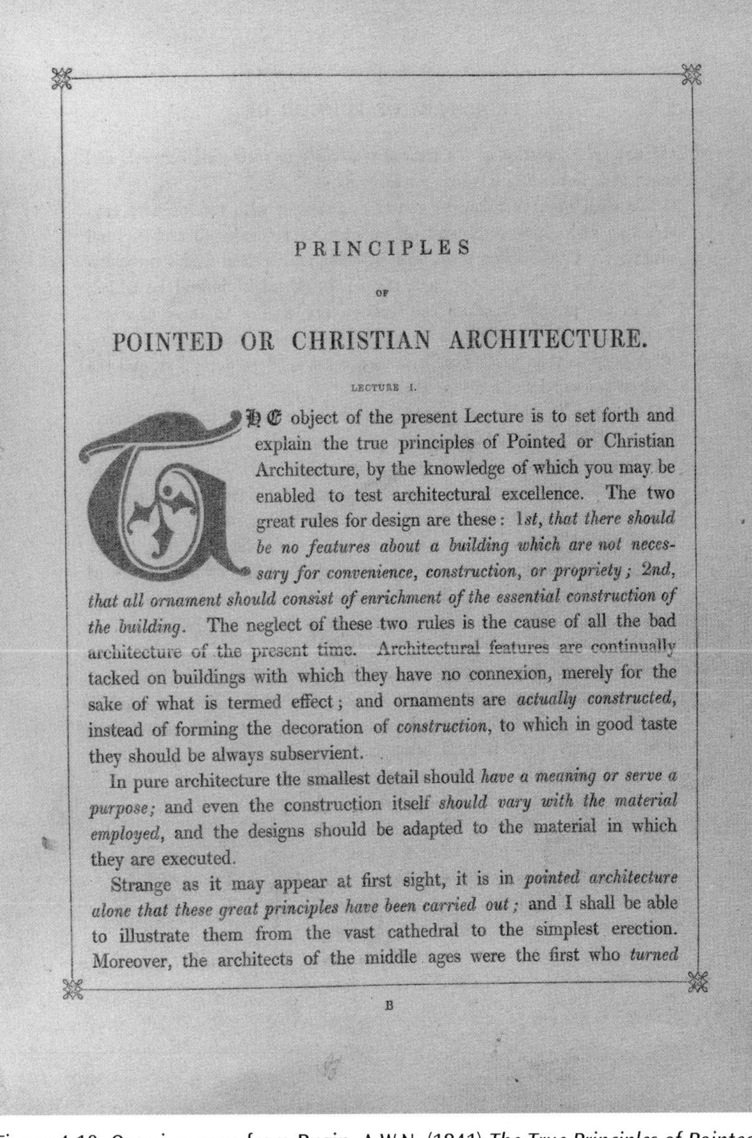

PRINCIPLES

OF

POINTED OR CHRISTIAN ARCHITECTURE.

LECTURE I.

THE object of the present Lecture is to set forth and explain the true principles of Pointed or Christian Architecture, by the knowledge of which you may be enabled to test architectural excellence. The two great rules for design are these: *1st, that there should be no features about a building which are not necessary for convenience, construction, or propriety; 2nd, that all ornament should consist of enrichment of the essential construction of the building.* The neglect of these two rules is the cause of all the bad architecture of the present time. Architectural features are continually tacked on buildings with which they have no connexion, merely for the sake of what is termed effect; and ornaments are *actually constructed,* instead of forming the decoration of *construction,* to which in good taste they should be always subservient.

In pure architecture the smallest detail should *have a meaning or serve a purpose;* and even the construction itself *should vary with the material employed,* and the designs should be adapted to the material in which they are executed.

Strange as it may appear at first sight, it is in *pointed architecture alone that these great principles have been carried out;* and I shall be able to illustrate them from the vast cathedral to the simplest erection. Moreover, the architects of the middle ages were the first who *turned*

B

Figure 4.10 Opening page from Pugin, A.W.N. (1841) *The True Principles of Pointed or Christian Architecture*, London, John Weale. British Library, London, 786.k.29. Photo:

However, *True Principles*, unlike *Contrasts*, also sets out a theory of architectural design. The main points are laid out in the opening paragraphs (see Figure 4.10). Let us look at the words Pugin uses in stipulating the first of his two rules. 'Convenience' means the building's function or purpose, while 'construction' refers to its structure. 'Propriety' he defines as follows: 'What I mean by propriety is this, that the external and internal appearance of an edifice should be illustrative of and in accordance with the purpose for which it is destined' (p. 42). Look back at Reading 4.1, where Pugin says that the different parts of a church should be decorated according to their purpose ('each portion ... was destined for a particular use, to which their ... decoration perfectly corresponded'). We have already mentioned that there was a long tradition of theoretical writing on classical architecture. In classical theory beauty (or aesthetics) plays an important part but, significantly, Pugin replaces this with his concept of propriety.

Once again, Pugin is here insisting on architecture's moral dimension. Architecture cannot be worthy, he says, unless it is appropriate for the social function for which it is being used.

Pugin's second rule makes a distinction between the structure of the building and its decoration. This had not generally been a concern for classical architects. In the classical system the main emphasis was on proportions and geometry, and whether elements were structural or ornamental or both was seen as secondary to the overall compositional framework. Columns, for example, were both load-bearing and decorative, but classical architects had no problem with using **pilasters** (these are effectively flattened columns placed against walls; they perform no structural purpose but are introduced purely for their visual effect). Pugin was interested in even the most humble and basic elements of building: 'Bolts, nails and rivets, so far from being unsightly are beautiful studs and busy enrichments, if properly treated' (p. 21) (see Plate 2.4.14).

Activity Look at Figures 4.11–12, depicting **flying buttresses** and roof structures, respectively. These were drawn by Pugin to demonstrate his architectural principles. What is Pugin trying to show in each case?

Discussion The caption to Figure 4.11 tells us that the **buttresses** of St Paul's cathedral are concealed, while those of the medieval example are revealed. Pugin lambasted St Paul's because, as he wrote, 'one half of the edifice is built to conceal the other' (p. 6). In Pugin's terms the screen walls were not necessary in terms of either convenience, construction or propriety. Furthermore, by hiding the buttresses in this way the stonework could not 'admit of the great principle of decorating utility': Pugin's second rule (p. 6). This is in contrast to the medieval church, where the decoration and structure of the building are united.

Figure 4.12 reveals similar ideas. In the three medieval examples the essential 'pointed' construction of the roof is left exposed and is decorated. In the modern roof, at top right, the triangular frame is hidden by the flat plaster ceiling, which has a rectangular patterned decoration.

Taken together, Pugin's ideas in *True Principles* comprise an argument for architecture to be legible. It should be apparent what the building is made of, how it stands up, how it is ornamented, what its function is and what the different parts are. These ideas were subsequently referred to by the designers of the late nineteenth-century Arts and Crafts Movement as 'honesty' in building or 'truth to materials': terms which nicely encapsulate Pugin's dual ethical and architectural approach. In the twentieth century the Modern Movement adopted the same approach and labelled it **functionalism**, summed up in the slogan 'form follows function'.

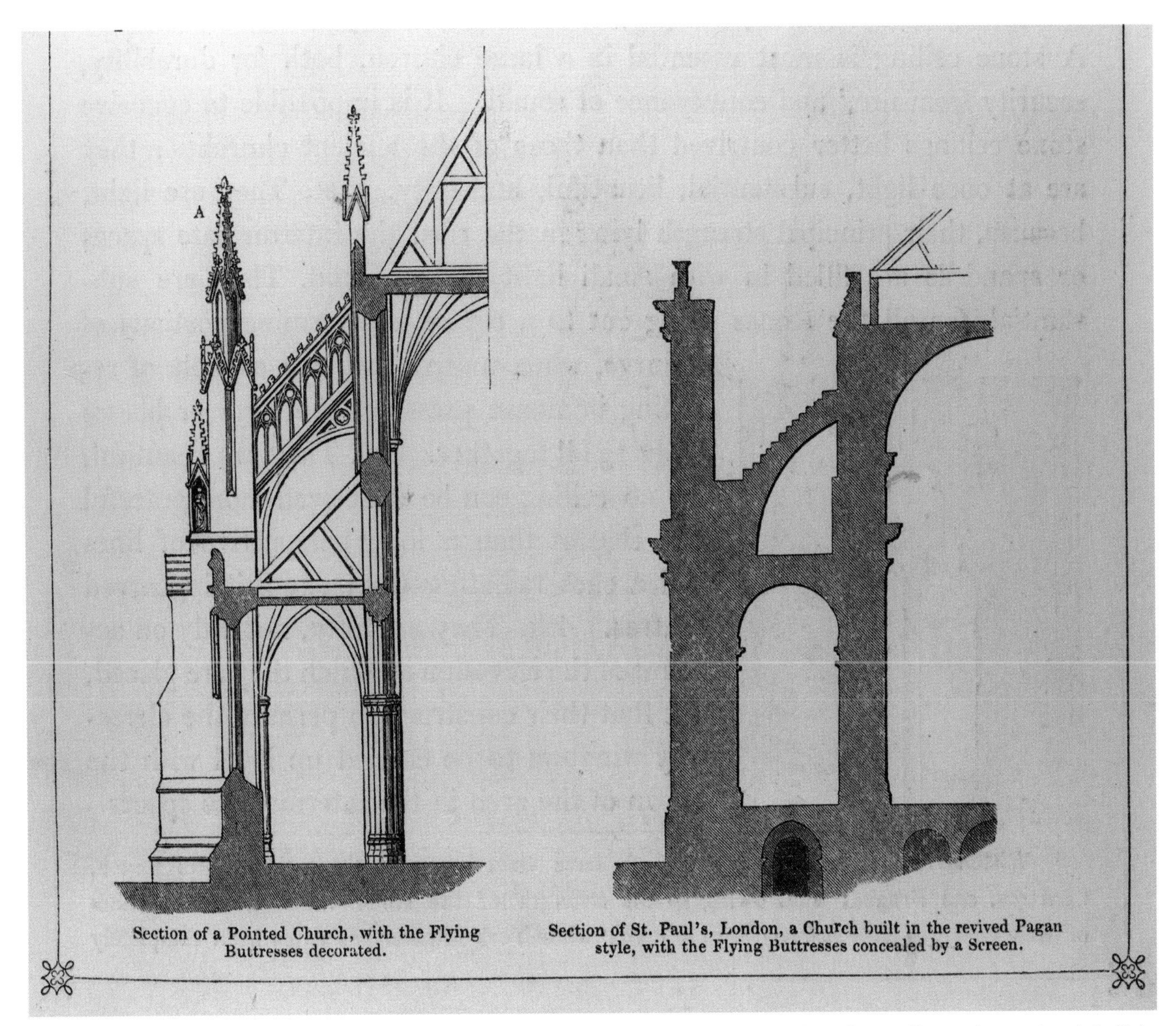

Figure 4.11 'Section of a Pointed Church, with the Flying Buttresses decorated' and 'Section of St Paul's, London, a Church built in the revived Pagan style, with the Flying Buttresses concealed by a Screen', from Pugin, A.W.N. (1841) *The True Principles of Pointed or Christian Architecture*, London, John Weale, p. 5, steel engraving. British Library, London, 786.k.29. Photo: © The British Library Board. All rights reserved.

Like the Palace of Westminster, then, Pugin's writings assert the claims of the Gothic style as the true national tradition of Britain. They reveal him to be not so much a dissenter as a radical traditionalist. He was a traditionalist in that he looked to a revival of medieval religion and society as the basis for a regenerated present, but he was also a radical in his architectural theories. Perhaps the most important among the latter was his insistence on the inter-relationship between human society and the environments it produces – an idea that has had a profound and lasting influence on succeeding generations.

Figure 4.12 Plate VI from Pugin, A.W.N. (1841) *The True Principles of Pointed or Christian Architecture*, London, John Weale, steel engraving. British Library, London, 786.k.29. Photo: © The British Library Board. All rights reserved.

4.3 PUGIN AND THE FURNISHING OF CATHOLIC CHURCHES

Kim Woods

Pugin's understanding of Gothic, his views on architecture and ecclesiastical furnishings and his own designs were all informed by the countless Gothic works of art that he studied first-hand. Through his travels in France, Germany, Belgium and the Netherlands from the 1830s to the 1850s, he familiarised himself with the Gothic world he was seeking to emulate. (So great was his aversion to the classical style associated with the Italian Renaissance that he visited Italy only once, in 1847.) In 1850, towards the end of his life, Pugin visited Lübeck in north Germany. This journey was undertaken in connection with a specific project, however: his treatise on **chancel screens** and **rood lofts** (published in 1851), for which he required real, Gothic examples. The spectacular carved wooden screen in Lübeck's cathedral was an obvious choice for Pugin to inspect.

The screen in Lübeck's cathedral divides the nave from the east end of the church (Figure 4.13). It was carved between 1470 and 1477 by Bernt Notke. In the centre is a statue of the crucified Christ. At the foot of the cross to the left kneels St Mary Magdalene, and to the right is a statue of the person who paid for this work, Bishop Albert Krummendiek, elected bishop of Lübeck in 1466. To either side are the Virgin Mary and St John the Evangelist who, together with Mary Magdalene, witnessed the crucifixion.

Through this open screen, or triumphal cross as it is sometimes called, a second, plainer screen can be glimpsed (Plate 2.4.15), set at the entrance of the chancel or choir. It is the triumphal cross, however, that offers a more spectacular glimpse of late Gothic sculpture.

The downward gaze of the Virgin is directed unnervingly at the viewer standing at the foot of the screen. The lifelike impression of the carved and painted figures is heightened by expressive postures, such as the twisting pose of Mary Magdalene, and realistic details: the raised veins in Christ's feet are picked out by using strips of leather stuck to the wood and then painted, while strips of parchment are used to simulate the cloth of Mary Magdalene's headdress (Plate 2.4.16). This dramatic re-enactment of the crucifixion in carved wood engages the viewer, invites emotional participation in the harrowing scene, and also delivers a reminder of the theological meaning of the crucifixion. At the far corners of the screen, carvings of Adam and Eve represent sinful humanity; behind them, almost hidden from view (but filmed on the DVD ROM), skeletons rise from the dead, a reference to the hope of victory over death through Christ's crucifixion and eventual resurrection. The portrait of Krummendiek, along with the inscription in Latin on the nave side of the ensemble, reminds viewers of the bishop's magnificent gesture in paying for this work of art and exhorts them to pray for his soul. Notke and his craftsmen also invested the work with their own religious aspirations, for when the figure of St John the Evangelist was restored in the 1970s, a parchment was found inside it that reads: 'In this year of grace 1472 Bernt Notke then made this work with the help of his journeymen ... Pray [to] God for their souls that they may find grace before God' (Svanberg and Qwarnström, 1998, p. 116). The note was evidently addressed to St John, through the medium of his statue that the craftsmen themselves had carved.

Pugin seems to have found Notke's stark approach hard to take, but he none the less wrote admiringly of it in *A Treatise on Chancel Screens*

Figure 4.13 Bernt Notke, Triumphal cross, 1470–7, oak. Lübeck cathedral. Photo: Helge Schenk, Hamburg.

and Rood Lofts: 'some of the images are rather barbarous, but the foliage and details are exquisitely wrought, and the whole design is most striking and original' (Pugin, 1851, p. 20).

A Treatise on Chancel Screens and Rood Lofts was the culmination of an ongoing controversy within the Roman Catholic church arising out of Pugin's ambition to reintroduce what he considered to be 'correct' pre-Reformation church furnishings into Britain's new Roman Catholic churches. In this final section of the chapter, we shall be looking at some of the traditional forms of religious art that Pugin wished to revive in his Roman Catholic churches, all based on pre-Reformation models and practices, and all in the Gothic style. We shall explore the reasons why religious art provoked such controversy, both in the nineteenth century and much earlier, during the Reformation of the sixteenth century.

Chancel screens and rood lofts

Activity Look carefully at Figure 4.14, a photograph of the screen that until 1967 used to divide the nave from the chancel in St Chad's Roman Catholic cathedral, Birmingham. Describe what you see, beginning at the top and working right down to ground-floor level, noting any sculptures that are present.

Discussion At the top of the photograph underneath the arch you can see the figure of Christ on the cross. At his feet are the Virgin Mary and St John the Evangelist. This carved group is placed on a kind of stand, supported by a gallery running from one side of the arch to the other. Below this gallery is an open screen composed of eight narrow columns and a central opening. There are statues on each of the eight columns and, if you look carefully, you will also see carvings between the bottom of the gallery and the top of the screen. Statues of angels are set above each end of the gallery.

Essentially, Pugin's screen in St Chad's cathedral revived a traditional structure that nearly every church in Britain would have had before the Reformation. The gallery was known as the rood loft. It was usually wide enough to walk on and was used to display candles and lamps. It was also sometimes used for reading the Gospels, and even to house the organ. It could generally be accessed via steps leading off the chancel arch. The rood loft supported the '**rood**' itself: the statue of Christ on the cross accompanied by the Virgin and St John. The '**rood screen**', as it is often called, divided the public part of the church from the choir, the area reserved for the priests where the high altar stood.

The modest screen at St Chad's was typical of the traditional chancel screens and rood lofts that would have been found in most British parish churches before the Reformation. In cathedrals and monastic churches the structures could sometimes be more complicated – we have already seen that in Lübeck's cathedral, Bernt Notke's rood images were supplemented by other statues and placed on a chancel arch entirely separate from the rood loft a few metres behind (Plate 2.4.17).

Pugin's enthusiasm for traditional rood screens was not invariably shared by the Roman Catholic clergy appointed to his new churches, including St Chad's. On 13 December 1840, Pugin wrote indignantly to a friend:

> Last week I received a letter from J. Hardman of Birmingham in great distress informing [me] that Dr W[iseman] [the recently appointed assistant to the bishop of Birmingham] had decided that the great Rood Screen of Birmingham was to be done away

Figure 4.14 Wooden rood screen separating nave from chancel (subsequently removed), St Chad's Roman Catholic cathedral, Birmingham, 1941. Unknown photographer. National Monuments Record, Swindon. Photo: reproduced by permission of English Heritage, NMR.

with [so th]at people might see better. I determined at once to resist this innovation and suffer any loss rather than agree – to abolish this ancient division between the priests and people – and accordingly I wrote down to J. Hardman that if the screen was altered I would at once resign my employment as architect of the building. I am resolved to build the real thing or nothing. Today I received a letter to say that he had agreed to allow the screen to remain.

But is not this state of things alarming. It is evident to me that Dr W. has no sympathy with the ancient Catholic England – and its ecclesiastical traditions. The objection to the screen was

> absurd. It is an *open* screen with only six slender **mullions** and as for expense, Mr Hardman has given five hundred pounds for the *purpose* of erecting this screen and the great Rood. It is evident to me that every good thing is to [be] fought for. I am fully resolved to carry out the real thing or resign. I will no longer consent to half measures. We must restore the ancient churches exactly as they existed in their glory.
>
> (Belcher, 2001–3, vol. 1, p. 174 [spelling modernised])

This letter reveals Pugin's uncompromising commitment to reviving the ancient Roman Catholic traditions of the pre-Reformation church, as well as hinting at Wiseman's objections to the rood screen: it was expensive and it reduced the visibility of the high altar. The rood screen at St Chad's was finally dismantled in 1967, as part of an internal reordering of the cathedral in response to the reforms of Popes John XXIII and Paul VI following the Second Vatican Council. (Like Wiseman in 1840, this council, known as Vatican II, placed modern priorities above the preservation of Roman Catholic tradition.) The rood cross was later suspended from the ceiling at the former site of the screen.

The dismantling of the St Chad's screen and the survival of the rood image of Christ are the precise reverse of what happened during the English Reformation. In the sixteenth century, the objections concerned not the separation of chancel, priest and altar from the nave and people, but the images on the rood loft itself. In January 1550, during the rule of Edward VI (son of Henry VIII), the Act for the Defacing of Images was passed. It was later reaffirmed by Elizabeth I in 1559. Another edict, passed in 1561, ordered the dismantling of rood lofts, but the screens beneath them often remained and sometimes do to this day. In the previous chapter you read Archbishop Grindal's injunctions of 1571, which included the order that 'the Rood lofts be taken down, and altered so, that the upper boards and timber thereof both behind and above, where the Rood lately did hang, and also the ... loft be quite taken down unto the cross beam' (see Reading 3.2).

Religious images were anathema within most Protestant traditions and virtually none dating from before the Reformation survive in England, although they continued to be important within the Roman Catholic church. A Protestant visitor to St Chad's at its consecration in 1841 would probably have been far more offended by the statues than by the controversial rood screen. To understand this, we need to look in more detail at the sort of art commonly found in churches before the Reformation, and at the purposes they were believed to serve.

Images and altarpieces

Most pre-Reformation churches in Britain would have contained a plethora of religious images, in addition to the images of Christ, the Virgin Mary and St John on the rood loft.

Activity Reread Roger Martyn's account of the Suffolk church of Long Melford before the Reformation (Reading 3.1 in the previous chapter). Make a list of the works of art he describes and where they were placed. Remember that this is sixteenth-century English, so you will need to refer to the glossary.

Discussion Martyn describes a carved wooden crucifixion altarpiece at the high altar, with statues (one representing the Trinity – in other words, God depicted as the Father, the Son and the Holy Ghost) in floor-to-ceiling carved niches to either side. There was another crucifixion altarpiece, this one perhaps painted, in his own family **chapel**, or **aisle** (to the south of the high altar), and statues of Christ as Saviour of the World and the Virgin with the dead Christ on her lap (an image known as a **pietà**), again placed in tall niches. In addition to the rood images, the 12 apostles were painted on the rood screen itself.

There were almost certainly many other images in the wealthy Long Melford church – in the late eighteenth century an alabaster relief carving of the Adoration of the **Magi** was discovered under the church floor there, presumably having been hidden during the Reformation to avoid its being destroyed, as the altarpieces and statues evidently were.

The dismantling of religious images in the Protestant church arose out of a fundamental disagreement about the purposes they served. Centuries earlier, Pope Gregory the Great (590–604 CE) first attempted to define and justify the function of religious art to Serenus, the bishop of Marseille. Bishop Serenus believed that such art might tempt Christians to worship images (i.e. indulge in idolatry) rather than God himself, and that this justified their destruction. We have already seen that the plea for prayer left by Notke and his assistants inside the statue of John the Evangelist at Lübeck's cathedral appears to blur the distinction between statue and saint. According to Pope Gregory, however, religious art had a value as a visual substitute for those who could not read: just as the literate minority learned through studying religious texts, so the illiterate majority learned through studying works of art.

For most of the period between 1559 and Pugin's own day, the Protestant church took the same line as Serenus in regarding religious images as potential idols that were best destroyed. Pugin was able to break with the English Protestant tradition of empty, imageless churches because Pope Gregory's justification of religious art retained its validity in the Roman Catholic church. He even acquired original Gothic images from Belgium, France and Germany, in order to re-create church interiors furnished in pre-Reformation style: many of the sculptures that formerly decorated the St Chad's rood screen are authentic Gothic works.

Lübeck escaped the destruction of the Reformation, and its churches can offer a glimpse of the sort of furnishings that might have decorated a pre-Reformation European church (though there would, of course, have been some regional variations). There is, for example, a spectacular carved wooden altarpiece with painted shutters in the Marienkirche (Church of Our Lady) in Lübeck that is reminiscent of the high altarpiece at Long Melford, albeit dedicated to the life of the Virgin rather than the crucifixion (Plate 2.4.18).

This altarpiece has movable shutters that fold over the central scene, a form known as a **triptych**, and it is unusual in having not just one set of shutters but two. The triptych's three stages of opening reflected the **liturgy** and calendar of the church year: it would have been fully opened on feast days such as Christmas and Easter, as Roger Martyn describes at Long Melford; perhaps half opened on Sundays, except in Lent and Advent (Plate 2.4.19), the two penitential seasons of the church calendar; and for the rest of the time it would probably have been closed (Plate 2.4.20).

The altarpieces in St Chad's were made to Pugin's own designs, but he acquired from abroad an authentic Gothic carved altarpiece, probably originally made in Brussels *c.*1510–20, for the **Lady Chapel** of one of his best-known churches, St Giles, Cheadle, consecrated in 1846 (Plate 2.4.22). Like the Long Melford high altarpiece, this is a crucifixion altarpiece with (on the left) the scene of Christ carrying the cross and (on the right) another subject found at Long Melford, the pietà. The altarpiece was evidently in poor condition when Pugin acquired it: the painted shutters were already missing and it was covered with thick gilding, probably to disguise the loss of the original paint and to cover up extensive restorations.

In addition to rood statues and altarpieces, fifteenth- and early sixteenth-century churches would also have been filled with statues placed by altars, against columns or pillars and in side chapels. In Reading 3.1 Roger Martyn makes no mention of statues of the Virgin and Child, yet they were so common that it is almost certain there would have been several at Long Melford. The cathedral at Lübeck has two stone statues of the Virgin and Child, one dating from around 1460 (Figure 4.15), the second dating from 1509 (Figure 4.16). Pugin donated an authentic late Gothic statue of the Virgin and Child to the Lady Chapel of St Chad's (Figure 4.17). We know from his letters that he paid £32 for it, which was rather a large sum at the time (Belcher, 2001–3, vol. 2, p. 278).

Rather than representing Mary as a humble mother, all three images show her crowned as queen of heaven. Nevertheless, the mood is one of relative informality, and the demeanour of the St Chad's statue is

Figure 4.15 Unknown artist, Virgin and Child, *c.*1460, stone. Lübeck cathedral. Photo: Helge Schenk, Hamburg.

Figure 4.16 Unknown artist, Virgin and Child, 1509, stone. Lübeck cathedral. Photo: Helge Schenk, Hamburg.

Figure 4.17 Unknown artist, Virgin and Child, *c.*1450, polychromed wood. St Chad's Roman Catholic cathedral, Birmingham. Photo: Malcolm Daisley, e-motif photography.

particularly cheerful, creating a certain human appeal. Pugin's statue of the Virgin and Child is reputed to have been the first image of the Virgin to be installed in a church in England for devotional purposes since the Reformation. Statues of the Virgin and saints were particular targets for sixteenth-century reformers, who had grave reservations about the elevated status of the Virgin Mary and of saints in the Roman Catholic church.

Reviving the past

Although pre-Reformation art and artefacts were sometimes installed in other buildings designed by Pugin, in general his practice was to use his study of Gothic church furnishings to make his own designs, which were in turn produced by a group of loyal collaborators. These included John Hardman, the Birmingham button manufacturer who financed the St Chad's rood screen. He produced metalwork and latterly also jewellery and stained glass for Pugin, using modern production methods that had more in common with the large-scale production of nineteenth-century manufacturing than with medieval workshop production – by the early 1850s he employed some 200 men on his stained-glass production. You can see some of this stained glass on the DVD ROM.

Many of Pugin's designs were based on original Gothic art and artefacts that he sketched on annual trips abroad. He also built up collections of original ecclesiastical art and furnishings in his home in Ramsgate and in Oscott College, a seminary in Birmingham where he was professor of ecclesiastical antiquities from 1837 until at least 1839 and perhaps longer. Still at Oscott is a small carved cupboard door with a carving of an angel dating from the fifteenth century and probably originally made in Utrecht in the Netherlands. It bears the inscription 'Hardman' on the back (Plate 2.4.23). Presumably it was used by Hardman as a model for his stained-glass designs, but it seems also to have been the basis for the Pugin-designed alabaster altar made for the side chapel of the Hospital Church of St John in Alton in the Midlands (Plate 2.4.24).

CONCLUSION

Pugin was a key figure in the Gothic Revival, a broad movement that favoured Gothic styles over the prevailing and long-standing taste for the classical. What made his dissenting attitude more than just a stylistic preference was his association of northern Gothic with national identity and with the cultural values of his own, revived Roman Catholic faith. There were some dissenters within the Anglican church who also championed Gothic architecture, pre-Reformation furnishings and liturgical practices. These included members of the Oxford Movement mentioned in Chapter 3 above, and their counterparts at Cambridge University, members of the **Camden Society**. It has even been argued that Pugin's ideas had greater impact in the Anglican church than in his own Roman Catholic church. During the controversy over St Chad's rood screen in 1840, Pugin commented: 'we nearly stand alone if we except the Oxford men, for among them I find full sympathy of feeling', and in the following year he noted: 'the Camden society at Cambryde [sic] are doing wonders in reviving Catholic ideas and taste in ecclesiastical matters. They lectured publicly on my last work and have recommended [it] in their printed works – which has increased the sale amazinly [sic]' (Belcher, 2001–3, vol. 1, pp. 175 and 293). Pugin's concerns remained a live issue for much of the nineteenth century and even into the twentieth century. Their legacy remains with us today.

Activity
You should allow about one and a half hours for this activity.

We would like you to end this chapter firstly by studying the DVD ROM 'St Chad's and Religious Art', which includes a virtual tour of key Gothic churches. You should work through the sections on 'Art and architecture' and 'Lübeck' and follow the 'Activities'.

Activity

To complement your virtual tour, we would like you to visit a nearby church. Make sure that it is either Anglican (or Episcopalian if you live in Scotland) or Roman Catholic, as non-conformist churches tend to have a very different set of architectural traditions.

Using a church guide, or whatever information is available to you, try to answer the following questions:

1. Is this building Gothic, or classical, or neither? If Gothic, is it original medieval Gothic, or a nineteenth-century revival of the Gothic tradition?
2. If this is a church dating from before the sixteenth century, are there any defaced images within the church? Look particularly for headless statues set within the architecture, or obvious gaps where statues used to be (empty niches, for example).
3. Are there any nineteenth-century Gothic furnishings or artworks in the church? Look, for example, at the pulpit, altar or choir stalls.
4. Is there a rood screen or, if this is an old church, any traces of where the rood screen might have been? Check whether there is any evidence of a door or stairs leading off the chancel arch to give access to the rood screen.

Note that churches are now often kept locked, and you may have to ask to gain access.

REFERENCES

Belcher, M. (1987) *A.W.N. Pugin: An Annotated Critical Bibliography*, London and New York, Mansell.

Belcher, M. (2001–3) (ed.) *The Collected Letters of A.W.N. Pugin*, 2 vols, Oxford, Oxford University Press.

Cannadine, D., Riding, C. and Riding, J. (eds) (2000) *The Houses of Parliament: History, Art, Architecture*, London, Merrell.

Eastlake, C.L. (1872) *A History of the Gothic Revival: An Attempt to Show how the Taste for Mediaeval Architecture ... has been Encouraged and Developed*, London, Longman.

Fell, B.H. and Mackenzie, K.R. (1994) *The Houses of Parliament: A Guide to the Palace of Westminster* (15th edn), London, HMSO.

Ferrey, B. (1978 [1861]) *Recollections of A.N. Welby Pugin, and his Father, Augustus Pugin*, London, Stanford (edited C. and J. Wainwright), London, Scolar Press.

Pugin, A.W.N. (1835) *A Letter to A.W. Hakewill, Architect, in Answer to his Reflections on the Style for Rebuilding the Houses of Parliament*, Salisbury, W.B. Brodie and Co.

Pugin, A.W.N. (2003 [1841]) *Contrasts: Or, a Parallel between the Noble Edifices of the Fourteenth and Fifteenth Centuries and Similar Buildings of the Present Day; Shewing the Present Decay of Taste* (2nd edn; 1st edn 1836) (intro. T. Brittain-Catlin), Reading, Spire Books.

Pugin, A.W.N. (2003 [1841]) *The True Principles of Pointed or Christian Architecture Set Forth* (intro. T. Brittain-Catlin), Reading, Spire Books.

Pugin, A.W.N. (2005 [1851]) *A Treatise on Chancel Screens and Rood Lofts* (ed. R. O'Donnell), Leominster, Gracewing.

Svanberg, J. and Qwarnström, A. (1998) *Saint George and the Dragon*, Stockholm, Rabén Prisma.

FURTHER READING

Atterbury, P. and Wainwright, C. (1994) *Pugin: A Gothic Passion*, New Haven, CN and London, Yale University Press in association with the Victoria & Albert Museum.

Brooks, C. (1999) *The Gothic Revival*, London, Phaidon Press.

Conway, H. and Roenisch, R. (2005) *Understanding Architecture: An Introduction to Architecture and Architectural History*, London, Routledge.

Fleming, J., Honour, H. and Pevsner, N. (1998) *Penguin Dictionary of Architecture and Landscape Architecture* (5th edn), Harmondsworth, Penguin.

Hill, R. (2007) *God's Architect: Pugin and the Building of Romantic Britain*, London, Allen Lane.

RESOURCES

Reading 4.1 On the present degraded state of ecclesiastical buildings

I will now proceed to examine the present state of ancient Ecclesiastical buildings, after three centuries of mingled devastation, neglect, and vile repair, have passed over them.

In the first place, I will commence with the cathedrals, the most splendid monuments of past days which remain, and, therefore, the most deserving of first consideration.

...

When these gigantic churches were erected, each portion of them was destined for a particular use, to which their arrangement and decoration perfectly corresponded. Thus the choir was appropriated solely to the ecclesiastics, who each filled their respective stalls; the nave was calculated for the immense congregation of the people, who, without reference to rank or wealth, were promiscuously mixed in the public worship of God; while the aisles afforded ample space for the solemn processions of the clergy.

The various chapels, each with its altar, were served by different priests, who at successive hours of the morning, commencing at six, said masses, that all classes and occupations might be enabled to devote some portion of the day to religious duties. The **cloisters** formed a quiet and sheltered deambulatory [aisle] for the meditation of the ecclesiastics; and the **chapter-house** was a noble chamber, where they frequently met and settled on spiritual and temporal affairs relating to their office.

These churches were closed only for a few hours during the night, in order that they might form the place from whence private prayers and supplications might continually be offered up. But of what use are these churches now? do their doors stand ever open to admit the devout? No; excepting the brief space of time set apart twice a-day to keep up the form of worship, the gates are fast closed, nor is it possible to obtain admittance within the edifice without a fee to the guardian of the keys. Ask the reason of this, and the answer will be, that if the churches were left open they would be completely defaced, and even become the scene of the grossest pollutions. If this be true, which I fear it is, what, I ask, must be the moral and religious state of a country, where the churches are obliged to be fastened up to prevent their being desecrated and destroyed by the people? how must the ancient devotion and piety have departed? Indeed, so utterly are all feelings of private devotion lost in these churches, that were an individual to kneel in any other time than that actually set apart for Divine service, or in any other part of the edifice but that which is inclosed, he would be considered as a person not sound in his intellects, and probably be ordered out of the building. No; cathedrals are visited from far different motives, by the different classes of persons who go to them. The first are those who, being connected with or living near a cathedral, attend regularly every Sunday by rote; the second are those who, not having any taste for prayers, but who have some ear for music, drop in, as it is termed, to hear the anthem; the third class are persons who go to see the church. They are tourists; they go to see everything that is to be seen; therefore they see the church, – *id est*, they walk round, read the epitaphs, think it very pretty, very romantic, very old, suppose it was built in superstitious times, pace the length of the nave, write their names on a pillar, and whisk out, as they have a great deal more to see and very little time.

...

Few are there who, amid the general change and destruction they have undergone, can conjure up in their minds the glories of their departed greatness, and who, while they bitterly despise the heartless throng that gaze about the sacred aisles, mourn for the remembrance of those ages of faith now passed and gone, which produced minds to conceive and zeal to execute such mighty, glorious works. 'Tis such minds as these that feel acutely the barren, meagre, and inappropriate use to which these edifices have been put; and to them does the neat and modern churchman appear truly despicable, as he trips from the door to the vestry, goes through the prayers, then returns from the vestry to the door, forming the greatest contrast of all with the noble works which surround him. What part has he, I say, what connexion of soul with the ecclesiastic of ancient days? Do we see him, when the public service is concluded, kneeling in silent devotion in the quiet retreat of some chapel? Do we see him perambulating in study and contemplation those vaulted cloisters, which were erected solely for the meditation of ecclesiastical persons? No; he only enters the church when his duty compels him; he quits it the instant he is able; he regards the fabric but as the source of his income; he lives by religion – 'tis his trade. And yet these men of cold and callous hearts, insensible to every spark of ancient zeal and devotion, will dare to speak with contempt and ridicule of those glorious spirits by whose mighty minds and liberal hearts those establishments have been founded, and from whose pious munificence they derive every shilling they possess.

Source: A.W.N. Pugin (1841) *The True Principles of Pointed or Christian Architecture*, reprinted in Pugin, *Contrasts and The True Principles of Pointed or Christian Architecture* (intro. T. Brittain-Catlin), Reading, Spire Books, 2003, pp. 35–7.

Reading 4.2 The Commissioners' churches

Yes; the erection of churches, like all that was produced by zeal or art in ancient days, has dwindled down into a mere trade. No longer is the sanctity of the undertaking considered, or is the noblest composition of the architect, or the most curious skill of the artificer, to be employed in its erection; but the minimum it can be done for is calculated from allowing a trifling sum to the room occupied for each sitting; and the outline of the building, and each window, moulding, and ornament, must be made to correspond with this miserable pittance.

...

The Church commissioners ... require a structure as plain as possible, which can be built for a trifling sum, and of small dimensions, both for economy and facilities of hearing the preacher, the sermon being the only part of the service considered; and I hesitate not to say, that a more meagre, miserable display of architectural skill never was made, nor more improprieties and absurdities committed, than in the mass of paltry churches erected under the auspices of the commissioners, and which are to be found scattered over every modern portion of the metropolis and its neighbourhood – a disgrace to the age, both on the score of their composition, and the miserable sums that have been allotted for their construction.

No kind of propriety or fitness has been considered in their composition. Some have porticoes of Greek temples, surmounted by steeples of miserable outline and worse detail. Others are a mixture of distorted Greek and Roman buildings; and a host have been built in perfectly nondescript styles, forming the most offensive masses of building. In some cases, the architect has endeavoured to give the shell the appearance of an ancient pointed church, and, by dint of disguising all the internal arrangements, something like an old exterior has been obtained; but when the interior is seen the whole illusion vanishes, and we discover that what had somewhat the appearance of an old Catholic church, is, in reality, nothing but a modern preaching-house, with all its galleries, pews, and other fittings. In fine, so impossible is it to make a grand design suitable to the meagreness of the present worship, that to produce any effect at all, the churches are designed to represent any thing but what they really are; and hence, all the host of absurdities and incongruities, in form and decoration, which abound in modern places built for religious worship.

...

In conclusion, ... when luxury is everywhere on the increase, and means and money more plentiful than ever, to see the paltry buildings erected everywhere for religious worship, and the neglected state of the ancient churches, it argues a total want of religious zeal, and a tepidity towards the glory of Divine worship, as disgraceful to the nation, as it must be offensive to the Almighty.

Source: A.W.N. Pugin (1841) *The True Principles of Pointed or Christian Architecture*, reprinted in Pugin, *Contrasts and The True Principles of Pointed or Christian Architecture* (intro. T. Brittain-Catlin), Reading, Spire Books, 2003, pp. 49–50 (footnote omitted).

5 IRELAND: THE INVENTION OF TRADITION

Anne Laurence with a contribution by Richard Danson Brown

INTRODUCTION		151
5.1	HISTORY AND TRADITION	153
5.2	THE INVENTION OF TRADITION	154
5.3	IRISH NATIONALISMS	157
	Political nationalism	158
	Cultural nationalism	160
5.4	THE EASTER RISING OF 1916	164
	'Easter 1916'	167
5.5	AFTER EASTER 1916	169
5.6	RETURN TO THE BUILT HERITAGE OF IRELAND	172
5.7	TRADITION AND DISSENT: THE INVENTION OF TRADITION	174
REFERENCES		175
RESOURCES		176
	Reading 5.1	176
	Reading 5.2	180
	Reading 5.3	181
	Reading 5.4	182
	Reading 5.5	183
	Chronology	185
	Media notes	185

MATERIALS YOU WILL NEED

- DVD Video: Ireland

AIMS

This chapter will:

- provide you with an introduction to the history of the struggle in the nineteenth century for an Irish state independent of British rule
- show you how ideas about the Irish past were mobilised by nationalists to give credibility to their cause
- show you how these ideas persisted and informed policy relating to the conservation of Ireland's historic buildings and sites after 1922
- demonstrate how historians can apply a general theory (in this case Eric Hobsbawm's and Terence Ranger's 'invention of tradition') to a variety of historical periods
- help you to develop your skills in reading primary and secondary historical writing and in using video material for academic study.

INTRODUCTION

Pearse, Patrick/Pádraig (1879–1916): A schoolteacher, member of the Gaelic League and Irish Republican Brotherhood, and author of the Proclamation of the Irish Republic in 1916, Pearse was executed for his part in the Easter Rising.

Connolly, James (1868–1916): A Scottish trade union activist and commander of the Irish Citizen Army in 1916. He was executed for his part in the Easter Rising.

On Easter Monday 1916 around 1,600 members of the Irish Volunteers and the Citizen Army marched out to seize agreed points in Dublin. Their commanders, Pádraig (Patrick) Pearse and James Connolly, made their headquarters the General Post Office (GPO) in Sackville (now O'Connell) Street. Outside the GPO was posted a declaration from 'The Provisional Government of the Irish Republic' which began with the words:

> Irishmen and Irishwomen: In the name of God and of the dead generations from which she receives her old tradition of nationhood, Ireland, through us, summons her children to her flag and strikes for her freedom.
>
> (Jeffery, 1999, p. 82)

After six days' fighting, the wrecking of much of central Dublin, looting, disruption, the deaths of 132 soldiers and policemen, 318 civilians and 64 rebels, and with 397 solders and policemen and 2,217 civilians wounded, Pearse ordered the surrender of his troops. Subsequently the number of fatalities was increased by the execution of 15 rebels (Fitzpatrick, 1989, p. 239). (Note that although the events of Easter 1916 are variously referred to as a rising, a rebellion or a war of independence, the active participants are usually referred to as rebels.) Figures 5.1 and 5.2 reproduce photographs taken at the time.

The Easter Rising was the culmination of demands for self-rule for Ireland which had been voiced from the late eighteenth century onwards. These demands were fuelled by the belief that government from London was oppressive, and by resentment at the advantages enjoyed by Anglo-Irish landlords. Since the 1880s the agitation had become more militant, better organised and increasingly republican (i.e. calling for an elected head of state rather than a hereditary monarch).

In 1922, 26 of Ireland's 32 counties became a state independent of Britain, and for much of the rest of the twentieth century its governments were dominated by politicians steeped in the traditions of the old **nationalist** movement. Both before and after independence, Irish nationalist politicians relied heavily on reference to an immemorial Irish past, chiefly one which emphasised the heroic, independent, culturally distinct Irish in contrast to the exploitative foreignness of the English who had governed Ireland for centuries.

This chapter is primarily concerned with republican nationalist views of the past, but it was not only supporters of an independent Ireland who mobilised tradition in support of their cause. The unionist movement (which at the time was by no means confined to the north of Ireland, and was not exclusively Protestant) had also drawn extensively on a vision of the Irish past in opposing the nationalists: before 1922

Figure 5.1 'Irish Rebellion, May, 1916. Sackville Street in flames. A photograph taken by a "Daily Sketch" photographer under fire', 1916. Unknown photographer. Imperial War Museum, London, Q 82364. Photo: reproduced with permission of The Trustees of the Imperial War Museum.

unionists wanted Ireland to remain part of the United Kingdom; after that they dedicated themselves to a campaign to retain British rule over the six counties of Northern Ireland. Although in this chapter we shall not be discussing the role of religion in these movements, the nationalist movement (which in the nineteenth century had some Protestant supporters) increasingly identified itself with Catholicism, while the new Irish state favoured the Catholic church and its religious and moral values over other denominations.

The Easter Rising is a focal point for this chapter. We shall look back at the ideas of the past – the traditions – that informed the republican nationalists who took control of the GPO in 1916. We shall also look at how a particular vision of the past influenced politicians after 1922 in setting priorities for the conservation of historic monuments in Ireland. Underlying this study is the idea that the kinds of tradition that are mobilised for polemical purposes sometimes have more to do with contemporary politics than with research in the archives.

Note that you are strongly advised to refer to the Media notes (which include a chronology and glossary) while working through this chapter, and especially while viewing the DVD Video.

Figure 5.2 British troops at a makeshift barricade in a Dublin street during The Easter Uprising, April 1916. Unknown photographer. Photo: Popperfoto/Alamy. Like many images of the Rising, this may have been a scene staged for the camera.

5.1 HISTORY AND TRADITION

Through your reading of earlier chapters in this course, you should be familiar with the idea that we can know the past only through the materials left behind and that we need to learn to interpret those materials; as Trevor Fear puts it in Book 1, Chapter 1 on Cleopatra, history is 'a maze of opinion, contradiction and hearsay'. Many of the materials of the past have themselves been interpreted , consciously and unconsciously, for good and bad reasons, before they reach us, so it is important for us to understand the processes that mould them. You have seen in Book 1 how the reputations of historical figures such as Cleopatra, the Dalai Lama and Stalin have fared at the hands of later commentators. The chapter on Stalin also introduces the idea of how we use evidence to create an account of past events and how myths may not draw much on evidence but may affect the actions and beliefs of individuals and societies.

In the current book you have encountered a variety of different kinds of tradition, some of them long established, like those of Christianity, while others, like Pugin's use of medieval precedents, have adapted traditions for new uses. In Chapter 3 John Wolffe makes the point that there may be different views about what constitutes tradition, while in Chapter 4 you saw how there may be a choice of architectural traditions to draw on (in that case, Gothic, Elizabethan or Tudor).

The interplay of tradition and dissent that you considered in relation to English Christianity (and that is apparent in many religions) can also be discerned in the ways in which states and nations (or nascent states and nascent nations) use tradition to give themselves legitimacy. Many political and religious movements use tradition to validate themselves; the traditions they draw on are not necessarily those understood by historians through a dispassionate analysis of the past, but are specific interpretations of the past invoked for a particular purpose. For example, Hitler called his state the Third Reich in order to draw on the idea of the past glories of Germany: the First Reich was the ancient German Holy Roman empire and the Second Reich the state created by the unification of Germany in 1871. Accounts of the past are moulded by people and movements in the present to serve their own needs. One way we may describe this is as 'the invention of tradition', using the word invention to mean not something conjured out of nothing, but something crafted.

On the face of it the phrase might seem to be disrespectful, but once we start to look at how tradition can be used, you can see that it is an accurate description for a process, an example of which is the annual service at the Cenotaph in London on Remembrance Sunday. This began in 1919 as a commemoration on the anniversary of the Armistice that ended the First World War (11 November) and was largely confined to the armed services. In 1945 it was moved to the nearest Sunday to 11 November, and military and naval participants have since been joined by representatives of civilian groups such as the merchant navy, London Transport and by relatives of service men and women killed in recent conflicts.

5.2 THE INVENTION OF TRADITION

The phrase 'the invention of tradition' is particularly associated with a book of essays published in 1983 with that title, edited by two distinguished historians, Eric Hobsbawm and Terence Ranger.

Activity Turn to Reading 5.1, an extract from Eric Hobsbawm's 'Introduction: inventing traditions'. Read the passage quickly and don't take detailed notes. If necessary, reread it before considering the following:

1 List some of the author's examples of 'invented traditions'.

2 Which examples do not necessarily draw on some idea of a historic past?

3 Which circumstances particularly give rise to invented traditions?

4 Which examples does Hobsbawm give of states using invented traditions?

Discussion

1 Examples of 'invented tradition' are the pageantry surrounding the British monarchy; the Festival of Nine Lessons and Carols; the royal Christmas broadcast; the customs associated with the FA Cup Final in England; Charles Barry's and Augustus Pugin's design of the Gothic Houses of Parliament at Westminster in the 1840s and 1850s, and the exact reconstruction of the House of Commons after it was bombed in the Second World War.

2 Those that don't necessarily draw on a historic past are the Cup Final; traditions following the French Revolution in 1789 (I hope you picked this up from paragraph 3); the British national anthem; mythical figures such as Marianne and John Bull.

3 I hope for this answer you alighted on paragraphs 4, 8 and 12: in circumstances where 'a rapid transformation of society weakens or destroys the social patterns for which "old" traditions had been designed'; in the confirmation of 'citizens' membership of states'; and in the creation of new nations.

4 Hobsbawm cites flags; semi-fictional founding fathers and mothers (such as Boadicea); Marianne and Uncle Sam; anthems and emblems.

This extract is not easy to read, but I hope that the idea of 'invented tradition' makes sense to you. The term is not used to denigrate the value of relying on ancient precedents but, rather, to suggest that many things we take for granted about the past may not be quite what they seem. Let me give you another example. The Open University was founded in 1969, but its graduates collect their degrees wearing academic gowns whose design is based on those worn by students in sixteenth- and seventeenth-century Oxford and Cambridge.

Let us for a moment reflect on what kind of historical writing this is. Hobsbawm is not recounting the causes of a series of events or tracking the emergence of ideas. Rather, he is developing an argument about how the past is used by societies. This is a reflective rather than a discursive piece, offering us a way of thinking about how ideas are used in societies and giving us some tools for analysis. It is very different in character from the extract from Robert Conquest's book on Stalin or the extract from Robert Grigor Suny's essay discussing the Stalinist purges which you read in connection with Book 1, Chapter 5. Both of these historians deal with a specific place and time. There are ideas in their writings which might be applicable to other societies at other periods, but that is not the basic purpose of their work. Writings such as Hobsbawm's are just as much 'history' as those of Conquest or Suny, but they are intended to challenge our preconceptions by taking a general thesis or idea and applying it to a variety of different historical situations – notice that the examples Hobsbawm uses are drawn from a wide range of times and places.

Activity With these ideas in mind, watch 'Ireland' on the DVD Video. If you are not familiar with the terms used in the programme, you will find them in the Media notes at the end of this chapter. You may want to take notes and to review sections of the programme in order to answer the following questions:

1 What is the general argument of the programme?
2 Which examples of 'invented tradition' can you see in the programme?
3 Which idea of the historic past animated Irish nationalists?
4 What evidence is used in the programme to support its argument?

Discussion

1 The programme's general thesis is that the Irish nationalist movement in the nineteenth century self-consciously drew on a set of symbols (harps, round towers, wolfhounds, etc.) that represented an ancient and purely Irish past untainted by the culture of English and Scots settlers who arrived in various waves from the twelfth century onwards. Following the creation of the **Irish Free State** in 1922, Irish governments, short of funds, gave priority to the preservation of neolithic and early Christian sites which celebrated the antiquity and separateness of Ireland's past. They also preserved a few notable Dublin landmarks, and restored the General Post Office, the seat of the 1916 Rising. Large country houses built, for the most part, by the Anglo-Irish were seen as relics of colonial oppression and were left to decay, as was Dublin Castle (seat of the English viceroy) and the Royal Hospital Kilmainham (seat of the commander of the army in Ireland before 1922). With greater prosperity and the wider view of Europe that followed Ireland becoming a member of the European Union in 1973, attitudes have begun to change. It has become possible to see the buildings of eighteenth-century Ireland not as expressions of colonial exploitation but as celebrations of Irish craftsmanship. The nub of the programme lies in the idea that it is possible to chart the attitudes of a nation to its history by looking at what it chooses to preserve of the past and what it chooses to neglect.
2 Two very conspicuous examples come to mind: that of the round tower built to commemorate Daniel O'Connell, and the reconstruction of Newgrange.
3 Nationalists referred to an idea of the Irish past in which the English and Scots were absent. So, in particular, nationalists looked back to prehistory with Newgrange; to the period of the high kings meeting at Tara; and to the glories of the Christian monastic tradition, begun with St Patrick, as represented by Cashel – Ireland having been one of the earliest lands outside the Roman empire to be converted to Christianity.
4 The evidence we have used for this programme is the country's surviving built heritage, but we are also concerned with what has *not* survived and why. We have used quotations from debates in the Irish parliament, the **Dáil**. Each of the speakers in the programme refers to different kinds of historical sources. For the most part they corroborate each other's views but there are some minor differences between them. Brian Murphy, in particular, provides anecdotes both of his own experience in the Irish civil service and from unnamed others.

I shall return later in this chapter to the connections between the preservation of the built heritage in Ireland and the ideas put forward by Eric Hobsbawm, but I hope that you are beginning to get the idea that what we see of the historic past around us is the product of both conscious and unconscious ideas about the past. Judgements about what to preserve, conserve, adapt, neglect and demolish are made not simply on aesthetic grounds but as a result of deeply felt ideas about which aspects of the past should be represented. So what we see of the past may be highly selective.

To give you a better idea of the background to the specific instance we've chosen to look at in the DVD Video, the next section provides an introduction to the history of Irish nationalism.

5.3 IRISH NATIONALISMS

I have used the terms 'Irish nationalists' as if referring to a homogenous group of people and 'Irish nationalism' as if this were a single set of ideas. In fact, Irish nationalism came in a wide variety of shades of opinion, drawing support from people from many different backgrounds. It would probably be more appropriate to talk of Irish nationalist movements in the plural, so varied and complicated were the groups of people who espoused the cause of an Ireland independent of rule from London.

In contemporary Ireland, nationalism survives in two forms, not entirely compatible with one another:

- the movement (expressed in a variety of political and paramilitary organisations) dedicated to reuniting the six counties that make up Northern Ireland (which is part of the United Kingdom) with the 26 counties that make up the Republic of Ireland
- the political parties in the Republic of Ireland that grew out of the nationalist struggle in the nineteenth and early twentieth centuries to secure independence from the United Kingdom, which was achieved by the treaty of 1921. Between 1922 (when the treaty came into effect) and 1999 the Irish constitution made territorial claims to the six counties. Under the terms of the Anglo-Irish Agreement of 1998 the constitution was amended the following year to express a desire for the peaceful political unification of the island subject to the consent of the people of Northern Ireland.

Both manifestations of nationalism have strong links with the Catholic church and avowedly republican (i.e. anti-monarchist) policies. In the next section I want to look at the origins of Irish nationalism and at how nationalists mobilised the past to support their claims. I shall refer in particular to people mentioned in the DVD Video. You may find it useful to consult the chronology in the Media notes as you work through this section.

Political nationalism

The rising that took place in Dublin on Easter Monday 1916 was the culmination of a long period during which Irish nationalism changed and matured and developed into a republican movement. Since the late eighteenth century there had been concern among Irish patriots – both Protestants and Catholics – that government from London and in the interests of the Anglo-Irish landlords was oppressive. Historically Catholics had suffered many restrictions not only to their civil rights, but also to their access to education and their ability to own and transfer property.

In the early nineteenth century a campaign for **Catholic emancipation** burgeoned. Daniel O'Connell (1775–1847), a lawyer, mobilised a mass movement in favour of extending to Catholics the civil rights that Protestants had, a campaign that reached fruition in 1829 with the Catholic Emancipation Act. This act made nationalism much less attractive to many Protestants. Subsequently O'Connell, now one of the 100 Irish MPs who sat at Westminster, devoted himself to campaigning to repeal the **Act of Union** between Britain and Ireland. As with his Catholic emancipation campaign, he made use of mass meetings and in 1843 evoked the spirit of the high kings of ancient Ireland in a meeting of over 500,000 people at their historic seat, the Hill of Tara (as you saw in the DVD Video; see also Figure 5.3). O'Connell's aim was to secure for Ireland political independence by peaceful means, a campaign that was derailed both by divisions within the movement and by the Irish famine of 1845–51. His importance was signified after his death by the magnificent monument erected for him in the Catholic necropolis at Glasnevin. While he had evoked the traditions of the Irish high kings at Tara, his admirers summoned up the tradition of early Irish Christianity by erecting in his memory a vast monument in the form of an early medieval Irish round monastic tower, as you saw in the DVD Video.

In 1845 the first signs of potato blight heralded a famine that lasted for some six years and led to the death or emigration to the USA, Canada, Australia and other parts of the British empire of over a million Irish men and women, chiefly from the poorest, Irish-speaking regions of the west. This catastrophe totally changed the character of Irish politics. Hitherto, nationalists had looked for self-government within the British empire. The famine energised republicanism, with militant movements emerging in both Ireland (the **Irish Republican Brotherhood**) and America (**Fenians**). These movements regarded the ownership of land by Irish people as central to the spirit of an Ireland free of British rule and mounted an all-out campaign against **Anglo-Irish** landlords, drawing much of their support from farming people. The famine affected Catholics more than Protestants and led to a stronger association between militant nationalism and Catholicism.

Figure 5.3 Unknown artist, *Meeting to demonstrate in favour of the repeal of the Act of Union at Tara*, 1843, engraving. Photo: Time Life Pictures/Mansell/Getty Images.

However, many land reformers concentrated on highly localised protests about rents and evictions and the attempts of Anglo-Irish landlords to introduce modern farming methods. The Land War of 1879–82 was a period of intensified agrarian unrest when, in the face of declining prices for agricultural produce, tenants demanded rent reductions and withheld their rent payments, following which many of them were evicted by their landlords. It was not until the 1880s that the Land League, the principal organisation lobbying for land reform, threw in its lot with the nationalists and demanded self-government for Ireland. From 1870 onwards the Westminster Parliament passed a series of acts which had the effect of allowing tenants to purchase the land they occupied and reducing the size of landlords' estates. The most important of these were the Wyndham Land Act of 1903, which compensated landlords with cash and dealt with a number of grievances arising from earlier legislation, and the Land Act of 1909, which introduced compulsory purchase for estates where agreement could not be reached between vendor and purchaser. Yet there were limits to the possibilities of an alliance between the land reformers and nationalists. Many nationalists dreamed of a return, once British landlordism had been eradicated, to the forms of communal landholding and egalitarian agricultural practices of ancient Irish society, while large numbers of agricultural tenants simply wanted to join the property-owning bourgeoisie by securing exclusive ownership of their land.

Parnell, Charles Stewart (1846–1891): The first president of the Land League and leader of the Irish Parliamentary party. He united a disparate alliance of supporters for Home Rule in Ireland and was able to convert the Liberal leader in the House of Commons, W.E. Gladstone, to the cause. His political career ended in disgrace in 1890 when he was cited as co-respondent in a divorce case.

Gladstone, William Ewart (1809–1898): Liberal prime minister in 1868–74, 1880–5, 1886 and 1892–4. He became a convert to the cause of Irish Home Rule in 1885.

You can consult the online version of the Oxford Dictionary of National Biography (ODNB) *through the course website.*

Throughout the later nineteenth century the movement for Home Rule for Ireland gathered strength, but most of those espousing the policy regarded it as something to be adopted within the framework of the British empire. Charles Stewart Parnell was able to unite a disparate alliance of Home Rule supporters and to convert W.E. Gladstone to the cause when the Irish MPs controlled the balance of power between the Conservatives and Liberals in the House of Commons. From 1885 onwards, Gladstone's support placed Home Rule at the centre of British politics. The campaign culminated in 1913 with the Liberal government under Herbert Asquith introducing the third Home Rule Bill (known as the Government of Ireland Bill), despite rising protests and violence from unionists (those who wanted to retain full parliamentary union with Britain), especially Protestants in the north of Ireland. The bill was passed in May 1914, with important issues concerning partition left unresolved. But all further action was suspended with the outbreak, in August, of the First World War.

Cultural nationalism

Daniel O'Connell's efforts were largely concerned with achieving administrative and social reforms through political means. You'll remember that in the DVD Video Professor Comerford contrasts O'Connell's indifference to culture with Thomas Davis's interest in it. Thomas Davis (1814–1845), and a group of others known as **'Young Ireland'**, founded *The Nation* newspaper in 1842 to campaign for the preservation and encouragement of a distinctively Irish folk culture which they saw as essential to the existence of a sense of nationhood among the Irish. Young Ireland was resolutely non-sectarian (Davis himself was a Protestant) and looked for a common vision of the Irish nation inspired by its past that everyone, regardless of their denomination, could share. For them, national independence carried with it the prospect of moral reform and the uplifting of the souls of the Irish people. Davis wrote extensively about Ireland's Celtic past and, in *The Nation*, published the works of more scholarly historical figures such as George Petrie. Davis also campaigned for education about Ireland's past and for the preservation of its monuments – presciently, he wrote in protest against the construction of a road through the prehistoric remains at Newgrange (Mulvey, 'Thomas Davis', *Oxford Dictionary of National Biography*).

For much of the nineteenth century cultural nationalists shared one common goal: to establish that the peoples of Ireland had a rich and ancient culture which justified their sense of nationhood. But cultural nationalism was made up of different strands, some of which are exemplified in the lives of George Petrie (1790–1866), antiquary and architect of the tower commemorating Daniel O'Connell at Glasnevin

Hyde, Douglas (1860–1949): The first president of the Gaelic League and later the first president of Ireland (1938–45).

Yeats, William Butler (1865–1939): Irish poet, playwright and member of the Irish Senate (1922–8).

Antiquity
language
literature

cemetery; Douglas Hyde (1860–1949), first president of the **Gaelic League** and later president of Ireland; and William Butler Yeats (1865–1939), poet and a leading member of the Anglo-Irish literary revival. Petrie represented the antiquarian interest, Hyde the language revival and Yeats the literary revival.

Petrie believed that Ireland's claim to nationhood rested on its immemorial religion and culture. He had a passionate desire to know more about the Irish past, taking the view that Irish civilisation had been destroyed by the English and that it was essential to understand what had been lost by studying the landscape, place names, bardic writings and antiquities (see Figure 5.4). He held that social unrest was caused by ignorance and that revealing the wealth of Ireland's history and culture would bring a new age of civilisation. He also wanted to separate historical fact from myth, pioneered the 'scientific' study of archaeology in Ireland, ran the historical section of the Irish Ordnance Survey, and bought for the Royal Irish Academy many items that are now treasures of the National Museum of Ireland. He was a tireless worker who published learned articles on both the monastic origins of the round towers and the history of the Hill of Tara (Murray, 2004).

While Petrie concentrated on antiquities, a parallel movement to revive the Irish language emerged. Douglas Hyde was one of a group of scholars who, in 1893, founded the Gaelic League (Conradh na Gaelige) to revive the language. Its use had started to decline significantly after the establishment in 1831 of a nationwide system of elementary education under which all teaching was carried out in the English language. Numbers of Irish speakers were further depleted by the deaths and emigration of so many of them as a result of the famine. The Gaelic League was one among several European organisations promoting language as one of a set of essential and distinctive cultural characteristics (folk culture, national dress, oral culture, etc.) in order to support the claims to political independence of nations suppressed by the dominant political cultures of Germany, Austro-Hungary, Russia and England (Boyce, 2004). Hyde was elected the League's first president and in 1902 he expressed his ideal:

> The Gaelic League has the best possible reason for believing that if Ireland is to become a really cultured country, and an artistic country, she must cease to imitate, and must take up the thread of her own past, and develop from within upon native lines. The moment Ireland broke with her own Gaelic past (and that is only a few score years ago), she fell away hopelessly from all intellectual and artistic effort. She lost her musical instruments, she lost her music, she lost her games, she lost her language and popular literature, and with her language she lost her intellectuality.
>
> (O'Day and Stevenson, 1992, p. 134)

Figure 5.4 J. and H.S. Storer after Petrie, *Mount Cashell, Co. of Tipperary*, engraving published by Sherwood & Co, 1 July 1824. Royal Irish Academy, Dublin. Photo: © By permission of the Royal Irish Academy. As well as his antiquarian activities, Petrie was an accomplished artist both of Irish landscapes and of the historic remains he wanted to record. Many of his paintings were engraved for reproduction in the new tourist guidebooks that started to appear in the early nineteenth century.

Activity Turn to Reading 5.2, an extract from a Gaelic League pamphlet by Reverend M.P. O'Hickey. What vision of the past is expounded in this document?

Discussion O'Hickey sees two different pasts. The first and earliest – 'the dim and distant', 'the very dawn of authentic history' – was the Irish-speaking past. The later one, much of it less than a century old, was the English-speaking past. For O'Hickey, language and history are completely inseparable. The Irish language (he uses the term Gaelic) carries the nation's past and, by extension, its culture, its 'polity and jurisprudence'. The English-speaking past blotted out centuries of history. Language is 'the surest and most powerful bond of a distinctive nationality'. Other Gaelic League documents advocated not merely the preservation of the Irish language, but the extension of its use both as a spoken tongue and as a modern literary language (Fahy, *c.*1890, p. 1).

O'Hickey was convinced by an ideal of a glorious Irish past before English became the language of much of Ireland. I say 'ideal' because since at least the early Middle Ages, Ireland had been a multilingual society. The Christian missionaries brought Latin, while the Anglo-Normans who arrived in the twelfth century brought French and English, with French later giving way to English as the language of government and the law. Debates in the Irish parliament were conducted in English, which meant that the Irish political elite was largely bilingual. So we should beware of taking at face value the pronouncements of a group of people who had an avowed policy of promoting the use of the Irish language and its role in the past.

One of the most important aspects of studying history is the need to respect the evidence of the past. We cannot know the past directly because we cannot experience it in person, but we can use the remnants of the past – archaeological remains, the relics of material culture, written documents and, for more recent periods, film, TV and electronic media – as evidence for the events, developments and beliefs of the past. To use this material we need to come to it with open but informed minds. We have questions we want to ask of it, but we cannot require that it prove a case. We also need to understand the circumstances that created it and the preconceptions of its creators.

Hyde had always insisted that the Gaelic League should avoid any sort of political or sectarian commitments, but his younger followers were not so squeamish. His campaign to revive the Irish language and its traditions had helped to galvanise the movement for a complete separation of Ireland from Britain during the bitter controversy over Home Rule. Hyde's repudiation of any political aim aroused impatience among his younger followers, and in 1915 he resigned his presidency of the League.

Gregory, Lady (Isabella) Augusta (1852–1932): A playwright and co-founder with W.B. Yeats of the Abbey Theatre, Dublin. She was also the chatelaine of Coole Park.

W.B. Yeats is the most famous member of the Anglo-Irish literary revival. With Lady Gregory, he founded the Abbey Theatre in Dublin in 1904. This movement was not completely separate from either the language revival movement or the political nationalists. Yeats was involved in the Gaelic League, while Thomas MacDonagh, one of the signatories of the 1916 Proclamation (see section 5.4), had a play performed at the Abbey Theatre. The aim of many of those active in the Anglo-Irish revival was to revive and reinterpret in English the culture of Gaelic Ireland, especially its mythology and in particular the legend of Cú Chulainn (whose statue in the GPO you saw in the DVD Video), a hero to both Catholics and Protestants.

Synge, John Millington (1871–1909): The Irish author of plays such as *The Playboy of the Western World,* Synge was a friend of W.B. Yeats and a director of the Abbey Theatre from 1904.

However, Catholic morality gave rise to dissension between the predominantly middle- and upper-class literary revivalists and the nationalists from a lower social class. Yeats's play *The Countess Cathleen*, produced at the Abbey Theatre in 1899, in which Countess Cathleen agrees to sell her soul to save famine-stricken peasants, outraged Catholic sensibilities. J.M. Synge's plays *In the Shadow of the Glen* (1903) and *The Playboy of the Western World* (1908) further deepened the division. The first portrayed an unfaithful wife; the second caused riots because it created a local hero out of a boy who was believed to have killed his father and then deflated him when it was proved that he had not in fact committed murder. For nationalists and Gaelic enthusiasts, literature and the theatre were primarily vehicles of propaganda to be used for the creation of, or in order to re-create, traditional Irish culture: a culture that was Gaelic, Catholic, morally pure and rural.

I hope you can see that each of the different strands of cultural nationalism described here used references to a distinctively Irish past as justification for the claim to Ireland's status as a nation. It was hoped that an appeal to a common Gaelic past would unite Irish men and women of all religions. And, for a brief period, this seemed to have worked. Yet the success of the nationalist movement ultimately came about through the igniting on Easter Monday 1916 of the sense that here were two opposing cultures: the Catholic Irish Gael set against the Protestant Anglo-Saxon.

5.4 THE EASTER RISING OF 1916

A truism of Irish history is that England's necessity was Ireland's opportunity. At the outbreak of war between Britain and Germany in 1914, Irishmen volunteered for the British army in large numbers and by 1916 some 150,000 had enlisted. Enthusiasm for enlistment was partly a consequence of high unemployment, but some nationalists saw it as a way of attaining the same standing within the British empire enjoyed by other members such as Australia and Canada (Boyce, 1994). Republican nationalists, however, regarded the war as a British affair and made contact with Germany, from whom they received a shipment of arms. The war had destabilised the constitutional nationalists and strengthened the position of the radicals, especially as there was a possibility that British Conservatives (who were closely allied with unionists) might not honour the Home Rule Act of 1914. A further concern was the prospect of conscription (introduced in Britain in 1916) being extended to Ireland.

We've seen how the Easter Rising broke out in Dublin in 1916 (Figure 5.5). The rebels comprised an alliance of republican nationalists (the IRB), labour activists (the Irish Citizen Army) and opponents of any Home Rule proposal that involved partition (the Irish Volunteers). Patrick Pearse, a schoolteacher much influenced by the Gaelic League, with a passion for Irish literature and language, and a preoccupation with sacrifice and redemption, was the moving spirit behind both the start of the uprising and the Proclamation of the Republic of Ireland.

Figure 5.5 'Sinn Féin 1916: inside the General Post Office, Dublin', 1916, postcard. Unknown photographer. Photo: © The Print Collector/Alamy. Postcards depicting scenes of the Easter Rising were sold in Dublin.

Activity Turn to Reading 5.3, the Proclamation of the Republic of Ireland. First, think about what kind of document this is by answering the following questions:

1 Who wrote it?

2 Who was the intended audience?

3 When was it written?

Now consider:

4 What type of document is it (public, private, official, published, etc.)?

5 What is its historical context?

6 What comments can you make on specific points in the text?

Discussion

1 It was written by Patrick Pearse.

2 It was intended to be read by the people of Ireland.

3 It was made public in 1916.

4 It's a public declaration by a group of rebels of the justice of their cause.

5 It was the document that justified the rising orchestrated by the Irish Republican Brotherhood with the assistance of the Irish Volunteers and the Irish Citizen Army as a prelude to seizing control of the government of Ireland from the British and declaring an independent republic.

6 It drew heavily on both religious ideas and an idea of the past ('dead generations') to establish the legitimacy of the rebels' claims to be representing the best interests of the people of Ireland. And note the reference to assistance from America and Europe. But it was also forward-looking in that it proposed to give Catholics and Protestants equal civil rights and to include women in the franchise.

Activity How does the Proclamation evoke the past?

Discussion The first paragraph refers to 'the dead generations from which [Ireland] receives her old tradition of nationhood'. In the second paragraph Pearse speaks of 'the long usurpation' of the English and to six rebellions in the last 300 years (it's not clear precisely which rebellions Pearse is referring to here).

The Proclamation is an extremely important document but, by itself, it doesn't tell us much about what effect it had. You know from the introduction to this chapter that the Proclamation led to much fighting in 1916 (look at the casualty figures), when nationalist volunteers were pitched against British troops. After six days the rebels surrendered. The Rising had not, as they had hoped, set the whole country alight. Indeed the *Irish Times*, unsympathetic to the nationalists, reported that most of the people who were in Sackville Street at the time the Proclamation was posted 'paid little attention to the doings of the rebels and preferred the more practical process of looting' (*Irish Times*, 6 May 1916). An account written some time later by a British government official, the secretary of the GPO, suggests that the government was probably using the *Irish Times* to downplay the impact of the Rising:

> Safe as we felt, in the presence of our own [British] troops, there was enough in the streets of Dublin that night of wild passion and fierce hope to convince the most careless of us that the country stood on the edge of some abyss, and as dark fell the thought recurred oftener than one wishes that this sudden outbreak was formidable, and might be timed to coincide with some German stroke, possibly an invasion.
>
> (Jeffery, 1999, p. 112)

Following the Rising, the British authorities sentenced 90 of the rebels to death. Seventy-five of the sentences were commuted to penal servitude, but 15 executions were actually carried out at Portobello Barracks and Kilmainham Gaol. These deaths made a great impact upon Ireland; they provided the hero-martyrs that persuaded the majority that British rule in Ireland was untenable.

Activity Turn to Reading 5.4, Yeats's letter to Lady Gregory.

What is this document, and how useful is it as a source for the history of the Easter Rising?

Discussion This is a private letter. Since Yeats wasn't in Dublin at the time of the Rising and was writing with only hearsay accounts to hand, we cannot really say that this document is of direct use in our understanding of the events in Sackville Street during the week following Easter 1916. But it is of great use in our understanding of how people responded to those events. For example, Yeats's scepticism regarding the likelihood that the rebels would receive fair trials is an interesting comment on the British administration of Ireland at the time. (On a completely different tack, his letter also brings home the importance of the war front in Belgium.)

Although we may regard this letter as a private communication between Yeats and Lady Gregory, Yeats was a man acutely conscious of his place in history, as he was by this time a considerable international figure (Foster, 2003, pp. xix–xx). So it would be disingenuous to think that he believed his letters would never be seen by anyone other than his correspondents. This is not to say that he always wrote with an eye for posterity, but rather that we might regard a letter from a major public and literary figure in a different light from correspondence from someone rather less well known. And Yeats's letter is of considerable importance in terms of our understanding the poem he wrote soon afterwards.

'Easter 1916'

Richard Danson Brown

Gonne, Maud (1866–1953): An Irish nationalist. W.B. Yeats was unhappily in love with her. In 1904 she married John MacBride, who was executed in 1916 for his part in the Easter Rising.

'Easter 1916', is one of Yeats's most famous works. It is, as the title indicates, a poem explicitly tied to historical events. Yet it is also a text where the personal and the political intertwine; as we have seen, Yeats was always conscious of himself as a public figure, and the sense of public utterance is very strong in the work. It was a difficult poem for Yeats to write. On a personal level, he disliked many of the participants in the Rising – for instance, he was contemptuous of Pearse, and overtly hostile to John MacBride, the husband of the woman, Maud Gonne, that Yeats himself had unsuccessfully courted for many years (Foster, 2003, pp. 59–66).

Activity Turn to Reading 5.5, Yeats's poem 'Easter 1916', and read it at least twice. Then consider the following questions:

1 Would you characterise the poem as 'traditional', or dissenting, and why?

2 To what extent do you think the poem supports the Easter Rising?

Discussion I wouldn't pretend that these are easy questions to answer. Critics have debated the meaning of the poem ever since its first publication. But we can make sense of the poem in terms of Irish nationalism and our broader concern in this book with the dynamic between tradition and dissent.

1 'Easter 1916' shows both traditional and innovatory features. It's written in rhyming stanzas of differing lengths. Stanzas 1, 2 and 4 all use a refrain, 'All changed, changed utterly:/A terrible beauty is born.' These devices powerfully suggest that Yeats was writing within the

traditions of English poetry, following on from writers like Blake and Donne, where verse is an elegant arrangement of lines in stanzas. However, Yeats's poem also deviates from tradition. It uses many half-rhymes, such as 'gibe'/'club', 'lout'/'heart', 'stream'/'brim'. You might also have noticed Yeats's fondness for repetition. For example, in the first stanza the phrase 'polite meaningless words' is almost immediately repeated, underlining the contrast between normal existence and the 'terrible' and 'beautiful' change wrought by the Rising. These devices suggest that Yeats is here consciously modifying poetic tradition – I would say they enhance the public character of his poem, as the first stanza successfully mimics both the speaking voice of someone excited by breaking news and the hypnotic cadences of an orator. We should also recognise that the poem implicitly dissents from British rule in Ireland: paradoxically, this is a poem written in English which opposes English rule. As the final stanza puts it: 'Now and in time to be,/Wherever green is worn,/Are changed'. The implication is that the Rising has irrevocably changed Irish nationalists, giving them a forward momentum which is at once disturbing and intoxicating.

2 As his wording suggests, Yeats's attitude towards the Easter Rising is ambivalent. On the one hand, he pays generous tribute to men he disliked. For example, although MacBride remains 'A drunken, vainglorious lout', nevertheless 'He, too, has resigned his part/In the casual comedy'. (Another way of putting this might be: 'Although I hated your guts, I recognise, despite myself, that you did something significant.') On the other hand, the poem is extremely vague about what precisely the Rising achieved. MacBride 'has resigned his part/In the casual comedy' of the opening stanza, depicting the ordinary social intercourse of pre-Rising Dublin, but the poem resists drawing any clear-cut political moral from the events of 1916. Rather, in the fourth stanza it advances an elliptical symbolic and psychological account of human action. Yeats dwells on the pitfalls of fanaticism ('Too long a sacrifice/Can make a stone of the heart'), and the poem is notable for refusing to condemn the British state's execution of 'MacDonagh and MacBride/And Connolly and Pearse', even as it uses a heroic rhetoric to celebrate their deeds.

Perhaps unsurprisingly, Maud Gonne, who was much less ambivalent in her politics, disliked 'Easter 1916'. She wrote: 'it isn't worthy of you & above all it isn't worthy of the subject ... [you] know quite well that sacrifice has never turned a heart to stone & through it alone mankind can rise to God' (Foster, 2003, p. 63). Gonne would have preferred a more explicit poem of nationalist celebration and lament, but Yeats characteristically refused to simplify the paradoxical texture of his thought.

Reading the materials in this section, you may have been reminded of some of the issues surrounding Cleopatra in Book 1. In other words, we try to be objective and extract the truth about what happened in the past, but it is often difficult to set aside our own values when reading historical material. Although we know a great deal more about the events of 1916 than we do about those in Cleopatra's time, many people continue to hold strong views about past events, and their opinions are often derived from their present-day political or religious beliefs. That is why we set about reading historical documents systematically, to make sure we have established as much disinterested information as possible in order to assess their content.

We should also be mindful of the purpose *why* something was written. Yeats's letter to Lady Gregory is a very different kind of communication from that of his poem. The first is a private message; the second a public one. Yeats had been meditating on his poem since May 1916; he completed it four months later. As Richard Danson Brown suggests, in his discussion of 'Easter 1916' above, Yeats was profoundly affected by the transformation of his former republican antagonists into the heroes of the hour. Several of the men executed after the Rising had been among his fiercest critics at the Abbey Theatre.

5.5 AFTER EASTER 1916

After the Easter Rising was suppressed, the British government returned to its preoccupation with the war in France, where casualties were rising fast. It was not until the Armistice was declared in 1918 that the government could address itself to Ireland. The general election for the Westminster Parliament that year produced an overwhelming victory for **Sinn Féin** in Ireland, which gained over 40 per cent of the Irish votes and 73 MPs who declined to take their seats at Westminster. (Sinn Féin had been formed in 1907 as a broadly based, nationalist political party committed to independence from Britain.) Meanwhile, the police, the military and the notorious Black and Tans (recruited from demobilised soldiers) were rallied to suppress the guerrilla war waged by the increasingly militant and violent republican nationalists. The Irish Volunteers, now transformed into the Irish Republican Army (IRA), conducted a war of terror on people and buildings associated with British rule. The suppression of the 1916 Rising had not brought peace to Ireland: many of those who had been sceptical of republican nationalism were converted to the cause by the brutal treatment of the 1916 rebels and the harsh measures taken by the government to suppress the guerrilla War of Independence (1919–21).

In 1919 the first Dáil Éireann (Irish parliament) met. This assembly of Sinn Féin MPs was, surprisingly, allowed to sit for six months before being closed down by the British government. Despite the pressures of trying to run an alternative administration and a terrorist campaign, the nationalists did not forget their historicist claims. The Declaration of Independence, passed at the first meeting of the Dáil, includes the words: 'Whereas for seven hundred years the Irish people has never ceased to repudiate and has repeatedly protested in arms against foreign usurpation ...' (Mitchell and Ó Snodaigh, 1985, p. 57).

The Dáil provided a provisional nationalist administration which went some way towards assuming powers hitherto exercised by the British. This gave the nationalists a significant position from which to bargain when they sat down at the conference table with the British in 1921 (Jackson, 1999, p. 253).

Collins, Michael (1890–1922): Organiser of Sinn Féin, chairman of the provisional Irish government in 1922, supporter of the Anglo-Irish Treaty and leader of the pro-Treaty Irish Free State army during the Irish civil war. He was killed by anti-Treaty irregular forces.

The Anglo-Irish peace treaty of 1921 proposed the division of Ireland into a 26-county 'free state' and a six-county province which was to remain part of the United Kingdom. The departure of British forces from Ireland in 1922 led to a civil war that lasted until 1923, fought between republicans who opposed the treaty and nationalists who supported it. Heroes of the earlier struggle against British rule adopted different views towards the treaty. Eamon de Valera opposed it; other republicans declared they would shoot members of the Dáil on sight. This they did in 1922 when they killed Michael Collins, leader of the Irish Free State (pro-treaty) forces. (You may have seen the 1996 film of Collins's life, starring Liam Neeson in the title role.)

The civil war was brought to an end by a ceasefire in May 1923, the Free State government having had to resort to the kinds of tactics used by the British government in order to suppress the opponents of the treaty. The new state, established in 1922, had to set about repairing the damage inflicted by the civil war and resorted to a conscious policy of Gaelicisation. Legislation was passed to ensure that the Irish language was taught in all schools and Irish cultural activities were actively promoted. In 1921 the National Programme Conference on Primary Education had declared that a primary aim of education was to 'revive the ancient life of Ireland as a Gaelic state, Gaelic in language, and Gaelic and Christian in its ideals', and that the chief aim of teaching Irish history was 'to inculcate national pride and self-respect ... by showing that the Irish race has fulfilled a great mission in the advancement of civilization' (quoted in Foster, 1989, p. 518).

But how had matters changed between 1916 and 1923? The ancient and distinctively Irish past still provided a frame of reference for the nationalists. However, by 1923 there was a new history to nourish the creation myth for the foundation of the Irish state: the tale of the heroes of 1916 and the War of Independence supplied the Irish people with tales of local struggles that allowed everyone to identify themselves with emergent nationalism. Think back to Book 1, Chapter 5 on Stalin, where you considered what a myth is. If you look at the most comprehensive *Oxford English Dictionary* you will find that one of the meanings given for the word myth is: 'A traditional story, typically involving supernatural beings or forces, which embodies and provides an explanation, aetiology [study of causes], or justification for something such as the early history of a society, a religious belief or ritual, or a natural phenomenon'. And in Book 1, Chapter 7 on the Dalai Lama, Helen Waterhouse makes the point that both history and myth are ways of making sense of the world around us.

As you saw in earlier chapters of this course, you can search the Oxford English Dictionary *online through the course website.*

Figure 5.6 Sir John Lavery, *Lady Lavery as Cathleen Ní Houlihan*, also known as 'Killarney', 1923, oil on canvas, 75.5 x 62.5 cm. The National Gallery of Ireland, Dublin. Photo: Courtesy of the National Gallery of Ireland. © Central Bank of Ireland. Lady Lavery was an American who became an ardent Irish nationalist. Cathleen Ní Houlihan, a mythical Irish heroine and the subject of Yeats's play of that name, is generally depicted as an old woman who needs the help of young Irish men willing to fight and die to free Ireland. The harp that 'Cathleen' holds here is a traditional symbol of Irish nationhood.

Nationalists' emphasis on the past inevitably drew on the period of the earliest Irish legends, before the era of written history. From the early Middle Ages English had become the language of the ruling elite, while from the sixteenth century onwards Protestantism had become their religion. But the English language and the Protestant religion were not exclusive to the elite: many ordinary people who regarded themselves as Irish spoke no Irish and were not Roman Catholic. So the past that the educators of the Irish Free State wanted to promote was selective.

The history of more recent times was also problematic in the new state. The civil war was deeply divisive and for a considerable period

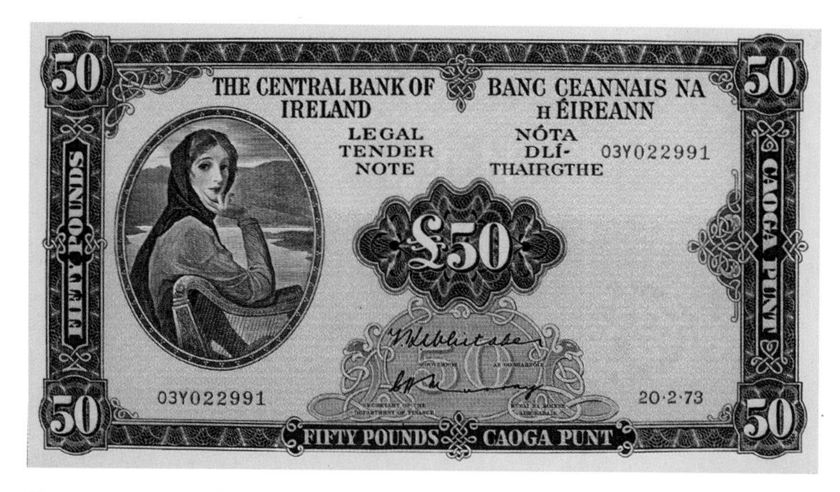

Figure 5.7 A £50 Irish Free State banknote, with the front showing Lady Lavery's portrait. Photo: Courtesy of the Central Bank of Ireland. The image of Cathleen Ní Houlihan has been used on a number of Irish banknotes.

afterwards was not the subject of serious historical writing: it was too contentious for that. While all nations require creation myths – in this case how the Irish people triumphed against British imperialism – the recovery from a civil war often requires a good deal of strategic forgetfulness in the interests of post-war reconstruction. The creation in Ireland during the nineteenth and twentieth centuries of a narrative of the past to justify the goal of an Irish state independent of British rule, and the development of a nationalist history of the independent Irish state, isn't the kind of history written by academics and published in scholarly journals; rather, it's a history of dramatic stories, murders, persecution, heroes and villains, colourful paintings, posters and banners, and sound-bites. And it doesn't matter how much academic historians who've studied the papers from the time might say that such and such a person wasn't quite a hero after all – the myths that give rise to a nation's sense of itself are difficult to disturb. The uses of history in current political discourse have little to do with academic scholarship and the work of professional historians.

5.6 RETURN TO THE BUILT HERITAGE OF IRELAND

Activity Watch 'Ireland' on the DVD Video again and think about what kind of past the governments of Ireland, following 1922, wanted to represent. Think about the phrases used by the speakers in the programme.

Discussion Did you notice the use of the phrases 'a land of saints and scholars' and 'ancient places and sacred spaces'? Here are neat slogans to characterise an Irish past which has nothing to do with Anglo-Irish landlords.

The point is made by Brian Murphy early on that the decision to rebuild the GPO, the Custom House and the Four Courts was pragmatic. The government needed places where citizens of the new state could buy stamps, pay their taxes and go to law. But the materials used for the reconstruction had to be of Irish origin; the contrast between the English Portland stone of the original Custom House and the greyer Irish limestone used to rebuild it is a conspicuous reminder of this policy. The two architecturally significant buildings that represented British military power (the Royal Hospital Kilmainham) and British political power (Dublin Castle) were simply abandoned. Note that de Valera had the foresight not to allow Dublin Castle to be demolished.

The use of the harp as a symbol for the new state was on the one hand a reference to nineteenth-century nationalism, but, on the other, also a reference to the harpists of the ancient high kings.

Did you also note that the Ancient Monuments Act of 1929 was designed only to protect buildings dating from before 1700? And that neolithic Ireland (in the form of Newgrange) was of more significance in the 1950s than any eighteenth-century building? Terence Dooley tells us that some 300 private country houses were destroyed during the period 1916–23. We do not know whether this was the consequence of a genuine collapse of law enforcement or of the new Irish government turning a blind eye to the activities of local republicans. Undoubtedly agricultural political interests militated against the kind of high culture and landlord ascendancy represented in the eighteenth-century country house.

The phrase ‘reversing Cromwell’s policy’ used in the DVD Video refers to the ownership of land, and in many nationalists’ eyes it was the Cromwellian conquest of Ireland in the seventeenth century that instituted the Protestant ascendancy in its most virulent form. In fact the transfer of land from Irish Catholics to people of English and Scots origin had started long before the Cromwellian invasion.

One aspect of this discussion I would like you to think about particularly is that tradition may not just be about preservation; it can also be about neglect or indifference. It is difficult to distinguish between deliberate, ideologically-driven neglect, and the neglect that comes from lack of money to carry out costly restorations. Certainly, as you saw in the DVD Video, the Irish government between 1922 and 1973 (when Ireland joined the European Union) could not afford to embark on many major building restorations, but all governments make choices about where their priorities lie and what will be electorally popular.

Activity What evidence does the DVD Video provide for a recent change of attitude to Ireland’s past?

Discussion The adaptation of St Mary’s church into a bar, the transformation of the Royal Hospital Kilmainham into an art gallery and the opening to the public of Dublin Castle show how former objections to preserving the relics of the British government and Protestant ascendancy are being set aside. Previously these buildings were neglected.

The comments made about O’Kelly’s restoration of Newgrange suggest that had the work been done now it would have been done differently, not for any ideological reasons but because archaeologists’ attitudes to reconstructions have changed.

The preservation of Castletown House flew in the face of orthodoxy at the time, but the building is now in the charge of a government department and regarded as one of the finest examples of eighteenth-century Irish craftsmanship. Conservers of such buildings no longer attract criticism as lackeys of landlordism.

Several of the speakers in the DVD Video refer to the way in which Irish people have 'moved on'. Brian Murphy suggests that an important consideration in promoting this change was that Ireland's membership of the EU brought much greater prosperity to the country, took Irish people to other parts of Europe and increased the numbers of foreign visitors to Ireland. Undoubtedly, the passage of time has also had an effect. The revolutionaries of the 1910s and 1920s are no longer living, and their descendants are more alive to the glories of Irish craftsmanship than to the wrongs of Anglo-Irish landlordism.

5.7 TRADITION AND DISSENT: THE INVENTION OF TRADITION

I hope that you can see how tradition has been mobilised to build a nationalist ideology in Ireland. But you will have noticed that it is a selective view of the past, and to this extent it conforms to the idea of the invention of tradition. The vision of the Irish past that is advanced is not a scientifically dispassionate one.

Activity Turn again to Reading 5.1. How does our discussion of Ireland relate to Hobsbawm's observations?

Discussion We can see elements of all three of Hobsbawm's types of tradition in the examples we have looked at. In the first instance a common sense of a Gaelic past was a form of cohesion for Irish nationalists in the nineteenth century. The prehistoric and early Christian past undoubtedly gave Irish people a sense of nationhood, both political and cultural, to justify their existence as a state. And the education policies of the new state certainly used a particular vision of the Irish past to socialise its young citizens.

There are, visible in the DVD Video, other kinds of invented tradition. Did you notice that the Royal Hospital Kilmainham (now the Museum of Modern Art) and St Mary's church (now Keating's Bar) are both built in the classical style, drawing on Roman and Italian Renaissance architectural models? As you saw in Chapter 4, Pugin's enthusiasm for the Gothic style was a reaction against the eighteenth-century passion for classicism.

The final paragraph in Reading 5.1 refers to language. Hobsbawm's observation about the teaching of the Flemish language in Belgium is just as applicable to Irish, which has had to find words for telephones, exhaust pipes, self-service petrol stations, computers, multi-storey car-parks, iPods and all the paraphernalia of modern life in a language which survived chiefly in a rural, agricultural society.

The study of these so-called invented traditions has proved to be a fruitful avenue of enquiry for historians. Their studies have not simply debunked accepted ideas about the past; they have also told us a good deal about the cultures that have created these traditions. So we have been concerned here with the ways in which the past may be presented in different ways to serve different purposes, not in the sense of wilfully misleading but in the sense of giving greater emphasis to some elements of the past than others in order to create a narrative that explains certain things about the present or satisfies certain needs in it. For example, it may be useful to stress the antiquity of state institutions in order to promote a sense of stability, or to emphasise the ability of institutions to adapt to meet new challenges. I have said very little about dissent here, but we need to remind ourselves of the dissent of those against whom the nationalists were reacting: the dissent of unionists, and the dissent of those who had a different vision of the Irish past.

REFERENCES

Boyce, D.G. (1994) 'Ireland & the First World War', *History Ireland*, vol. 2 (autumn), pp. 48–53.

Boyce, D.G. (2004) 'Ireland's Celtic heroes' in Boyce, D.G. and Swift, R. (eds) *Problems and Perspectives in Irish History since 1800: Essays in Honour of Patrick Buckland*, Dublin, Four Courts Press, pp. 196–216.

Fahy, F.A. (*c.* 1890) *A Gaelic League Catechism*, London, Gaelic League of London.

Fitzpatrick, D. (1989) 'Ireland since 1870' in Foster, R. (ed.) *The Oxford Illustrated History of Ireland*, Oxford, Oxford University Press, pp. 213–74.

Foster, R.F. (1989) *Modern Ireland 1600–1972*, Harmondsworth, Penguin.

Foster, R.F. (2003) *W.B. Yeats: A Life*, vol. 2: *The Arch Poet*, Oxford, Oxford University Press.

Hobsbawm, E. and Ranger, T. (eds) (1983) *The Invention of Tradition*, Cambridge, Cambridge University Press.

Jackson, A. (1999) *Ireland 1798–1998: Politics and War*, Oxford, Blackwell.

Jeffery, K. (ed.) (1999) *The Sinn Féin Rebellion as They Saw It*, Dublin, Irish Academic Press.

Mitchell, A. and Ó Snodaigh, P. (1985) *Irish Political Documents, 1916–49*, Dublin, Irish Academic Press.

Mulvey, H. 'Thomas Davis', *Oxford Dictionary of National Biography*, http://www.oxforddnb.com/view/article/7294?docPos=3 (Accessed March 2008).

Murray, P. (2004) *George Petrie (1760–1866): The Rediscovery of Ireland's Past*, Kinsale, Gandon Editions.

O'Day, A. and Stevenson, J. (eds) (1992) *Irish Historical Documents since 1800*, Dublin, Gill and Macmillan.

RESOURCES

Reading 5.1 Hobsbawm, Inventing traditions

This is the introduction to a highly influential volume of essays that was published following a conference on 'the invention of tradition'. Other essays deal with such topics as the emergence of the distinctive traditions of the Scottish Highlands in the nineteenth century; the development of rituals around the British monarchy, and the emergence of traditions in colonial Africa.

1 Nothing appears more ancient, and linked to an immemorial past, than the pageantry which surrounds British monarchy in its public ceremonial manifestations. Yet ... in its modern form it is the product of the late nineteenth and twentieth centuries. 'Traditions' which appear or claim to be old are often quite recent in origin and sometimes invented. Anyone familiar with the colleges of ancient British universities will be able to think of the institution of such 'traditions' on a local scale, though some – like the annual Festival of Nine Lessons and Carols in the chapel of King's College, Cambridge on Christmas Eve – may become generalized through the modern mass medium of radio. This observation formed the starting-point of a conference organized by the historical journal *Past & Present*, which in turn forms the basis of the present book.

2 The term 'invented traditions' is used in a broad, but not imprecise sense. It includes both 'traditions' actually invented, constructed and formally instituted and those emerging in a less easily traceable manner within a brief and dateable period – a matter of a few years perhaps – and establishing themselves with great rapidity. The royal Christmas broadcast in Britain (instituted in 1932) is an example of the first; the appearance and development of the practices associated with the Cup Final in British Association Football, of the second. It is evident that not all of them are equally permanent, but it is their appearance and establishment rather than their chances of survival which are our primary concern.

3 'Invented tradition' is taken to mean a set of practices, normally governed by overtly or tacitly accepted rules and of a ritual or symbolic nature, which seek to inculcate certain values and norms of behaviour by repetition, which automatically implies continuity with the past. In fact, where possible, they normally attempt to establish continuity with a suitable historic past. A striking example is the deliberate choice of a Gothic style for the nineteenth-century rebuilding of the British parliament, and the equally deliberate decision after World War II to rebuild the parliamentary chamber on exactly the same basic plan as before. The historic past into which the new tradition is inserted need not be lengthy, stretching back into the assumed mists of time. Revolutions and 'progressive movements' which break with the past, by definition, have their own relevant past, though it may be cut off at a certain date, such as 1789. However, insofar as there is such reference to a historic past, the peculiarity of 'invented' traditions is that the continuity with it is largely factitious.

In short, they are responses to novel situations which take the form of reference to old situations, or which establish their own past by quasi-obligatory repetition. It is the contrast between the constant change and innovation of the modern world and the attempt to structure at least some parts of social life within it as unchanging and invariant, that makes the 'invention of tradition' so interesting for historians of the past two centuries ...

4 There is probably no time and place with which historians are concerned which has not seen the 'invention' of tradition ... However, we should expect it to occur more frequently when a rapid transformation of society weakens or destroys the social patterns for which 'old' traditions had been designed, producing new ones to which they were not applicable, or when such old traditions and their institutional carriers and promulgators no longer prove sufficiently adaptable and flexible, or are otherwise eliminated: in short, when there are sufficiently large and rapid changes on the demand or the supply side. Such changes have been particularly significant in the past 200 years ...

5 More interesting [than the adaptation of old traditions], from our point of view, is the use of ancient materials to construct invented traditions of a novel type for quite novel purposes. A large store of such materials is accumulated in the past of any society, and an elaborate language of symbolic practice and communications is always available. Sometimes new traditions could be readily grafted on old ones, sometimes they could be devised by borrowing from the well-supplied warehouses of official ritual, symbolism and moral exhortation – religion and princely pomp, folklore and freemasonry (itself an earlier invented tradition of great symbolic force). Thus the development of Swiss nationalism, concomitant with the formation of the modern federal state in the nineteenth century, has been brilliantly studied by Rudolf Braun, ... in a country where its modernization has not been set back by association with Nazi abuses. Existing customary traditional practices – folksong, physical contests, marksmanship – were ... supplemented by new songs in the same idiom, often composed by schoolmasters, transferred to a choral repertoire whose content was patriotic-progressive ... The statutes of the Federal Song Festival – are we not reminded of the eisteddfodau? – declare its object to be 'the development and improvement of the people's singing, the awakening of more elevated sentiments for God, Freedom and Country, union and fraternization of the friends of Art and the Fatherland'. (The word 'improvement' introduces the characteristic note of nineteenth-century progress.) ...

6 It is clear that plenty of political institutions, ideological movements and groups – not least in nationalism – were so unprecedented that even historic continuity had to be invented, for

example by creating an ancient past beyond effective historical continuity, either by semi-fiction (Boadicea, Vercingetorix, Arminius the Cheruscan) or by forgery (Ossian, the Czech medieval manuscripts). It is also clear that entirely new symbols and devices came into existence as part of national movements and states, such as the national anthem (of which the British in 1740 seems to be the earliest), the national flag (still largely a variation on the French revolutionary tricolour, evolved 1790–4), or the personification of 'the nation' in symbol or image, either official, as with Marianne [in France] and Germania, or unofficial, as in the cartoon stereotypes of [the English] John Bull, the lean Yankee Uncle Sam and the 'German Michel'....

7 In the private lives of most people ... even the invented traditions of the nineteenth and twentieth centuries occupied or occupy a much smaller place than old traditions do in, say, old agrarian societies. ...

8 However, this generalization does not apply in the field of what might be called the public life of the citizen ... There is no real sign of weakening in the neo-traditional practices associated ... with the citizens' membership of states. Indeed most of the occasions when people become conscious of citizenship as such remain associated with symbols and semi-ritual practices (for instance, elections), most of which are historically novel and largely invented: flags, images, ceremonies and music. Insofar as the invented traditions of the era since the industrial and French revolutions have filled a permanent gap – at all events up to the present – it would seem to be in this field ...

9 What benefit can historians derive from the study of the invention of tradition?

10 First and foremost, it may be suggested that they are important symptoms and therefore indicators of problems which might not otherwise be recognized, and developments which are otherwise difficult to identify and to date. They are evidence. The transformation of German nationalism from its old liberal to its new imperialist-expansionist pattern is more exactly illuminated by the rapid replacement of the old black-red-gold colours by the new black-white-red ones (especially by the 1890s) among the German gymnastic movement, than by official statements of authorities or spokesmen for organizations. The history of the British football cup finals tells us something about the development of an urban working-class culture which more conventional data and sources do not. By the same token, the study of invented traditions cannot be separated from the wider study of the history of society, nor can it expect to advance much beyond the mere discovery of such practices unless it is integrated into a wider study.

11 Second, it throws a considerable light on the human relation to the past, and therefore on the historian's own subject and craft. For all invented traditions, so far as possible, use history as a legitimator of action and cement of group cohesion. Frequently it becomes the actual symbol of struggle ... Even revolutionary movements backed their innovations by references to a 'people's past' ..., to traditions of revolution ... and to its own heroes and martyrs. James Connolly's *Labour in Irish History* [1910] exemplifies this union of themes excellently. The element of invention is particularly clear here, since the history of nation, state or movement is not what has actually been preserved in popular memory, but what has been selected, written, pictured, popularized and institutionalized by those whose function it is to do so. Oral historians have frequently observed how in the actual memories of the old the General Strike of 1926 plays a more modest and less dramatic part than interviewers anticipated. ... Yet all historians, whatever else their objectives, are engaged with this process inasmuch as they contribute, consciously or not, to the creation, dismantling and restructuring of images of the past which belong not only to the world of specialist investigation but to the public sphere of man as a political being. They might as well be aware of this dimension of their activities.

12 In this connection, one specific interest of 'invented traditions' for, at all events, modern and contemporary historians ought to be singled out. They are highly relevant to that comparatively recent historical innovation, the 'nation', with its associated phenomena: nationalism, the nation-state, national symbols, histories and the rest. All these rest on exercises in social engineering which are often deliberate and always innovative, if only because historical novelty implies innovation. Israeli and Palestinian nationalism or nations must be novel, whatever the historic continuities of Jews or Middle Eastern Muslims, since the very concept of territorial states of the currently standard type in their region was barely thought of a century ago, and hardly became a serious prospect before the end of World War I. Standard national languages, to be learned in schools and written, let alone spoken, by more than a smallish élite, are largely constructs of varying, but often brief, age. As a French historian of Flemish language observed, quite correctly, the Flemish taught in Belgium today is not the language which the mothers and grandmothers of Flanders spoke to their children: in short, it is only metaphorically but not literally a 'mother-tongue'. We should not be misled by a curious, but understandable, paradox: modern nations and all their impedimenta generally claim to be the opposite of novel, namely rooted in the remotest antiquity, and the opposite of constructed, namely human communities so 'natural' as to require no definition other than self-assertion.... And just because so much of what subjectively makes up the modern 'nation' consists of such

constructs and is associated with appropriate and, in general, fairly recent symbols or suitably tailored discourse (such as 'national history'), the national phenomenon cannot be adequately investigated without careful attention to the 'invention of tradition'.

Source: E. Hobsbawm, 'Introduction: inventing traditions', from E. Hobsbawm and T. Ranger (eds) (1983) *The Invention of Tradition*, Cambridge, Cambridge University Press (reprinted Cambridge, Canto, 1995, pp. 1–14; footnote omitted).

Reading 5.2

The Ideals of the Gaelic League, 1898

This pamphlet was based on a lecture given on behalf of the Gaelic League in Dublin in 1898.

Amongst the essentials of nationality, understood aright, none is more fundamental, none more important, none strikes deeper roots, none is more far-reaching in its results, than a national language. ...

But a nation's language is more – much more – than a mere element of nationality. It is its most striking symbol – the one invincible barrier against disintegration. A distinct language is the surest and most powerful bond of a distinctive nationality: its most effective bulwark; the most certain – indeed, the only certain – guarantee of its continuance and perpetuation. But a nation's language, thus regarded, should not be looked at merely in itself. It should be looked at in conjunction with all that it imports, holds and enshrines – all that it carries down the stream of time from the dim and distant, the storied and centuried past. It should be regarded as the vehicle of the people's history; the key to their polity and jurisprudence; the mirror in which their mind, manner and customs are reflected; the shrine of their legends, myths, beliefs and superstitions; the repository of their literature; the only reliable index to the national life of the past. For all this, and much more, a people's language is.

When did our English-speaking history begin? For most of us, not much more than a century ago; for very many of us, not much more than a half-century ago; and for a not inconsiderable number – well over half a million – it has not begun at all. Our Gaelic-speaking history, on the other hand, goes back through a long series of centuries, back to the very dawn of authentic history, and probably far beyond it. ... Shall we cut ourselves adrift from our Gaelic past, with all its wealth of tradition, of proud memories, of glorious literature – blot out centuries of our history, and appear before the world as a people whose history began a century or two ago?

Michael Patrick O'Hickey (1860–1917) was appointed Professor of Irish, St Patrick's College, Maynooth in 1896 and dismissed in 1908 for advocating publicly that Irish be a compulsory entry requirement to the newly founded National University of Ireland. This was later achieved.

Source: Rev. M.P. O'Hickey (1898) *The True National Idea*, London, Gaelic League pamphlet no. 1, p. 2.

Reading 5.3

Proclamation of the Republic of Ireland, April 1916

The proclamation was drafted by Patrick Pearse with suggestions from other members of the military council of the Irish Republican Brotherhood. It was read on the steps of the GPO in Dublin on Easter Monday (24 April) 1916 by Pearse as commander-in-chief of the insurgents and president of the provisional government of the Irish Republic.

The Provisional Government of the Irish Republic to the People of Ireland,

Irishmen and Irishwomen: In the name of God and of the dead generations from which she receives her old tradition of nationhood, Ireland, through us, summons her children to her flag and strikes for her freedom. Having organised and trained her manhood through her secret revolutionary organisation, the Irish Republican Brotherhood, and through her open military organisations, the Irish Volunteers, and the Irish Citizen Army, having patiently perfected her discipline, having resolutely waited for the right moment to reveal itself, she now seizes that moment, and, supported by her exiled children in America and by gallant allies in Europe [the IRB had received a shipment of arms from Germany], but relying in the first on her own strength, she strikes in full confidence of victory.

We declare the right of the people of Ireland to the ownership of Ireland, and to the unfettered control of Irish destinies, to be sovereign and indefeasible. The long usurpation of that right by a foreign people and government has not extinguished the right, nor can it ever be extinguished except by the destruction of the Irish people. In every generation the Irish people have asserted their right to national freedom and sovereignty; six times during the past three hundred years they have asserted it in arms. Standing on that fundamental right and again asserting it in arms in the face of the world, we hereby proclaim the Irish republic as a sovereign independent state, and we pledge our lives and the lives of our comrades-in-arms to the cause of its freedom, of its welfare, and of its exaltation among the nations.

The Irish republic is entitled to, and hereby claims, the allegiance of every Irishman and Irishwoman. The republic guarantees religious and civil liberty, equal rights and equal opportunities to all its citizens, and declares its resolve to pursue the happiness and prosperity of all its parts, cherishing all the children of the nation equally, and oblivious of the differences carefully fostered by an alien government, which have divided a minority [Protestants] from the majority [Catholics] in the past.

Women did not have the vote anywhere in Britain or Ireland, though from 1894 they could vote in and stand for local council elections in England and Wales.

Until our arms have brought the opportune moment for the establishment of a permanent national government, representative of the whole people of Ireland, and elected by the suffrages of all her men and women, the Provisional Government, hereby constituted, will administer the civil and military affairs of the republic in trust for the people. We place the cause of the Irish republic under the protection of the Most High God, whose blessing we invoke upon our arms, and we pray that no one who serves that cause will dishonour it by cowardice, inhumanity, or rapine. In this supreme hour the Irish nation must, by its valour and discipline, and by the readiness of its children to sacrifice themselves for the common good, prove itself worthy of the august destiny to which it is called.

Signed on behalf of the provisional government,

Thomas J. Clarke, Sean MacDiarmada, Thomas MacDonagh, Pádraig Pearse, Eamonn Ceannt, James Connolly, Joseph Plunkett

Source: A. Mitchell and P. Ó Snodaigh (eds) (1985) *Irish Political Documents 1916–1949*, Dublin, Irish Academic Press, pp. 17–18.

Reading 5.4 Yeats's response to the Easter Rising, 1916

Royal Societies Club, St James's Street, [London] S.W.

Thursday [11 May 1916]

My dear Lady Gregory,

William Thomas Cosgrave (1880–1965) was joint founder, with Arthur Griffith, of Sinn Féin. In 1916 he fought with the Dublin Volunteers, was captured and condemned to death. The sentence was commuted to life imprisonment and he was released from gaol in 1917. Cosgrave later became the first president of the Executive Council of the Irish Free State (1922–32).

Douglas (later Earl) Haig (1861–1928), was commander-in-chief of the British forces in Europe in the First World War.

The Dublin tragedy has been a great sorrow and anxiety. Cosgrave, whom I saw a few months ago in connection with the Municipal Gallery project and found our best supporter, has got many years' imprisonment and today I see that an old friend Henry Dixon – unless there are two of the name – who began with me the whole work of the literary movement has been shot in a barrack yard without trial of any kind. I have little doubt there have been many miscarriages of justice. The wife of the Belgian Minister of War told me a few days ago that three British officers had told her that the command of the British army in France should be made over to the French generals, and that French generals have told her that they await with great anxiety the result of the coming German attack on the English lines because of the incompetence of the English Higher Command as a whole. Haig however they believed in – he was recommended by the French for the post. I see therefore no reason to believe that the delicate instrument of Justice is being worked with precision in Dublin. I am trying to write a poem on the men executed – 'terrible beauty has been born again'. If the English Conservative party had made a declaration that they did not intend to rescind the Home Rule Bill there would have been no Rebellion. I had no idea that any public event could so deeply move me – and I am very despondent about the future. At the moment I feel that all the work of years has been overturned, all the bringing together of classes, all the freeing of Irish literature and criticism from politics. Maud Gonne reminds me she saw the ruined houses about O'Connell Street and the wounded and dying lying about the streets, in the first few days of the war. I perfectly remember the vision and my making light of it and saying that if a true vision at all it could only have a symbolised meaning. This is the only letter I have had from her since she knew of the Rebellion. I have sent her the papers every day. I do not yet know what she feels about her husband [John MacBride]'s death. Her letter was written before she heard of it. Her main thought seems to be 'tragic dignity has returned to Ireland'. She had been told by two members of the Irish Party that 'Home Rule was betrayed'. She thinks now that the sacrifice has made it safe. She is coming to London

Count George Plunkett (1851–1948), curator of the National Museum in Dublin, was the father of Joseph Plunkett who was executed in 1916 for his part in the Rising.

if she can get a passport, but I doubt her getting one. Indeed I shall be glad if she does not come yet – it is better for her to go on nursing the French wounded till the trials are over. How strange that old Count Plunkett and his wife and three sons should all be drawn into the net.

Yours

W.B. Yeats

Source: W.B. Yeats to Lady Gregory, in A. Wade (ed.) (1954) *The Letters of W.B. Yeats*, London, Rupert Hart-Davis, pp. 612–14.

Reading 5.5

W.B. Yeats, 'Easter, 1916'

I have met them at close of day
Coming with vivid faces
From counter or desk among grey
Eighteenth-century houses.
5 I have passed with a nod of the head
Or polite meaningless words,
Or have lingered awhile and said
Polite meaningless words,
And thought before I had done
10 Of a mocking tale or a gibe
To please a companion
Around the fire at the club,
Being certain that they and I
But lived where motley is worn:
15 All changed, changed utterly:
A terrible beauty is born.

That woman's days were spent
In ignorant good-will,
Her nights in argument
20 Until her voice grew shrill.
What voice more sweet than hers
When, young and beautiful,
She rode to harriers?
This man had kept a school
25 And rode our wingèd horse;
This other his helper and friend
Was coming into his force;
He might have won fame in the end,
So sensitive his nature seemed,
30 So daring and sweet his thought.
This other man I had dreamed
A drunken, vainglorious lout.
He had done most bitter wrong
To some who are near my heart,

35 Yet I number him in the song;
He, too, has resigned his part
In the casual comedy;
He, too, has been changed in his turn,
Transformed utterly:
40 A terrible beauty is born.

Hearts with one purpose alone
Through summer and winter seem
Enchanted to a stone
To trouble the living stream.
45 The horse that comes from the road.
The rider, the birds that range
From cloud to tumbling cloud,
Minute by minute they change;
A shadow of cloud on the stream
50 Changes minute by minute;
A horse-hoof slides on the brim,
And a horse plashes within it;
The long-legged moor-hens dive,
And hens to moor-cocks call;
55 Minute by minute they live:
The stone's in the midst of all.

Too long a sacrifice
Can make a stone of the heart.
O when may it suffice?
60 That is Heaven's part, our part
To murmur name upon name,
As a mother names her child
When sleep at last has come
On limbs that had run wild.
65 What is it but nightfall?
No, no, not night but death;
Was it needless death after all?
For England may keep faith
For all that is done and said.
70 We know their dream; enough
To know they dreamed and are dead;
And what if excess of love
Bewildered them till they died?
I write it out in a verse –
75 MacDonagh and MacBride
And Connolly and Pearse

Now and in time to be,
Wherever green is worn,
Are changed, changed utterly:
80 A terrible beauty is born.

September 25, 1916

Source: From *English Literature Online* website, available through the course website.

Media notes

Chronology

3200 BCE	Construction of Newgrange
3rd century CE	Legendary king Cormac Mac Airt sat at Tara; the site remained an important meeting place with religious significance until the 11th century
4th century	Kings of Munster had a fortified palace at Cashel
5th century	Life and mission of St Patrick; Cashel became the seat of a bishop
12th century	Arrival of Anglo-Normans from England
16th century	Henry VIII, king of England, declared supreme head of the (Protestant) Church of Ireland and king of Ireland; land confiscated from Catholic Irish and given to English settlers
17th century	Further confiscation of land from Irish Catholic lords, lands granted to Protestant English and Scots settlers; rebellion of Catholic Irish against English rule in 1641 contributed to outbreak of civil war in England; victors of English civil war arrived under Oliver Cromwell to suppress the war in Ireland; further confiscations of land from Catholics and grants to English Protestants Construction of Royal Hospital Kilmainham; Irish support for James II following William III's assumption of the English crown led to further confiscations of land from Irish Catholics.
18th century	Legislation to limit Catholic ownership of land or occupation of public office introduced 1704; Relief Acts 1770s onwards; construction of Castletown House 1720s; 1796–9 nationalist uprising supported by French
1800	Act of Union with Great Britain. Irish parliament abolished; from 1801 Ireland represented by 100 MPs at Westminster
1829	Catholic Emancipation Act

1831	Establishment of national system of elementary education using only the English language
1845–51	Famine
1858	Irish Republican Brotherhood formed
1873	Home Rule League founded
1879–82	Land War, a period of intensified agrarian unrest when, in the face of declining prices for agricultural produce, tenants demanded rent reductions and withheld their rent, leading to evictions by landlords
1886	First Home Rule Bill
1893	Gaelic League founded
1903	Wyndham Land Act modified earlier land acts, compensating landlords with cash and dealing with a number of grievances arising from earlier legislation
1909	Land Act which introduced compulsory purchase for estates where agreement could not be reached between vendor and purchaser
1914	Home Rule Bill passed in House of Commons as Government of Ireland Bill, further progress deferred because of outbreak of the First World War
1916	Irish Republic proclaimed (24 April): Easter Rising (24–9 April)
1918	End of First World War General election: 73 Sinn Féin MPs elected to Westminster Parliament (including Constance Markievicz as first woman MP), but refused to take their seats.
1919	Meeting of Sinn Féin MPs (lacking 36 who were in prison) as Dáil Éireann: adoption of provisional constitution, declaration of independence
1919–21	War of Independence between Irish nationalists and British
1921	Anglo-Irish peace treaty, approved by Dáil (parliament). Irish Free State created of 26 counties; 6 counties of Northern Ireland remained under British rule
1922–23	Civil war between pro-treaty (nationalist) and anti-treaty (republican) forces
1923	Irregulars ordered to cease hostilities
1929	Completion of restoration of GPO; Irish Monuments Act

1937	Constitution of Republic of Ireland replaced that of Irish Free State
1939	Ireland's declaration of neutrality at outbreak of Second World War
1973	Republic of Ireland joined European Community
1998	Anglo-Irish Agreement
1999	Republic of Ireland amended constitution, replacing territorial claims to 6 counties by desire for a united Ireland through the consent of the population of Northern Ireland
2007	First power-sharing executive for Northern Ireland comprising the Democratic Unionist Party and Sinn Féin

Glossary for the DVD Video

Anglo-Irish the descendants of English settlers who occupied land confiscated from the Roman Catholic Irish, especially *c.*1560–1700. They dominated the government of Ireland.

Anglo-Normans descendants of the Norman invaders of England who colonised Ireland in the twelfth century CE.

Auxiliaries (Ireland) a specially raised force created in 1920, made up of former British army officers who were attached to the Royal Irish Constabulary (RIC). Unlike the Black and Tans, they dressed in RIC uniforms or in military khaki.

Black and Tans members of the Royal Irish Constabulary (RIC) recruited in Britain from 1919, so called because there was a shortage of RIC bottle-green uniforms and so they were dressed in a mixture of clothing. Members were mainly ex-servicemen, who served for no more than eight months at a time.

built heritage buildings, roads and other features of man-made landscapes constructed in past times.

Cashel, Co. Tipperary the rock here marked the headquarters of kings of the province of Munster in south-west Ireland from the fourth century CE. It was visited by St Patrick, who made it a bishopric. In the twelfth century it became the seat of an archbishop. The cathedral was taken over by the Protestant Church of Ireland in 1540, but it fell into ruin by the eighteenth century.

Castletown House, Co. Kildare built *c.*1722 for William Conolly, the speaker of the Irish House of Commons and reputedly the richest man in Ireland at the time. It remained in the hands of Conolly's descendants until 1965. It was then restored by

Desmond Guinness and the Irish Georgian Society, and was transferred to the ownership of the state in 1994.

Catholic emancipation the campaign to give all Roman Catholics in Britain and Ireland civil rights, which achieved success in 1829, allowing Catholics to sit in Parliament and hold most high offices.

Cormac's chapel a twelfth-century Romanesque chapel at Cashel in Ireland.

Cromwell's policy a reference to the expropriation of large amounts of land from Irish Catholics and its transfer to Protestant owners following the invasion and conquest of Ireland in 1649–51 by English forces under the command of Oliver Cromwell. He is popularly regarded as a hero in English history, but as a villain among Roman Catholics in Ireland because of the murder of civilians at Drogheda and Wexford in 1649.

Cú Chulainn a mythical Irish leader who was said to have been bound upright while he was dying. He appealed to the nationalists as a Celtic Irish hero, and to Unionists as an Ulsterman defending Ulster from attacks from the south.

Custom House, Dublin the headquarters of customs and excise administration until 1922. It was designed by James Gandon in the 1780s.

Dáil the lower legislative house in the Irish parliament (the upper house is the Senate).

Davis, Thomas (1814–45) a journalist and leader of the Young Ireland movement.

de Valera, Eamon (1882–1975) president of the nationalist party Sinn Féin from 1917, De Valera was elected president of the Dáil (lower house in the Irish parliament) in 1919. He opposed the Anglo-Irish Treaty of 1922, founded the Fianna Fáil party in 1926, and was president of the Irish Republic 1959–73.

Dublin Castle the seat of British administration in Ireland until 1922.

Four Courts the combined High Court and Central Criminal Courts in Dublin, designed in 1776–1802 by James Gandon.

Gandon, James (1743–1820) the architect of Dublin's Four Courts (constructed in 1776–1802) and Custom House (built in the 1780s).

General Post Office (Dublin) the centre of the Easter Rising in 1916, located in Sackville (now O'Connell) Street in Dublin. The building was designed in 1814–18 by Francis Johnson and restored in 1929 after its destruction in 1916.

Glasnevin a Roman Catholic cemetery in the Dublin suburbs, opened in 1832. It was the burial site of many nationalist heroes.

Irish Civil War (1922–23) the war between pro- and anti-treaty Irish nationalists.

Irish Free State the independent state of Ireland, established under the Anglo-Irish Treaty of 1922.

Irish Revolution a term denoting the succession of struggles for Irish independence between 1916 and 1922.

Irish War of Independence (1919–22) the war between the Irish Nationalists and the British that was concluded by the Anglo-Irish Treaty of 1921.

Johnson, Francis (1760–1829) the architect of the General Post Office in Dublin (1814–18).

Land Acts (Ireland) legislation passed between 1870 and 1923, initially intended to give tenants the right to buy the land they rented, but later permitting the compulsory purchase and finally the expropriation of land from landlords.

Moore, Thomas (1779–1852) a writer of patriotic Irish poetry.

nationalist in Ireland, this term refers to anyone who seeks Irish self-determination. It has been used to denote a variety of different political parties and positions.

Newgrange, Co. Meath a huge neolithic passage tomb, dating from *c.*3200 BCE. This is the oldest known astronomically aligned man-made structure in the world.

O'Connell, Daniel ('the Liberator') (1775–1847) the leader of the campaign in Ireland for Catholic emancipation, O'Connell was later leader of the campaign movement to repeal the Act of Union with Britain. He developed the use of mass political campaigns.

O'Kelley, Professor Michael (1915–82) a professor at Cork University, he was responsible for excavations at Newgrange and the restoration of the structures there.

Office of Public Works (Ireland) the official department responsible for the maintenance of government buildings in Ireland.

Palladian this refers to the approach adopted by Andrea Palladio (1508–80), the Italian architect who revived the classical style of architecture.

Petrie, George (1790–1866) a journalist, antiquary, archaeologist, architect and painter, Petrie was inspired by a desire to know more about the Irish past, taking the view that Irish civilisation had been destroyed by England. He provided a scholarly foundation for the study of Gaelic antiquity and established that round towers were monastic buildings.

Robinson, Sir William (1645–1712) the surveyor-general of Ireland and architect of the Royal Hospital Kilmainham (1680), St Mary's church, Dublin (1700–04) and other public works.

Royal Hospital Kilmainham built in the later seventeenth century, this was a refuge for wounded, disabled and aged soldiers and the headquarters of the British army in Ireland. In 1988–91 it was converted into the Irish Museum of Modern Art.

St Patrick (373–463 CE) the patron saint of Ireland and leader of the Christian mission to Ireland in 432 CE.

Tara, Hill of, Co. Meath the legendary meeting place of the Irish high kings in antiquity.

Tone, (Theobald) Wolfe (1763–98) leader of the United Irishmen, a revolutionary movement inspired by the French Revolution. Tone was executed for his part in the 1798 rising.

Young Ireland a movement of cultural nationalism led by Thomas Davis (1814–45).

6 TRADITION AND DISSENT IN MUSIC: DMITRI SHOSTAKOVICH

Fiona Richards

INTRODUCTION		**193**
	Tradition and dissent in music	193
6.1	**INTRODUCING THE STRING QUARTET**	**195**
	What is chamber music?	196
	What is a string quartet?	199
	Being a member of a string quartet	201
6.2	**INTRODUCING SHOSTAKOVICH**	**203**
	Setting Shostakovich in context	203
6.3	**TRADITION AND DISSENT IN THE STRING QUARTETS OF SHOSTAKOVICH**	**207**
	The first movement	207
	The second movement: biography and dissent in music	209
	The third movement	214
	The fourth movement	215
	Performance traditions: rehearsing and performing Shostakovich's string quartets	216
6.4	**SHOSTAKOVICH AND JEWISHNESS IN MUSIC**	**217**
	Klezmer	219
	Shostakovich Piano Trio No. 2	220
CONCLUSION		**221**
REFERENCES		**222**
RESOURCES		**223**
	Reading 6.1	223
	Reading 6.2	224

MATERIALS YOU WILL NEED

- Audio CD: Shostakovich
- DVD Video: Shostakovich

AIMS

This chapter will:

- introduce you to the life and music of an important twentieth-century composer
- give you an overview of the musical background to the Soviet period and, through the music of Shostakovich, introduce the relationship between culture and politics, tradition and dissent
- explain some traditional musical structures and genres, in particular the Classical string quartet
- consider music in rehearsal and performance.

INTRODUCTION

The aim of this chapter is to explore what the terms 'tradition' and 'dissent' mean in musical terms, and in particular as they relate to the Russian composer Dmitri Shostakovich (1906–75). A series of issues will be explored through a number of short musical extracts drawn from a range of styles, but primarily from case studies taken from the string quartets of Shostakovich.

Music drawn from four of his fifteen quartets was recorded for this course in January 2006, following a very successful festival of Russian chamber music at the Royal Northern College of Music in Manchester that subsequently won a South Bank Award. We filmed four different student groups, the Diamond, Navarra, Heath, and Myrios quartets, and your work in this chapter will focus largely on these ensembles (in musical terms, an **ensemble** is a small group of musicians) and the music they play:

The Diamond Quartet playing String Quartet no. 2: first movement

The Heath Quartet playing String Quartet no. 7: second movement

The Navarra Quartet playing String Quartet no. 3: second and third movements

The Myrios Quartet playing String Quartet no. 9: last movement

The DVD Video has been structured in such a way that you can watch it through as a complete programme, but it has also been divided into scenes for specific use within the chapter. While much of the film features extracts played in rehearsal, there are two 'performances' by the Navarra Quartet which were filmed under different conditions.

Tradition and dissent in music

From the chapters you have already studied in Book 2, you should have a good understanding of the words 'tradition' and 'dissent' and be able to apply them to different disciplines within the arts. For example, in Chapter 2 you looked at the ways in which poets build on traditions established by preceding generations of writers. You will find a similar approach adopted in this chapter on music, which looks at traditional musical practices, both in terms of forms and performance.

In music, the word 'tradition' can be understood to mean many different things. Here is a list of some of the issues that this word might raise:

- unbroken musical traditions passed on through time and place
- the revival and reinvention of traditions
- how musical tradition is transmitted

- **ethnography** (collecting folk and other musical materials) and the preservation of tradition
- the creation, establishing and dissolving of musical traditions.

Below you can see some of the different ways in which three twentieth-century composers have described what they understand by the word 'tradition'. It may help to know that the quotation from Ernst Krenek (1900–91) refers to the fact that many composers adhere to compositional procedures established in the past, for example musical forms such as the **opera** aria that you studied in Book 1, Chapter 6. Igor Stravinsky's (1882–1971) description of tradition as not simply 'handed down' recalls the phrase used by Paul Muldoon in his interview for 'What am I? Beasts and tradition' on the Audio CD for Chapter 2.

> Tradition, then, is the continuity of ideas expressed through the repetition of procedures.
>
> (Krenek, 1962, p. 27)

> I am merely very prudent with the word, for it now seems to imply 'that which resembles the past' – the reason, incidentally, why no good artist is very happy when his work is described as 'traditional'. In fact, the true tradition-making work may not resemble the past at all, and especially not the immediate past, which is the only one most people are able to hear. Tradition is generic; it is not simply 'handed down', fathers to sons, but undergoes a life process: it is born, grows, matures, declines, and is reborn, perhaps.
>
> (Stravinsky, in conversation with Robert Craft, 1960, p. 33)

> I venture to credit myself with having written truly new music which, being based on tradition, is destined to become tradition.
>
> (Schoenberg, 1984, p. 174)

Activity Make a list of three or four types of music that relate to the word 'tradition' as used above. (To get you started, note that a hymn might be regarded as a type of musical tradition.)

Discussion There is no definitive answer to this question, and every individual will come up with different possibilities and a range of traditions. These are some of the examples that I thought of:

- Christmas carols: these are handed down over time and traditionally sung in December
- folk songs
- the tradition of playing particular concerts in specific venues, for example the Last Night of the Proms at the Albert Hall in London and the New Year's Day concert that takes place every year in Vienna (see Figure 6.1)
- songs that are taken out of their original context and transformed into a new tradition, for example 'You'll Never Walk Alone', originally a song from the 1945 musical *Carousel* and now the anthem of Liverpool Football Club.

Figure 6.1 Willi Boskosvsky conducts the New Year's Day concert, *c.*1964. Photographed by Charlotte Till-Borchardt. Musikverein, Vienna. Photo: The Historical Archives of the Vienna Philharmonic.

From the examples given above you will see that there is no such thing as a static and unchanging tradition. Any artistic tradition (and you have addressed this in your work so far in Book 2) is always receptive to outside influence and is therefore always evolving and changing. As you saw in Chapter 2 with regard to poetry, no artistic form can exist by just repeating traditional formulae. The same is true of music: there has to be innovation in order to keep an art form alive.

6.1 INTRODUCING THE STRING QUARTET

Activity Start your week's work by listening to some of the music of Shostakovich. Find 'Perfomance 2' on the DVD Video. This is a filmed performance of the third movement of Shostakovich's String Quartet No. 3, written in 1946. Watch the DVD performance twice and then answer the questions below.

I would recommend that you first watch the performance straight through. As you watch for the second time, you can stop the DVD whenever you want in order to help you to answer the questions.

Some of these questions may seem very simple, but they will help you to establish early on a notion of what a string quartet is.

1 How many players are in the quartet?
2 Which instruments make up the ensemble? Choose from one of the following options:
   - two violins, a cello and a double bass
   - three violins and a cello
   - two violins, a viola and a cello.
3 How are the players seated?
4 Is the music fast or slow?
5 Is any particular instrument dominant?
6 How are the players communicating with one another?

Discussion

1 There are four players in the quartet. This always remains standard.
2 The ensemble is made up of two violins, a viola (a slightly larger and lower-pitched instrument than the violin) and a cello. This also always remains standard in a string quartet: it is the traditional make-up of the group.
3 The players sit in a slightly curved line, so that the highest pitched instrument (violin) is on one side and the lowest pitched (cello) on the other. In this particular case they sit as follows, from left to right: first violin (Xander van Vliet), second violin (Marije Ploemacher), viola (Simone van der Giessen) and cello (Nathaniel Boyd). While many quartets sit in this formation (in order of pitch), some do not, as you will notice later in the chapter. The formation is largely down to the personal preference of group members.
4 The music is fast, passionate and intense.
5 No particular instrument dominates the movement as a whole: every member of the ensemble is equally important. However, you may have noticed that there are moments when different individuals seem to have a more significant role.
6 There are many different ways in which the players communicate with one another. They use eye contact, they watch one another's bows and they are 'led' by the first violinist, Xander. This particular group are very physical in the way in which they play, with much unspoken interplay between the four students.

What is chamber music?

'Chamber music' is the name given to a range of music written for small groups to play, rather than a full orchestra. Initially chamber music was intended for performance under domestic circumstances, for example in a drawing room or a small hall in front of a small audience. It is music of an intimate character, originally played and heard in private rooms, hence the term signifies 'music to be played in a chamber'.

Activity Think back to Chapter 6 on 'The Diva' in Book 1. Which music example might fall into the category of chamber music as described above?

Discussion The madrigals you heard in Book 1, Chapter 6 might be an example of vocal chamber music, as opposed to opera, which is a large-scale, grand music genre for public performance in front of a large audience, or to Madonna's stadium pop, produced by a huge cast of players.

Traditional classical instrumental examples include the string quartet, the wind quintet (five wind instruments: flute, oboe, clarinet, bassoon and French horn), the wind octet (eight wind instruments: two oboes, two clarinets, two bassoons and two French horns) and the **piano trio** (for piano, violin and cello).

Figure 6.2 The Florestan Trio, 2004. Photographed by Richard Lewisohn. Photo: The Florestan Trio.

Figure 6.3 Coldplay in performance at Madison Square Garden, New York, 2005. Photographed by Mick Hutson. Photo: Mick Hutson/Redferns.

Activity Turn to Reading 6.1, a passage written by the musician Susan Tomes, the pianist in the Florestan Trio (a well-known and very successful piano trio – see Figure 6.2). Here she tries to establish what chamber music is. As you read, highlight the phrases or words that strike you as summing up the characteristic features of chamber music.

Discussion The phrases I highlighted were:

> 'truest portraits of themselves, their most intimate thoughts and feelings'
>
> 'no sense of showing off such as might occur in solo repertoire'
>
> 'wonderful conversation between people with meaningful things to say'
>
> 'everyone was vital'
>
> 'Groups are alternative families, with their different characters'
>
> 'They listen, they react, they wait, they surge forward, they bounce off one another's ideas. They each represent some different facet of human nature'
>
> 'a chamber group is like a family whose members always say, in music, different and interesting things'

While you may have highlighted different areas, or longer passages, I hope you would agree with me that the essence of this passage is that chamber music is intimate music played by musicians, whether in classical or popular music situations, who interact with one another and have important things

Figure 6.4 ABBA in performance, 1970s. Photographed by Michael Ochs. Photo: Michael Ochs Archive/Redferns.

to say in musical terms. As you work though this chapter, you will hear, on the DVD Video, students returning to the idea of 'family' and sharing intimate thoughts and feelings. I hope you will be persuaded that chamber music is not difficult and aimed at just a small group of listeners, but that it offers something really special.

Activity What does the Navarra Quartet in performance have in common with the groups shown in Figures 6.3 and 6.4?

Discussion It is clear that each of these groups shares the musical intimacy described above. In every case you can see the interplay between them. They stand or sit close together and work as an ensemble.

What is a string quartet?

At the start of this section you were introduced to the string quartet as a group, or ensemble, and what the four members of the group play. Now you will move a stage further and look at the string quartet as a genre (that is, as a musical *type*). The string quartet, and its particular type of chamber music, originated in what is called the **Classical period** of western music, roughly 1760–1820. This period saw a great flourishing of chamber music, written for both string and wind

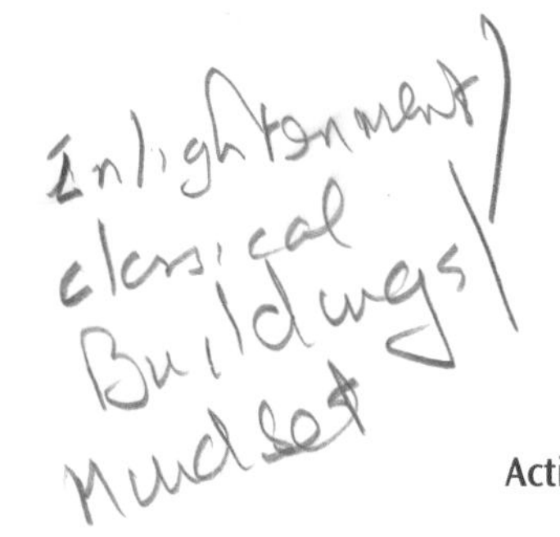

instruments and sometimes for combinations of the two, as well as music including a piano. It is called the Classical period because of the stylistic features of the music, which you will consider in the next activity.

Activity

Find track 8 on the Audio CD, and listen to the piece twice. This is a movement from a wind octet by Wolfgang Amadeus Mozart (1756–1791). It is scored for eight wind instruments, as described above. It is included here so that you can hear an example of wind chamber music as well as the string chamber music that dominates the chapter.

What words can you find to describe the 'style' of this music? Think about the character of the music, its melodies (tunes), chords (harmonies) and overall feel.

Discussion

The music moves in regular sections, composed of clear-cut musical phrases. The **melody** is graceful and simple, with a basic accompaniment pattern. The **harmony** is also simple (you may have noticed that very few chords are used) and the overall feel is one of elegance and poise. Its style is typical of what is called the Viennese Classical style and it uses one of the traditional structures of the period: the **minuet and trio**, which we will return to later in this chapter. A minuet and trio is a simple dance movement in three-time. The minuet is played first, followed by a contrasting trio before a return to the minuet. The two most famous composers of this type of music during the period were Joseph Haydn (1732–1809) and Mozart, and to a certain extent Ludwig van Beethoven (1770–1827), though his music tends to move away from the contained simplicity of this piece by Mozart.

Activity

Now find scene 1, 'What is a string quartet?', on the DVD Video. Watch this through once or twice without making any notes. Then watch it again and answer the following questions:

1. How many movements make up a traditional string quartet?
2. Can you briefly describe the different movements?
3. Traditionally, what is the function of the different instruments within the group?
4. How does the Beethoven extract you hear match the description of Classical style above?

Discussion

1. There are four movements in a traditional string quartet. This is also true of a traditional **symphony**. Some of the quartets by Shostakovich stick to the traditional four-movement structure. However, there are others where he dissents from the norm, writing five movements (for example Quartet No. 3), or uses one movement only (Quartet No. 8).
2. The first movement is fast (described by the cellist as 'Allegro', an Italian word used traditionally in music to denote a fast, sometimes merry movement). The second movement is slow. The third movement is a 'minuet and trio', or a scherzo. The fourth movement is another fast one, usually quicker than the first. In the DVD passage you heard examples of these different types of movement, each taken from a different quartet by Shostakovich.

3 Traditionally, the cello has the bass line, the first violin the tune and the second violin and viola take inner melodies to fill out the texture. However, if you think back to the Shostakovich quartet you heard at the beginning of this section you will recall that here this was not the case. On the contrary, in this example every instrument played an equally important and varying role.

4 The short Beethoven extract you hear has clear-cut phrases and simple melodies.

Being a member of a string quartet

The next scene of the DVD Video, scene 2, 'Being a member of a string quartet', introduces you to some of the issues that arise for four musicians working closely together for many hours a day. Watch this section through twice. The second time you watch it, make notes comparing the views of the Navarra and Heath Quartets and then read on.

This is an interesting sequence. Both quartets talk about the fact that relationships are important in such an intimate working environment. However, the two quartets have quite different opinions. The Navarra believe that strong personal relationships are as important as musical ones, while the Heath talk about the significance of their musical relationships as being much stronger than their friendships and mention some famous quartets – the Hungarian and the Amadeus – who actually disliked one another. (Since this DVD was made the Heath quartet has changed its personnel; it now has a different second violinist.) Both groups talk about teamwork as being essential to the success of a good string quartet, and it becomes clear through the discussion that it is crucial to have a strong leader in the first violinist. You will notice particularly with the Navarra Quartet that the leader, Xander, is very vocal and a real driving force. You might liken the relationships between the four string players to those in a team sport. The first violin is akin to the captain of the football team, while the inner instruments are the midfield players and perhaps the cellist is the goalkeeper.

Now watch scene 3 of the DVD Video, entitled 'The importance of good instruments'. In this section members of the Navarra Quartet talk about stringed instruments. You will hear them describe the instrument played by the second violinist, Marije, as 'very powerful', and indeed she and the viola player Simone (the 'midfield') are the powerhouse of the group in terms of the sheer volume of sound they can produce. Marije tells you that she plays a Guadagnini made in 1757. Traditionally, the best violins were made in Italy during the late seventeenth and eighteenth centuries (see Figure 6.5), and she is fortunate to have this on loan. This particular instrument was owned by the virtuoso Adolph Brodsky (1851–1929) and used by him in the 1881 premiere of Pyotr Il'yich Tchaikovsky's (1840–1893) violin **concerto** (a concerto is a piece of music for a solo instrument or instruments and orchestra, usually in three movements, slow-fast-slow; you can hear an extract of a concerto on track 9 of the Audio CD). Brodsky was the leader of Manchester's Hallé orchestra from 1895 and the principal of the Royal Northern College of Music (RNCM); hence the fact that this marvellous violin is now owned by the music college and loaned to gifted students. Figure 6.6 shows you the important parts of the violin so that you can recognise these later in the chapter.

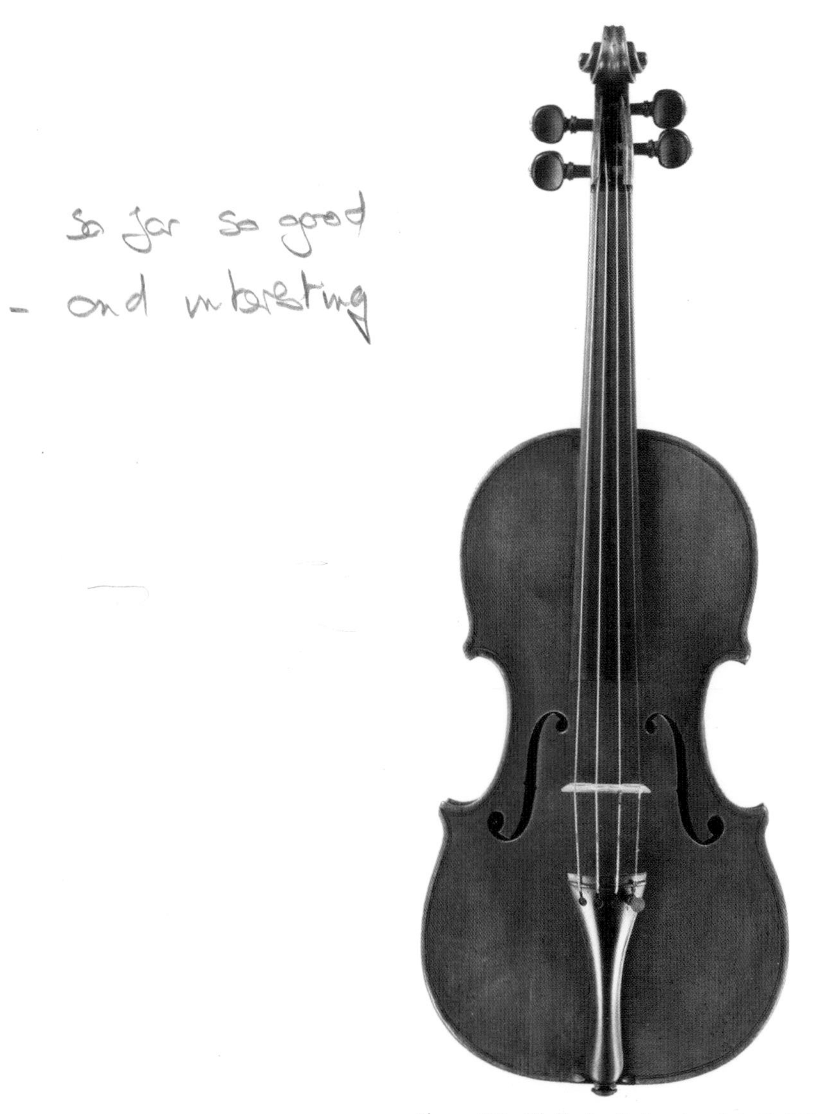

Figure 6.5 Violin by G. Guadagnini, *C.* 1753. Clarissa Bruce, Royal Academy of Music. Photo: © Royal Academy of Music Coll/Lebrecht.

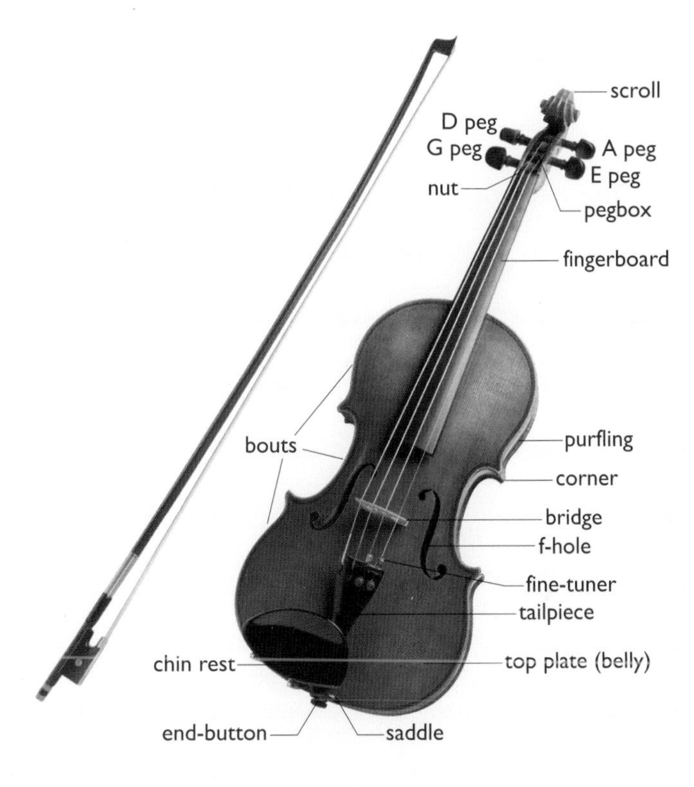

Figure 6.6 Diagram of the modern violin.

6.2 INTRODUCING SHOSTAKOVICH

Setting Shostakovich in context

The Russian composer Dmitri Shostakovich has been chosen for study in this book as he is an example of a composer who both adhered to musical traditions and dissented from them. Like John Donne, whom you encountered in Chapter 2, Shostakovich provides an original twist on an old theme. He has also been chosen because of his ability to dissent in a somewhat different way, in that through his music he challenged Stalin's dictatorship (see Book 1, Chapter 5). His musical works include 15 symphonies, 15 string quartets and 36 film scores, as well as many other pieces. You will hear some of his most striking and varied works during the course of this week's study.

Born on 25 September 1906 in St Petersburg, Shostakovich was one of the most significant composers of the twentieth century. He began piano lessons at the age of nine, and in 1919 entered what was then known as the Petrograd Conservatory (now the St Petersburg Conservatory) to study piano and also composition, working with another important Russian composer, Aleksandr Glazunov

(1865–1936). In 1923 he married Nina Vasilevna Varzar, with whom he went on to have two children, but in 1924 he suffered malnutrition and tuberculosis and had to suspend his musical studies to work as a cinema pianist in order to support himself and his wife.

A few years later, in 1926, Shostakovich's first major work, his Symphony No. 1, was premiered in Leningrad (now St Petersburg) and received with great acclaim. A year later his Symphony No. 2, 'To October', was commissioned to mark the tenth anniversary of the Russian Revolution.

Shostakovich now turned to music for the stage, working first on the opera *The Nose* (1928), on the ballet *The Golden Age* (1930) and then on a major piece, the opera *Lady Macbeth of the Mtsensk District*. The latter was first produced in 1934 in Leningrad and in Moscow, but in 1936 it was publicly denounced in the official government newspaper *Pravda*, where it was described as 'muddle instead of music' and as not meeting Soviet ideals, where music was expected to be rousing, simple and tuneful, in order to demonstrate public happiness and allegiance to the state, and not to challenge or include dissonance:

> From the very first moment of the opera the listener is flabbergasted by the deliberately dissonant, muddled stream of sounds. Snatches of melody, embryos of a musical phrase drown, struggle free and disappear again in the din, the grinding, the squealing. To follow this 'music' is difficult, to remember it is impossible.
>
> (Quoted in Shostakovich, 1979, p. xxix)

Shostakovich's Symphony No. 5, completed in 1937, saw him returning to traditional structural symphonic methods, abandoning the more radical aspects of his two operas. In part this was to satisfy the critics, though its finale was hardly the bold statement preferred at the time.

Despite these earlier public criticisms, in 1940 Shostakovich received the Stalin Prize for his Piano Quintet. The next few years saw the composer responding to the events of the Second World War in musical terms. For example, in 1941 he composed his Symphony No. 7, the 'Leningrad', dedicated to a city that was besieged at the time. In 1942 the score of this work was smuggled out of Russia and conducted by the famous Arturo Toscanini (1867–1957) as a symbol of resistance against Nazism, and in 1943 Shostakovich moved to Moscow to teach at the Conservatory there. His music continued to provoke extreme reactions and some adverse public reviews. In particular his Symphony No. 8 (1943) was called 'repulsive', and his Symphony No. 9 (1945) 'grotesque' and an inappropriate reflection of the celebratory national mood at the end of the Second World War. Shostakovich also continued to produce works in a very traditional format, such as the String Quartet No. 2 (1944) and pieces making use

Figure 6.7 Dmitri Shostakovich working on a score, *c.* 1945–7. Unknown photographer. Photo: © Lebrecht Music and Arts.

of Jewish elements, such as the Piano Trio No. 2 (1944), which, as you will discover later in the chapter, could be viewed as musical expressions of dissent.

In 1948 Shostakovich, along with a number of composers, found himself suffering under the cultural purges of the Stalin regime, accused of writing music that was **atonal**, dissonant and 'formalistic'. Perhaps the culmination of this repression came in 1953, following Shostakovich's Symphony No. 10, in which he expressed his feelings of oppression with a grim second movement intended as a depiction of Stalin. Once again this incited extreme criticism, with the official Composers' Union decrying it as being antipathetic to the ideals of Soviet music.

Figure 6.8 Dmitri Shostakovich at the piano, 1960. Unknown photographer. Photo: © RIA Novosti/Lebrecht.

In 1954 the composer's wife died suddenly. Two years later he married Margarita Andreevna Kajnova, an activist in the Young Communist League, though this marriage did not last long and the composer continued to mourn his first wife. He wrote several chamber works expressing his grief. You will hear one of these, the String Quartet No. 7 (1960), on the DVD Video.

The last years of Shostakovich's life were focused on further new symphonies and string quartets, in between bouts of illness before his death in 1975. After his death a provocative book entitled *Testimony* was published in 1979. Claiming to be the official and revelatory memoirs of the composer, as edited by his friend Solomon Volkov, this book has continued to prove a controversial text. You will study some extracts from it later in the chapter.

Activity

Drawing on the narrative above, put together a brief timeline for Shostakovich that you can refer to as you progress through this chapter. This will help you to maintain a sense of what the composer wrote and how his music relates to historical and personal events. Make sure you include important dates, events and major musical works in your timeline.

If you wish, you can insert musical works, dates and events that are not included above by looking them up on *New Grove Dictionary of Music and Musicians* online. This is an extensive electronic resource accessed via the course website. Under the 'Grove' search engine you simply enter the name of the composer.

This is an activity you might work at and return to during the course of this chapter, as you become aware of other important dates and works.

Start like this:

1906 Shostakovich is born in St Petersburg

1919 Begins studies at the Petrograd Conservatory

6.3 TRADITION AND DISSENT IN THE STRING QUARTETS OF SHOSTAKOVICH

Exposition
Development
Recapitulation

The aim of this section of the chapter is to link the information in sections 6.1 and 6.2, bringing together your introduction to chamber music and the background to Shostakovich. Thus you will be introduced to five of Shostakovich's 15 string quartets, and will look at musical structure and at some of the ways in which Shostakovich adheres to or dissents from established formal structures. Different structures develop and form the basis of a musical language at different historical periods.

The first movement

Activity

Start your work in this section by watching the DVD Video, scene 4, the complete first movement of Shostakovich's String Quartet No. 2.

During the Classical period, virtually every piece of instrumental music that contained more than one movement traditionally used a structure known as '**sonata form**', or 'sonata principle'. Essentially this is a very simple idea. A musical sonata form movement is constructed in three parts: exposition, development and recapitulation, the three big structural moments you saw on the DVD. In the exposition two main melodic ideas are presented; in the development they are literally 'developed'; and in the recapitulation they are restated.

The Beethoven extract you heard earlier uses sonata form, and indeed many of Shostakovich's string quartets also use this traditional structure. The structure depends on certain other musical conventions.

A sonata form movement is in a **key**. Much of the music you will know – popular songs, classical music, hymns etc. – is based in a key (that is, it has a harmonic home within which most of the music is based). For example, a simple tune such as 'Old MacDonald had a farm' uses a major **key signature** and oscillates around a few main notes, as shown below.

Music example 1

Conventional classical music also uses a **time signature**. 'Old MacDonald' is in four-time. Look at the music example again as it appears below and this time note the dots that indicate a regular pulse of four beats in a **bar**. Try tapping the pulse as you sing the melody.

Music example 2

Activity On the DVD Video find scene 5, 'Sonata form' and watch this section. In it the first violinist, Samson Diamond, explains what sonata form is and the Diamond Quartet demonstrate the opening of the three sections. See if you can spot the similarities between the exposition and the recapitulation.

Now return to scene 4 on the DVD Video and listen to the opening of the first movement of Shostakovich's String Quartet No. 2, the exposition section only. Stop the DVD Video at the point where you see the word 'Exposition' appear.

This movement is in the key of A major (though you do not need to worry about this at all). Music example 3 on pp. 210–11 has been highlighted to show the part of the first violin. I have marked the starting points of the two melodies (remember that an exposition usually has two main tunes). List the principal differences between these two melodies.

Discussion The purpose of having two melodies is to have two contrasting ideas: light and shade, rising and falling, and so on. To me the differences here are quite striking. The first tune is very bold, purposeful and simple, with big leaps and forceful gestures. It announces the start of the piece of music. Because the first violin stands out as carrying this tune, it is very striking.

The second melody is very different. It has none of the boldness and leaps of the first; rather, it is more winding and intense.

The passage of score in Music example 3 is the opening of the exposition. Don't worry if you can't 'read' the score – you should be able to see that one line of the music, the first violin (here marked 'Violino I' and highlighted in a diferent colour), carries the tune and that the other instruments mainly play an accompanying role.

The exposition contains two radically contrasting melodies. In the development section these melodies are mixed up, changed, decorated and fragmented. This is the section where the composer can let his imagination loose. The recapitulation brings back the two melodies. In a traditional sonata form structure these recur in the order in which they started, i.e. tune 1, tune 2. However, Shostakovich somewhat dissents from this, in that he first hints at bringing back tune 1, though it is not yet recognisable as such, and then presents tune 2, before ending with a bold return to tune 1.

Activity Complete your work on the first movement by once again watching it through on the DVD Video, scene 4. Aim to hear the two main tunes and the differences between them. Also notice the dominance of the first violin. In Shostakovich's more traditional quartet movements this instrument is dominant, whereas in some of his more radical quartets all four instruments take melodic roles.

The second movement: biography and dissent in music

Significant moments of change and progress in the musical work of a composer are often associated with big life events, such as major political upheavals or personal crises. Shostakovich is a figure whose music often reflects what was happening around him, both in terms of his country and its regime and in terms of his own personal struggles. Many of Shostakovich's works can be associated with extra-musical events. For example, the String Quartet No. 3 (1946), which you heard earlier in this chapter, has been described thus:

> the horrors broached in the Third Quartet ... and the tight-lipped reticence with which it ends, can all be linked with the events and moods of the just-concluded Patriotic War [Second World War], and that may have been their immediate motivation. But they can be read in many other contexts as well. Some are personal. Some are political.
>
> (Richard Taruskin, quoted in Whittall, 2003, p. 110)

This part of the chapter looks at some of the ways in which Shostakovich's music reflects what was happening in his life. It includes some extracts from his controversial book of memoirs, *Testimony* (Shostakovich, 1979), which was mentioned at the end of section 6.2 There has been some controversy surrounding this book, most notably whether the words are actually the memoirs of the composer, or have been subject to heavy editing and alteration.

Music example 3

tenuto
p cresc.
marcatiss.
3
f
4
Melody 2
5
cresc.
ff

However, they do help to give us some idea of the political landscape against which Shostakovich was working.

Testimony opens with these lines:

> These are not memoirs about myself. These are memoirs about other people. Others will write about us. And naturally they'll lie through their teeth – but that's their business.
>
> One must speak the truth about the past or not at all. It's very hard to reminisce and it's worth doing only in the name of truth.
>
> Looking back, I see nothing but ruins, only mountains of corpses. And I do not wish to build new Potemkin villages on these ruins.
>
> Let's try to tell only the truth. It's difficult. I was an eyewitness to many events and they were important events. I knew many outstanding people. I'll try to tell what I know about them. I'll try not to color or falsify anything. This will be the testimony of an eyewitness.
>
> (Shostakovich, 1979, p. 3)

Whether or not a composer's biography affects the way in which we should hear his or her music is an interesting and always provocative question. Does it actually matter whether we know the historical and political background against which musical works were created? And are there some composers for whom that background is more relevant than others? In the case of Shostakovich, it is possible to listen to his music without knowledge of his biography, but the environment in which he was working affected his compositions to the extent that it can help to know a bit about them. Acquiring layers of knowledge about a composer and the background to a work can aid your understanding of the piece and alter your listening, so that you not only approach the work as a piece of music in an abstract sense, but also perceive it within its context. For instance, Shostakovich's String Quartet No. 7 was written at a harrowing time in his life, after the death of his first wife. Traditionally the slow movement of a quartet is the most expressive of the four movements, where the language of music is used to mean something. This is certainly the case here.

Activity On the DVD Video, find scenes 6 and 7, 'Meaning in music' and 'Shostakovich String Quartet No. 7', and watch these through. Here the Heath Quartet play the complete second movement of this work and talk about it. What makes this movement so poignant? And what special device does the composer use to help him create the sound he needs?

Discussion The combination of the very intense, slow, winding melody with the monotonous accompaniment creates the expressive poignancy of this movement. The special device used to help create the sound is a **mute**, a small object that dampens the vibrations and adds to the intensity of the movement (see Figures 6.9 and 6.10).

Figure 6.9 Violin mute on the bridge of the instrument. Photographed by Graham Salter. Photo: © Graham Salter/Lebrecht.

Figure 6.10 Violin mutes – brass and rubber. Photographed by Graham Salter. Photo: © Graham Salter/Lebrecht.

Activity Watch scene 8, 'The use of the mute', on the DVD Video. In this scene the Heath Quartet explain the function of the mute and show the difference between this intense slow movement and the fast movement that follows it.

So far we've looked at the first and second movements of a string quartet. To recap, the first movement is a fairly long, usually quite fast introductory movement with two main melodies. In the particular quartet you have just heard (No. 7), Shostakovich makes use of the traditional sonata form structure but also slightly alters it. The second movement is the slow movement, often used by Shostakovich as a means of expressing his most intimate thoughts and feelings.

The third movement

In the Classical period the third movement of a typical four-movement piece was always a minuet and trio. You heard such an example earlier in this chapter, in section 6.1, when you listened to the Mozart wind octet. A minuet and trio tends to be the frothier, lighter part of the piece, and in the Classical period was a formal minuet dance movement. Beethoven transformed this into a different, much quicker movement called a **scherzo** (Italian for joke) and sometimes moved its position within the symphony, placing it second.

Activity Find track 10 on the Audio CD, the complete third movement scherzo of Beethoven's Symphony No. 9. Listen to this, and then listen again to the Mozart minuet and trio on track 8 (although you need only listen to the opening of this). Track 10 is a long movement.

How do these movements differ, and in which ways are they similar?

Discussion These movements use the same time signature, i.e. they are both in three-time, and both are light-hearted in character. However, in many other ways they could not be more different. While you can count a steady one, two, three to the Mozart example, the Beethoven speeds along so that you feel only the first beat of the bar. Mozart's example is more poised and stately; Beethoven's is much more rousing, almost wild at times with its loud **timpani** interjections. Both composers tend to use this three-time movement as the third of their four-movement works. Shostakovich continued this tradition well into the twentieth century, taking the light-hearted, but also manic, elements of the scherzo and using it frequently in his instrumental music. However, his scherzi sometimes form the second movement of his four-movement works, and are not always in three-time.

We're going to listen to a scherzo from Shostakovich's String Quartet No. 3. In many ways this is a traditional scherzo movement, but straight away Shostakovich breaks with the traditional four-movement structure, in that he writes five movements in this piece, the second and third of which are scherzi. This is the second movement scherzo.

Activity Watch the performance of this scherzo on the DVD Video, Performance 1. Then answer the following two questions in a few words:

1 What does this movement take stylistically from the Mozart minuet you heard earlier?

2 What aspects make this different in character to both the Mozart minuet and the Beethoven scherzo?

Discussion

1 Like the Mozart example, this is a dance movement in three-time. The viola gives you a steady one, two, three pattern from the start. It has a lilting, light feel.

2 What makes this different, however, is the sense of melancholy and irony in the music. It is in no sense a frothy moment within the work,

but rather a much more intense affair than either the Mozart or the Beethoven. The melodies are quirky and twisting and there is a particularly strange and eerie section where all four players together pick out very quiet, **staccato** (detached) chords as shown below in Music example 4. Whereas both the Mozart and Beethoven examples were propelled along to their conclusion, this movement winds down into a ruminative, slow ending, before the next scherzo takes over – this one containing the wilder nature of the scherzo.

Music example 4

Activity Now watch scene 9 on the DVD Video, a short section showing you part of the wilder third scherzo (which is not in three-time) along with some commentary from the quartet on the nature of the music.

The fourth movement

In the Classical period a big four-movement work such as a symphony or a string quartet traditionally ended with something fast and showy, sometimes dramatic. Rather as a film might have a big denouement and conclusion, lengthy pieces of music similarly build to a grand ending.

Activity Listen to track 11 on the Audio CD, the last part of the last movement of Beethoven's Symphony No. 5. How does this extract meet the criteria above?

Discussion This is one of the most famous musical 'endings' created. Beethoven writes a grand conclusion in which all instruments of the orchestra play, repeating two chords over and over again to emphasise and re-emphasise the fact that this is the finale. If you play the track again, listen out for these repeated hammered chords.

Activity Now find scene 10, 'Shostakovich String Quartet No. 9', on the DVD Video and listen to the final section of Shostakovich's String Quartet No. 9, along with comments on the ending from the viola player, Michael Gurevich, in the Myrios Quartet. As you do so, note that here Shostakovich also ends with a massive, dramatic flourish.

Shostakovich did not always uphold this musical tradition of a grand conclusion. Many of his works have a sombre or ironic ending, which sometimes caused him difficulties politically, most particularly with the Symphony No. 9, where the light-hearted finale was not the grand celebration of the end of the Second World War expected by Stalin.

Performance traditions: rehearsing and performing Shostakovich's string quartets

The final part of this section shows you the Shostakovich quartets in rehearsal and in performance, focusing on the second and third movements of the String Quartet No. 3.

Activity First read the extract below, and then watch scene 11, 'Rehearsing and performing', on the DVD Video, a long piece that shows you the Navarra Quartet rehearsing the two scherzi from Shostakovich's String Quartet No. 3. What are the three main areas addressed by the group as they rehearse?

> R is for Rehearsal and Repetition
>
> Rehearsal and repetition. Curiously, these are the English and French words, respectively, for the same thing. What we call a rehearsal is 'une répétition' in France; I always thought it a poor description of a process that accounts for at least half of a musician's working life. I'm making a distinction here between private practice, which takes place alone, and rehearsal, which is a collective process undertaken by a group of players. For all of us, the time spent giving concerts is only the tip of the iceberg. Rehearsal occupies far more time and often more energy, partly because it thrusts the players into a minefield of diplomatic niceties. Firstly, it is often difficult to put into words one's sense of what the music means or how to make it expressive. In any group, there are always people better than others, or just quicker to find a form of words. This can drive others further into their shells, or force them to agree to something, just because they haven't yet figured out a way of countering it.
>
> (Tomes, 2006, pp. 99–100)

Discussion The three main areas addressed are:

- bow strokes
- balance
- intonation.

In their discussion of bow strokes the group focus on the ways in which they might achieve perfect ensemble, particularly in that eerie chordal section you heard earlier. The passage they discuss was shown in Music example 4.

Balance means achieving just the right distribution of sound across the group. (Sometimes one instrument might be too quiet and needs to project its sound more clearly.) Intonation means tuning – each person's instrument needs to be exactly in tune with the others' – and an interesting point made here is that any quartet will have its own intonation, depending on the four individuals who make up the group.

I hope you felt that this was a really fascinating insight into the ways in which an ensemble work together towards a performance.

In the final part of scene 11 on the DVD Video, there is a short extract of dialogue about the difference between performance and rehearsal.

Activity

Finally, watch the two scherzi in performance, DVD Video Performances 1 and 2. These movements should now seem a little more familiar to you, and you may recognise some of the passages rehearsed by the Navarra Quartet.

6.4 SHOSTAKOVICH AND JEWISHNESS IN MUSIC

One of the principal ways in which Shostakovich created a personal form of dissent from a regime he detested was by creating a body of music with strong Jewish elements and links. This section focuses on the appearance of Jewish elements and Jewish style in Shostakovich's music, and moves away from the string quartet to focus on a different chamber music combination: the piano trio.

Activity

Start by reading the section on Shostakovich and Jewishness in the memoirs previously mentioned, *Testimony*. You can find this reprinted as Reading 6.2. This is an emotive passage that quite clearly sets out the composer's opposition to Stalin's anti-Semitism: a dangerous political position to take at this time.

Now find tracks 12–19 on the Audio CD. These comprise three pieces of music that share certain characteristics.

The three pieces are:

1. Track 12.
   The song 'Tradition' from *Fiddler on the Roof*. (The film is set in 1910, at a time of unrest as Jews were forced from their homes. Another central theme is the loss of old traditions to industrialisation and mechanisation. The singer here, who played the lead part in the film, is Topol, a Russian Jew.)
2. Tracks 13–18 (these run continuously to give you the complete piece).
   Klezmer: piece of traditional music played at Jewish weddings or other gatherings (see below).
3. Track 19.
   Shostakovich, Piano Trio No. 2, last movement.

Listen to the three pieces one after the other, several times if necessary, and jot down what you think the musical similarities are. What are the common stylistic features?

Don't expect to come up with complex analyses. Any suggestions you make will provide a useful learning process.

Discussion The main point you should make is that all three examples, despite their differences, share a certain melodic style – that is, they all have tunes with a particular flavour.

The chief purpose of this section of the chapter is to introduce you to the notion of Jewishness in music, and the ways in which Shostakovich draws on Jewish elements. To understand the meaning of Jewish elements in Shostakovich's music you need to have an idea of the position of Jewish culture in the Soviet Union, particularly under the Stalin regime. The dominant ideological view during the composer's lifetime was that a distinctive Jewish culture was anti-Soviet, and therefore undesirable.

As you read at the start of this section, Shostakovich displayed a particular interest in Jewish subjects, both musical and non-musical, and this can be seen across his output. He used Jewish elements in three main periods in his life. The first, the years 1943–4, coincided with the war and with his encounter with a talented pupil, Venyamin Fleishman (1913–41). The second period, 1948–52, coincided with the years during which the Soviets attempted to destroy Jewish culture. Over 400 Jewish writers, artists and musicians were arrested and shot during this time. During this period Shostakovich wrote a number of significant works with Jewish elements, among them the song cycle *From Jewish Folk Poetry*, in which the use of Jewish folk poetry was in itself a dissident gesture. The third period covers 1959–63 and includes his Symphony No. 13, which sets five poems from Yevgeny Yevtushenko's (b. 1933) poem 'Babi Yar', a literary response to the massacre of Jews in occupied Kiev in 1941.

Shostakovich's Piano Trio No. 2 (if you recall, a piano trio is a chamber work scored for three solo instruments: violin, cello and piano) is a significant work on several counts. It stands at the centre of the composer's output in terms of its date – it was finished in the spring of 1944 – and grew out of both national and personal tragedy. Shostakovich had just completed the first movement when he learnt that his close friend Ivan Sollertinksy (1902–44), a writer and brilliant linguist, had died from a heart attack at the young age of 41. At the same time, Russia was suffering the effects of several years of war. The siege of Leningrad, during which 600,000 people had died, had come to an end in January 1944. The German army was in retreat from Russia, and revelations of the horrors of the death camps and the fate of Jews were beginning to surface. Shostakovich was chilled by stories that were emerging and this horror is evident in his Piano Trio No. 2. Shostakovich wrote this piece in memory of Sollertinsky, following in a tradition of elegiac Russian piano trios (those by Tchaikovsky, for example), but the music itself makes it clear that Shostakovich intended a memorial beyond that for the individual who was his friend.

Klezmer

The term **klezmer** is a Yiddish word originating in the **Ashkenazi** centre of central Europe. Around the fifteenth century a tradition of secular Jewish music was developed by travelling musicians known as klezmorim. The music is characterised by a four- or five-piece ensemble, traditionally consisting of lead violin, clarinet or another violin, **cimbalom** (a tuned percussion instrument played with hammers), bass or cello and occasionally a flute. At the beginning of the eighteenth century klezmer ensembles were exclusively male. The leader was the first violinist, who usually passed on the position to his son or son-in-law. Over the years the make-up of the group has varied and has become much more flexible depending on which players are available. Thus the trombone or the accordion might also feature in the ensemble (see Figure 6.11).

Figure 6.11 Klezmer musicians playing at a wedding in Israel, 2005. Photographed by Dan Porges. Photo: Dan Porges/ArenaPAL Picture Library.

Klezmer bands played at dances at weddings and at holy days. Their compositions were never published, but handed down to family successors within the band. The Holocaust largely destroyed klezmer music in Poland and it was suppressed in the Soviet Union. However, previously unknown music is still emerging from the former Soviet Union and many traditions have survived. There is also a strong tradition of klezmer in the USA.

Activity Listen to the klezmer extracts on tracks 13–18 of the Audio CD. You can hear it as a single, continuous track, but it is also divided into six tracks for ease of following. Below are six descriptions that match the six tracks which make up the piece of klezmer but are not shown to you in the correct order. Listen to the extract and then arrange the letters in the right order.

A Solid beat, violin tune, clarinet also playing, then dissolves into slower, expansive music.

B Slower, lower scoring, husky clarinet, gentle strumming.

C Free, expansive melody on violin. Slow.

D Violin and clarinet at higher pitch. Continued um-pah feel. Slight pause at end.

E Slightly quicker, definite um-pah feel. Interplay between clarinet and violin.

F Melody and um-pah return briefly before slow, quiet ending.

Discussion The box below shows you the six tracks with the descriptions in the right order.

Table 6.1

Track	Letter	Music description
13	C	Free, expansive melody on violin. Slow.
14	A	Solid beat, violin tune, clarinet also playing, then dissolves into slower, expansive music.
15	E	Slightly quicker, definite um-pah feel. Interplay between clarinet and violin.
16	D	Violin and clarinet at higher pitch. Continued um-pah feel. Slight pause at end.
17	B	Slower, lower scoring, husky clarinet, gentle strumming.
18	F	Melody and um-pah return briefly before slow, quiet ending.

The main thing to take away from this exercise is a sense of the four-square melody and um-pah accompaniment that feature in traditional klezmer.

Shostakovich Piano Trio No. 2

The movement from Shostakovich's Piano Trio No. 2 that you will shortly listen to is the finale, the last of four movements that make up this work. The finale brings together all the moods of the earlier movements of this work – the eerieness of the opening, the frantic irony of the second movement scherzo and the sombre mourning of the third movement **passacaglia**. While it was expected of Soviet composers that they should provide a joyous finale to resolve all tensions at the end of a musical composition, Shostakovich does no such thing in this work.

Activity Read the interpretations of the finale quoted below and then listen to the last movement in its entirety, on track 19 of the Audio CD.

> This movement is nothing less than a gruesome dance of death; its quiet ending is the stillness of the mass grave.
>
> (Huth, 2005)

> This movement has been interpreted as a representation of evil, of malice, of death itself, perhaps the forces that caused Sollertinsky's death. In this work personal and social feelings intermingle, and they are expressed in a Jewish idiom.
>
> (Braun, 1985, p. 76)

> This is *Klezmer*, the wild music of Jewish celebration, here grotesquely metamorphosed into an image of sustained destructive power. At the climax, the music breaks off into a swirling reminiscence of the first movement, as if, in the midst of this terrible vision, even the memory of a bleak past is to be cherished. And at the end the chords of the passacaglia come together with the eerie harmonics from the very opening, leaving the landscape as empty as when we entered it.
>
> (Philip, 2005)

This is a more challenging listening activity. Drawing on the klezmer music you heard earlier, and on the descriptions of Jewish elements used by Shostakovich, answer the following question:

What is it that gives this movement a Jewish inflection?

You will need to listen again to the whole movement, and then focus on the opening only (about the first minute of track 19).

Discussion

There are several ways in which Shostakovich incorporates Jewish elements into his music. He makes use of Jewish folk poetry, draws on well-known Jewish melodies and also creates his own melodies that show affiliation to Jewish melodies. What you can hear in this example is the same type of melody that characterises the extract of traditional klezmer music, as well as an emphasis on the solo violin and um-pah-like accompaniment. The meaning of these elements is often dissidence concealed: 'It is in fact a hidden language of resistance communicated to the listener aware of its subtle meaning' (Braun, 1985, p. 80). In other words, Shostakovich uses traditional musical material to dissent from prevailing political ideologies. In creating this eerie finale with its use of klezmer, he challenges the system in a subtle way.

CONCLUSION

The purpose of this chapter has been to introduce you to some ways in which music has traditions from which it also dissents, through a focus on the music of one particular composer. At the beginning of Book 2 you were introduced to the idea of a tradition as being something that is rooted in the past, but which can also change and develop. Shostakovich was chosen as the figure to study here as his music both adheres to traditional Classical musical structures and methods dating back to the eighteenth century, and also changes and develops these – something that was discussed in section 6.3. He also uses musical materials to dissent from the prevailing political ideologies of the Stalin regime, an added complexity that makes the composer and his music so fascinating to study and to hear. But perhaps the most important consideration is that Shostakovich left a rich body of music that offers much to the listener. I hope you leave this week's work with a better understanding of this powerfully expressive composer. If you wish to hear more of his music once your work on AA100 is complete, you might like to try listening to some of the symphonies.

REFERENCES

Braun, J. (1985) 'The double meaning of Jewish elements in Dmitri Shostakovich's music', *Musical Quarterly*, vol. 71, no. 1, pp. 68–80.

Huth, A. (2005) sleeve notes for Shostakovich Piano Trio 2, Beaux Arts Trio, Warner Classics, 2564 62514–2.

Krenek, E. (1962) 'Tradition in perspective', *Perspectives of New Music*, vol. 1, no. 1, autumn, pp. 27–38.

Philip, R. (2005) Programme notes, Florestan Festival, Peasmarsh, Sussex.

Schoenberg, A. (1984) *Style and Idea: Selected Writings* (ed. L. Stein; trans. L. Black), London, Faber and Faber.

Shostakovich, D. (1979) *Testimony: The Memoirs of Dmitri Shostakovich* (ed. S. Volkov; trans. A.W. Bouis), London, Faber and Faber.

Stravinsky, I. and Craft, R. (1960) *Memories and Commentaries*, London, Faber and Faber.

Tomes, S. (2006) *A Musician's Alphabet*, London, Faber.

Whittall, A. (2003) *Exploring Twentieth-Century Music: Tradition and Innovation*, Cambridge, Cambridge University Press.

RESOURCES

Reading 6.1 'C' is for chamber music

How to write about chamber music, the family of pieces that won my heart when I was a youngster, and which has been at the centre of my performing life? These days, when anyone alludes to the fact that chamber music is 'difficult' or 'elitist', I often recall that first effortless sense of liking. Our educational work as musicians tries to address the question of why young people don't naturally gravitate towards chamber music, and need to be gently and persuasively introduced to it. I'm ill-equipped for this kind of outreach work because I don't remember ever having had doubts about chamber music. Nobody had to use their imagination to convert me. I saw the point straight away, and took it for granted that everyone else did too.

'The point' was really that many composers used chamber music to give us the truest portraits of themselves, their most intimate thoughts and feelings. There was no sense of showing off such as might occur in solo repertoire; nor was there the multiplication of means and effects which sometimes makes orchestral music seem coarse. Instead, there was a wonderful conversation between people with meaningful things to say. With one person on each part, everyone was vital, and each player influenced the others in an unpredictable way. Playing chamber music was like digesting life in the company of a newly acquired family. At junior music college and on music courses, I always particularly looked forward to my chamber music sessions, which gradually overtook everything else in importance.

Now, I have an axe to grind about chamber groups and their difficulties in reaching large audiences. Everyone else tells us that our kind of music is less popular than symphonies and operas because it uses small forces and lacks impact. We are supposed to be philosophical about this and content ourselves with small audiences. However, if you look at the world of popular music you find that small groups are by far the dominant force, rulers of the airwaves and darlings of the media. From The Beatles and The Rolling Stones through The Beach Boys and ABBA to U2 and Coldplay – it's exactly these groups of a few individuals that audiences love most. ... I know teenagers who refer to someone in tones of reverence just because they are 'in a group'. Even a despised contemporary will acquire social cachet if they become a group member.

I find groups just as interesting as everyone else does. Groups are alternative families, with their different characters, their rows, their intimacy, their loyalty. We find the dynamic endlessly fascinating. The same principle works in all the successful TV sitcoms. ... Watching accomplished actors in these sitcoms is for me very much like watching a skilful group of chamber musicians at work. There's something musical about the **rhythm** and pace of their interactions.

They listen, they react, they wait, they surge forward, they bounce off one another's ideas. They each represent some different facet of human nature. They have to know when to be centre-stage, when to support, when to be in the background. There are only a few of them, and the audience doesn't want anyone to be added or subtracted; they tend to resent actors brought in to be someone's new partner or whatever. The integrity of the original group is really important to fans.

In other words, the 'chamber group' in the worlds of pop music and TV drama is actually the king. Actors and musicians are desperate to get into those groups because they know how powerful they will become as a part of it. The whole will become more than the sum of its parts. So why, in the world of classical music, are chamber groups not similarly idolised? We can play our instruments, we have years of experience, we spend time getting the mixture of players right, we're devoted to our art, and we have fantastic music to play. To continue the 'family' analogy, we could say that a chamber group is like a family whose members always say, in music, different and interesting things.

Source: Tomes, S. (2006) 'C is for chamber music', in Tomes, S., *A Musician's Alphabet*, London, Faber, pp. 15–18.

Reading 6.2 Extract from *Testimony*

This quality of Jewish folk music is close to my idea of what music should be. There should always be two layers in music. Jews were tormented for so long that they learned to hide their despair. They express despair in dance music.

All folk music is lovely, but I can say that Jewish folk music is unique. Many composers listened to it, including Russian composers, Mussorgsky, for instance. He carefully set down Jewish folk songs. Many of my works reflect my impressions of Jewish music.

This is not a purely musical issue, this is also a moral issue. I often test a person by his attitude toward Jews. In our day and age, any person with pretensions of decency cannot be anti-Semitic. This seems so obvious that it doesn't need saying, but I've had to argue the point for at least thirty years. Once after the war I was passing a bookstore and saw a volume with Jewish songs. I was always interested in Jewish folklore, and I thought the book would give the melodies, but it contained only the texts. It seemed to me that if I picked out several texts and set them to music, I would be able to tell about the fate of the Jewish people. It seemed an important thing to do, because I could see anti-Semitism growing all around me. But I couldn't have the cycle performed then, it was played for the first time much later, and later still I did an orchestral version of the work.

My parents considered anti-Semitism a shameful superstition, and in that sense I was given a singular upbringing. In my youth I came across anti-Semitism among my peers, who thought that Jews were getting preferential treatment. They didn't remember the pogroms, the ghettos, or the quotas. In those years it was almost a mark of sangfroid to speak of Jews with a mocking laugh. It was a kind of opposition to the authorities.

I never condoned an anti-Semitic tone, even then, and I didn't repeat anti-Semitic jokes that were popular then. But I was much gentler about this unworthy trait than I am now. Later I broke with even good friends if I saw that they had any anti-Semitic tendencies.

But even before the war, the attitude toward Jews had changed drastically. It turned out that we had far to go to achieve brotherhood. The Jews became the most persecuted and defenseless people of Europe. It was a return to the Middle Ages. Jews became a symbol for me. All of man's defenselessness was concentrated in them. After the war, I tried to convey that feeling in my music. It was a bad time for Jews then. In fact, it's always a bad time for them.

Despite all the Jews who perished in the camps, all I heard people saying was, 'The kikes went to Tashkent to fight.' And if they saw a Jew with military decorations, they called after him, 'Kike, where did you buy the medals?' That's when I wrote the Violin Concerto, the Jewish Cycle, and the Fourth Quartet.

Not one of these works could be performed then. They were heard only after Stalin's death. I still can't get used to it. The Fourth Symphony was played twenty-five years after I wrote it. There are compositions that have yet to be performed, and no one knows when they will be heard.

I'm very heartened by the reaction among young people to my feelings on the Jewish question. And I see that the Russian intelligentsia remains intractably opposed to anti-Semitism, and that the many years of trying to enforce anti-Semitism from above have not had any visible results ...

The last time I was in America I saw the film *Fiddler on the Roof* and here's what astounded me about it: the primary emotion is homesickness, you sense it in the music, the dancing, the color. Even though the motherland is a so-and-so, a bad, unloving country, more a stepmother than a mother. But people still miss her, and that loneliness made itself felt. I feel that loneliness was the most important aspect. It would be good if Jews could live peacefully and happily in Russia, where they were born. But we must never forget about the dangers of anti-Semitism and keep reminding others of it, because the infection is alive and who knows if it will ever disappear.

Source: Shostakovich (1979), pp. 156–8.

AFTERWORD

Carolyn Price

In this book we've aimed to build on and extend your experience of study in the Arts and Humanities. The first book in this course, *Reputations*, introduced two key skills:

- how to study and interpret works of art and historical documents
- how to undertake close reading of a literary text and close listening of pieces of music.

In this book, you'll have found many opportunities to develop these skills and to apply them in new contexts. You've also been introduced to some new skills, including:

- how to identify and evaluate philosophical arguments
- how to apply a general historical argument to a specific case
- how to use plans and drawings in understanding architectural designs.

You'll have further opportunities to practise all these skills later in the course.

The discussions in this book have taken you to some very different times and places – from classical Athens to Victorian London, and from the battle of Crécy to Stalin's Soviet Union. You'll certainly have noticed many contrasts, but I hope that you've also noticed some recurring patterns, relevant to our themes of tradition and dissent.

To help you reflect further, you may wish to end your work on this book by returning to the questions that I raised in the introduction. Here's an activity to help you do this.

Activity

Choose just one of the traditions discussed in this book – one that particularly interested you. For example, you might pick the Roman Catholic tradition in England, or the tradition of composing music for string quartets. Then, drawing on the material you have encountered in the book, consider the following questions:

1. Did this tradition remain static or did it change over time? Why?
2. Was this tradition renewed, revived, or even invented at a certain point in history? If so, why?
3. Did the tradition represent certain values to the people who adhered to it? What were they?
4. Did it provoke dissent? If so, why?
5. Was this tradition itself ever used to express dissent? If so, what suited it to that role?

As a follow-up, you might try asking these questions of other traditions described in this book, or of a tradition that you've encountered in your own life – for example, a tradition followed in your family or local community.

GLOSSARY

Act of Union (Ireland) the Act of 1800 which abolished the Irish parliament in Dublin and gave Ireland 100 MPs at Westminster.

aisles the two wings flanking the nave of a church, divided from it by a row of pillars.

altar a table or slab used for the celebration of Holy Communion.

altarpiece a painting, sculpture or other artwork placed above, behind or on an altar to form a backdrop.

Anglican church the official Protestant church of England and Wales after the Reformation.

Anglo-Irish the descendants of English settlers who occupied land confiscated from the Roman Catholic Irish, especially *c.*1560–1700. They dominated the government of Ireland.

anthropomorphism in the words of the *OED*, this means 'attributing a human personality to anything impersonal or irrational'. *The Faber Book of Beasts* is littered with examples – consider Alexander Pope's miniature verse 'Engraved on the Collar of a Dog': 'I am His Highness' dog at Kew;/Pray tell me, sir, whose dog are you?', in which human thoughts and attitudes are ascribed to dogs.

argument a set of claims (premises) intended to support or to prove some further claim (the conclusion). Some arguments are deductive arguments.

Arts and Crafts Movement a group dedicated to reviving craft traditions and improving standards of design in Victorian Britain. One of its best-known members was William Morris (1834–1896).

Ashkenazi Ashkenazi Jews, also called Ashkenazim, are descendants of Jewish people from Germany, Poland, Austria and eastern Europe. In historical times, Ashkenazi Jews usually spoke Yiddish or a Slavic language.

atonal not tonal, i.e. in no particular key.

bar a modular segment of music incorporating a fixed number of beats, as in the phrase 'three beats to the bar'. It is shown in notation by vertical 'barring'. The corresponding US term is 'measure'.

biting the bullet deciding not to change your position on a certain issue, while recognising that it has an implication that many people (including you, perhaps) find implausible.

box-pew fixed bench seating in a church with a wooden enclosure round it and a door for entry. Such fixtures were common in the eighteenth century.

buttress brick or stone work built up against a wall to provide additional strength, usually to counteract the outward thrust from a roof or upper storeys.

Camden Society a society founded in Cambridge in 1839 by J.M. Neale and B. Webb, dedicated to exploring the ecclesiastical antiquities and aesthetics of the English church.

Catholic emancipation the campaign to give all Roman Catholics in Britain and Ireland civil rights, which achieved success in 1829, allowing Catholics to sit in Parliament and hold most high offices.

central plan a design for a building which radiates out from a central point.

chancel or **choir** the east end of the church in which the altar is placed, traditionally reserved for the clergy and choir.

chancel screen a screen dividing the public part of the church from the choir. It supported the rood loft and rood statues.

chapel usually either a side sanctuary within a church; or a place of worship for Methodists, Presbyterians and other Protestant groups outside the Anglican church. The term is also sometimes used for non-parish churches within the Anglican church.

chapter-house the place in a cathedral or monastery where the ecclesiastics met to discuss their business.

cimbalom a Hungarian instrument consisting of a box over which strings are stretched, the performer playing them from front to back with beaters or hammers.

choir *see* chancel.

classical architecture so-called because it can be traced back to the ancient Greek and Romans, this style is based on the use of columns combined with round or square openings rather than the pointed ones of the Gothic style.

Classical music with a capital ‘C’, this term is commonly used to denote the period of music of Haydn and Mozart (the period preceding the Classical is known as Baroque, while the period following it is known as Romantic).

cloisters an open square linking the church and the other areas of a monastery.

conceit an elaborate and often far-fetched comparison of the kind used by John Donne in his poem ‘The Flea’.

concerto a musical composition, traditionally in three movements, for solo instrument(s) and orchestra.

conclusion the claim that an argument is used to argue for.

Dáil the lower legislative house in the Irish parliament (the upper house is the Senate).

deductive argument an argument that is intended to prove its conclusion; deductive arguments are supposed to be valid.

ensemble a group of singers or instrumentalists usually made up of one per part, for example instrumentalists playing chamber music.

entomology the scientific study of insects.

ethnography the collecting of folk and other musical materials.

fan vault a stone vaulted ceiling made up of concave-sided semi-cones. The ribs of the cones are decorated with raised lines which together give the appearance of fans.

Fenians the Irish-American republican movement linked with the Irish Republican Brotherhood in Ireland.

flying buttress (*see also* buttress) a high-level arch transmitting the thrust of a roof or vault from the upper part of a wall to an outer support or buttress – and hence 'flying' between the two parts of the building.

free verse verse which avoids traditional poetic devices such as rhyme and conventional metre, as in the poetry of D.H. Lawrence and Miroslav Holub. Free verse is sometimes referred to as *vers libre*, which is simply the same term in French.

functionalism the notion that the primary purpose of a building is its suitability for its purpose. The idea was originated by Pugin and the term was coined by the Modern movement.

Gaelic League an organisation founded in 1893 by a group of Gaelic scholars to promote the Irish language and Gaelic culture. It was initially without political aims, but became increasingly politicised from 1915 onwards.

Gothic architecture a style used in Europe during the Middle Ages, based on the use of the pointed arch and the vault, exemplified in medieval cathedrals.

Gothic Revival the reinterpretation of Gothic architecture, particularly in Victorian Britain.

harmony in music, the sounding together of notes to produce a chord.

Holy Communion the blessing and sharing of the bread and wine, the central act in Christian worship.

hyperbole, hyperbolic the language of deliberate exaggeration and overstatement.

image, imagery these words describe the capacity of literary language to represent objects, actions, feelings, etc. in different (not necessarily visual) terms. These aren't scientific terms, and are often used vaguely to describe a wide range of different things. The lines 'a few arms and legs/still twitched jerkily under the trees' (from Miroslav Holub's poem 'The Fly') and 'this/Our marriage bed, and marriage temple is' (from John Donne's poem 'The Flea') both contain images, but the first is a literal description, while the second fuses two complementary metaphors. This term can also mean an artistic representation such as a statue or painting.

imitation this is a complex term with many different meanings. In poetry, it means the process whereby a poet copies or adapts the work of someone that he or she admires, as in Alexander Pope's poem 'Imitation ... of Horace'.

Irish Free State the independent state of Ireland, established under the Anglo-Irish Treaty of 1922.

Irish Republican Brotherhood (IRB) the IRB emerged after an unsuccessful uprising against Britain in 1848 and was strongly supported by the American Fenian movement. It aimed actively to destroy British rule in Ireland and to establish an independent republic, by violence if necessary.

key this describes any piece of music where the melodies and harmonies are based on the notes of a major or minor scale. For example, a piece in the key of C major uses mainly the notes of the C major scale, and the harmonies are made up mainly from the notes of that scale. Most music which uses this system does not remain in one key for its whole duration but moves on to related keys.

key signature in musical notation, sharps or flats printed at the beginning of every stave to tell the player which key the piece is in.

klezmer this Yiddish term derives from the Hebrew word for musical instruments. It was first used by eastern European Jews in the seventeenth century to describe professional musicians, but it also refers to the traditional instrumental music they performed.

lady chapel a chapel dedicated to the Virgin Mary within a larger church.

Latin cross plan a design for a church based on a cross with a long stem consisting of three short 'arms' and a long nave.

liturgical calendar the different forms of worship used for the various Christian festivals.

liturgy the services used for formal worship within the church.

longitudinal plan a design for a building where a single long axis predominates, as in the Latin cross plan.

Magi the wise men who, according to the gospel of Matthew, came to worship the Christ Child shortly after his birth.

melody in music, a series of notes of different pitches played or sung after one another, also more commonly known as the tune.

minuet and trio traditionally the third movement of a Classical four-movement symphony, a stately dance in three time with a contrasting middle (trio) section.

Modern Movement an international style based on functionalism, dominant *c.*1930–60.

modus ponens a *modus ponens* argument is a valid deductive argument that follows the following pattern:

Premise 1: If [claim 1] is true, then [claim 2] is true
Premise 2: [Claim 1] is true.
Conclusion: So, [claim 2] is true

modus tollens a *modus tollens* argument is a valid deductive argument that follows the following pattern:

Premise 1: If [claim 1] is true, then [claim 2] is true.
Premise 2: [Claim 2] is not true.
Conclusion: So [claim 1] is not true.

moral traditionalism the view that tradition is the best source of moral beliefs.

moral rationalism the view that reason is the best source of moral beliefs.

mullion a vertical bar dividing a window or the lights of a screen.

mute in music, a device used to dampen the vibration of an instrument and thus to affect the tone.

nationalist in Ireland, this term refers to anyone who seeks Irish self-determination. It has been used to denote a variety of different political parties and positions.

nave the main part of the church, to the west of the crossing, where the congregation are traditionally seated.

neo-classicism a specific revival of the classicism of antiquity, dating from the mid-eighteenth century onwards.

opera an extended dramatic musical work in which singing takes the place of speech.

passacaglia an instrumental form of music constructed over a cyclically repeating bass line.

Perpendicular a form of Gothic architecture characterised by its slender proportions and elaborate decoration, common in England from the fourteenth to the sixteenth centuries.

personification a kind of metaphor which attributes human characteristics to inanimate objects or non-human creatures, e.g. 'My thoughtless hand'; 'A happy fly'.

piano trio a musical group comprising a piano, a violin and a cello. The term also refers to the music written for such a group.

Pietà an image of the Virgin Mary with the dead Christ in her lap.

pilaster a flattened rectangular column attached to and projecting only slightly from a wall.

premises a set of claims that are intended to support or to prove the conclusion of an argument.

protestantism the Christian churches which separated from the Catholic church in the sixteenth century, mainly in northern Europe.

pulpit a raised structure used by a preacher or reader in a church or chapel.

Reformation the religious movement of the sixteenth century which replaced the Catholic church with 'reformed', or Protestant, ones.

resurrection the belief that Christ rose from the dead after his crucifixion.

rhetorical describing uses of language which are artificial, where the speaker or writer has used the resources of language to maximise its effect.

rhythm the way that sounds of varying length and stress are grouped together in patterns.

Romantic/Romanticism an artistic movement of the late eighteenth and early nineteenth centuries which emphasised the individual and the power of the human imagination. Romantic poets such as William Blake and Percy Bysshe Shelley tended to position themselves as social outsiders, or even outcasts from society, and their work aimed to challenge and reform a complacent society.

rood the statue of Christ on the cross accompanied by the Virgin and St John, which was placed in the chancel arch of a church on the rood loft and chancel screen.

rood loft a gallery, usually wide enough to walk on, supporting the rood statues. It was also used to display candles and lamps, sometimes for reading the Gospels, and even to house the organ. It could generally be accessed via steps leading off the chancel arch.

rood screen the structure supporting the rood loft. In England this is often a partly open rather than a solid structure.

scherzo a lively piece of music, usually in triple time, often used as a movement in a sonata or symphony as a substitute for the more stately minuet and trio.

simile a formal comparison which is usually introduced by the words 'like' or 'as'. For example, the phrase 'Wings like bits of umbrella' formally compares the wings of bats to umbrellas, while the words 'umbrella winged bat' metaphorically describe bats' wings in terms of umbrellas.

Sinn Féin This was formed in 1907 as a broadly based nationalist political party. It subsequently became committed to independence from Britain but its founder, Arthur Griffith (1872–1922), was a cultural and economic nationalist rather than a republican.

sonata form one of the most important and most frequently used musical forms, in which the structure divides into three main sections: exposition, development and recapitulation.

sound a sound argument is both valid and has true premises. Only deductive arguments can be said to be sound (or unsound) in this sense.

staccato a musical term used to describe playing notes in a short, detached manner.

symphony the most important form of composition for an orchestra, consisting of three or most often four separate movements.

syntax the construction and ordering of sentences.

time signature in musical notation, a numerical sign placed after the clef and key signatures indicating the metre of the music.

timpani also known as kettledrums, these are tuned drums that produce notes of definite pitch and form a standard part of the symphony orchestra.

trabeated architecture architecture built using the post and lintel system of horizontal blocks resting on vertical supports, as in Greek temples. This is in contrast to arcuated architecture (used, for example, in the Gothic), whose structure is based on the use of arches.

triptych an altarpiece in three parts: a central section with one (or more) folding shutters to either side.

valid to say that an argument is valid is to say that, if the premises are true, you can be certain that the conclusion is true. Only deductive arguments can be said to be valid (or invalid) in this sense.

Young Ireland A movement of cultural nationalism led by Thomas Davis (1814–45).

ACKNOWLEDGEMENTS

Grateful acknowledgement is made to the following sources for permission to reproduce material in this book.

Chapter 2

Miroslav Holub, *Poems Before & After*. Translation © George Theiner. (Bloodaxe Books, 2006). www.bloodaxebooks.com

Holub, M. (1990) 'The Fly', © Miroslav Holub. Reproduced with permission from DILIA Theatrical, Literary and Audiovisual Agency. Translation © Stuart Friebert and Dana Hábová.

Chapter 3

Newman, J. H. (1852) 'The Second Spring: a sermon delivered to the First Provincial Council of Westminster, 1852', reprinted by permission of The National Institute of Newman Studies.

Chapter 5

Hobsbawm, E. 'Introduction: inventing traditions' in Hobsbawm, E. and Ranger, T. (eds) (1992) *The Invention of Tradition*, published by Cambridge University Press, reproduced with permission.

Chapter 6

Shostakovich, D., 'String Quartets 1-4', © Copyright by Boosey & Hawkes Music Publishers Ltd UK, British Commonwealth (ex Canada) and Eire.

INDEX

Page numbers in **bold** refer to figures.

ABBA in performance **199**

The Aberdeen Bestiary 57

Act of Uniformity (1559) 79

Aeschylus 36

Aesop's fables 45, 65

altarpieces, Pugin and Gothic architecture 120–1, 138–40

Amichai, Yehuda, 'A Dog After Love' 68

Anglican Church *see* Church of England

animal poetry, traditions in 42–54

anthologies, and *The Faber Book of Beasts* 54–8

anthropomorphism
- and Blake's 'The Fly' 44–5, 54
- and Donne's 'The Flea' 51
- and Holub's 'The Fly' 54
- and Lawrence's poetry 58–9
- and Whitman's 'A Noiseless Patient Spider' 65

antiquities, and Irish nationalism 161

architecture vi
- architectural writings 119–20
- Arts and Crafts Movement 120, 130
- Elizabethan 112, 113, 114
- Modern Movement 120, 130
- trabeated 128
- traditions in 153–4
- *see also* classical architecture; Gothic architecture; Pugin, Augustus

arguments, philosophical 13–16
- and the Socratic method of teaching and learning 26–7

Arts and Crafts Movement 120, 130

Athens
- democratic government 5–6
- Plato and Socrates in 5–6
- war with Sparta 6, 9

atonal music, and Shostakovich 205

Auden, W.H. 60, 61

balance, performing Shostakovich's string quartets 216

Barry, Charles 110
- design for the Palace of Westminster 109, 111, 114–19, **115**

Beethoven, Ludwig van 200, 207
- last movement of Symphony No. 5 215
- scherzo of Symphony No. 9 214, 215

Belcher, M. 137

beliefs *see* traditional beliefs

Bentham, Jeremy 127

bestiaries, medieval 57

the Bible, and English Christianity 75, 78, 80, 85, 87, 97

Birmingham
- church buildings 91–4, 96
  - St Chad's Roman Catholic Cathedral vi, 93–4, **94**, 110, 135–7, **136**, 139–40, **140**, 141–2
  - Oscott College 141

Blake, William 41, 42, 53
- engravings 47–8
- 'The Lamb' 46–7
- portrait of **47**
- Songs of Innocence and of Experience 46–7
- 'The Fly' 42, 43–8, 50, 56
  - anthropomorphism in 44–5, 54
  - engraved version of 48
  - and Holub's 'The Fly' 52, 54
  - personification in 44
  - poetic analogy in 46
  - poetic imagery in 44
  - rhyming words in 43–4
  - simile in 44
- 'The Tyger' 46–7, 48

blank verse, and free verse 53

Boleyn, Anne 78, 79

Bossy, J. 95

bow strokes, performing Shostakovich's string quartets 216

Braun, J. 221

Brighton, Chapel Royal 121–4

Brodsky, Adolph 202

Buckler, John Chessel 114

Burns, Robert, 'The Book-Worms' 68

Calydonian Hunt **18**

Camden Society 141–2

Catherine of Aragon 78

Catholicism
- Catholic Emancipation 158
- in England
  - eighteenth-century recusants 88
  - and the Elizabethan church 79, 80, 82
  - and the Gunpowder Plot 82–3
  - and James II 85
  - nineteenth-century revival 89, 93–6, 104–6, 109
  - and the Oxford Movement 90–1, 141
  - pre-Reformation 75–8, 80
  - and the Relief Act (1791) 109
  - restoration of (1553–58) 78, 80
- and Gothic architecture 109, 120–6
  - furnishing of Catholic churches 132–41
  - images and altarpieces 138–40
  - Latin cross church plan 124, **125**
- and Irish nationalism 151, 157, 158–60
- and other religious traditions 82

Vatican II reforms and rood screens 137
see also church buildings

cellos, and string quartets 196, 201

Cenotaph, London, Remembrance Sunday service 154

chamber music 196–9, 223–4
instruments 197
Mozart's wind octet 200–1
piano trios **197**, 197, 218

chancel screens
Lübeck cathedral 133–4, **134**
St Chad's Roman Catholic cathedral, Birmingham 135–7, **136**

Chappell, Tim, interview with 17, 28, 36–7

Charles I, King 84

Charles II, King 84, 85

Charles, Prince of Wales, on the Book of Common Prayer 84–5

Chigi Vase **12**

childhood experience, and Blake's 'The Fly' 43, 48

Christianity *see* English Christianity

church buildings 91–4
Birmingham 91–4, **94**
St Chad's Roman Catholic Cathedral vi, 93–4, **94**, 110, 135–7, **136**, 139–40, **140**, 141–2
box pews 124
Chapel Royal, Brighton 121–4
Long Melford, Suffolk **76**, **77**, 77–8, 99–100, 138, 139
Lübeck 110, 133–4, **134**, 135, 138, 139, **140**
and neo-classicism 121, 126
Pugin and Gothic architecture 121–6, 129–30
and 'Commissioners' churches 126, 146–7
and furnishings of Catholic churches 132–41, 141–2
Latin cross churches 124, **125**
St George's Chapel, Windsor 121–4
St Peter's Parish Church, Leeds **90**, 91
York **81**, 91, **92**, **93**

Church of England
Anglican religious societies 85
Book of Common Prayer 79, 80, 84–5
establishment of 79–83
Grindal's injunctions to churchwardens 80–2, 97, 100–2, 137
and Roman Catholicism 83–4
nineteenth-century 89, 90–1, 95, 96
and church building 125–6
seventeenth-century 84–5
Thirty-Nine Articles 79
Whitefield's criticisms of Anglican clergy 87–8, 97
see also church buildings; English Christianity; Protestantism

classical architecture 112
neo-classicism 121
Pugin's rejection of 109, 128, 130, 132–3
and the rebuilding of the Palace of Westminster 112, 113, 116
writings about 120

classical period of music 199–201

Coldplay in performance **198**

Coleridge, Samuel Taylor, 'The Rime of the Ancient Mariner' 65

Collins, Michael 170

communities
and pre-Reformation English Christianity 76, 77
and traditional beliefs 4, 5

conceits, poetic, and Donne's 'The Flea' 50, 51

concertos 202

conclusions, and philosophical arguments 13–14

Connolly, James 151

Cosgrave, William Thomas 182

courage
in Plato's *Laches* 41
as endurance 13–16
and Greek tradition 11–12
Nicias' definition of 16–17, 19, 20, 23, 25
Socrates' question 9–11
as the whole of virtue 18–19

Cranmer, Thomas, Archbishop of Canterbury 78

creation myths, in Ireland 171–2

Crécy, battle of (1346), and Holub's 'The Fly' 53

cultural nationalism in Ireland 160–4

Czechoslovakia, and Holub's poetry 51

Daedalus, mythical inventor and artist, statues of 20–2, **21**

the Dalai Lama 73

Davis, Thomas 160

de Valera, Eamon 170

deductive arguments 14–15

Diamond Quartet 193, 208

Diaper, William, from Oppian's *Halieuticks* 69

Disraeli, Benjamin 96

dissent, and tradition v, xi, 226

Donne, John 53
'A Jeat Ring sent' 51
portrait of **49**
and Shostakovich 203
'The Flea' 41, 42, 48–51, 54, 56, 60
as a conceit 50
form and syntax 48
and Holub's 'The Fly' 52
rhyme scheme 48
sexuality in 49–51

double entendres, in Donne's 'The Flea' 50

Dublin
Easter Rising (1916) in 151, **152**, 152, **153**, 164, **165**, 166
invented tradition and Dublin landmarks 156, 172–3

Duffy, Carol Ann 41

Duffy, Eamon, *The Stripping of the Altars: Traditional Religion in England c.1400–1580* 76–7

DVD material vii

Eastlake, Charles 113
education
 and cultural nationalism in Ireland 160, 161, 170
 the Socratic method of teaching and learning 26–7
Edward VI, King 78, 80, 137
Eighteenth Century Collections Online 86–7
Eliot, T.S. 55
Elizabeth I, Queen 79, 80, 82, 113, 137
Elizabethan architecture 112, 113, 114
endurance, courage as, in Plato's *Laches* 13–16
English Christianity v, vi, 71–106
 and core Christian teachings 74–5
 eighteenth-century 83–8
 Evangelical/Methodist movement 83, 85–8
 nineteenth-century 88–96
 pre-Reformation 75–8, 99–100
  and Gothic architecture 109, 138–40
 the Protestant Reformation 75, 78–83, 137
 see also church buildings; Church of England
entomology, and animal poetry 45
Estienne, Henri 29
ethnography, and musical tradition 194
Evangelical movement, and English Christianity 83, 85–8, 91, 97
The Faber Book of Beasts 39–69
 and the Audio CD 'What am I? Beasts and Tradition' 41, 54
 Blake's 'The Fly' 42, 43–8, 50, 56
 Donne's 'The Flea' 41, 42, 48–51, 54, 56, 60
 Holub's 'The Fly' 42, 51–4, 56, 58
 Lawrence poems in 57, 58–65
 using as an anthology 54–8
  alphabetical ordering in 56, 57
  contradictions in selection 57
  medieval bestiaries 57
  miniature anthologies 57–8, 68–9
The Faber Book of Contemporary Irish Poetry 55, 56

fan vaulting, and Perpendicular Gothic architecture 114
Fenians 158
Fiddler on the Roof, 'Tradition' from 217
First World War
 and Ireland 164, 169
 and Remembrance Sunday 154
Fleishman, Venyamin 218
Florestan trio **197**, 198
Fonthill Abbey, Wiltshire 117
Fox, George 84
Foxe, John *Book of Martyrs* 82
free verse
 and Holub's 'The Fly' 53, 54
 and Lawrence's poems 58
French Revolution (1789) 89, 112
Friebert, Stuart and Hábová, Dana, translation of Holub's 'The Fly' 53, 67
functionalism, and the Modern Movement in architecture 130

Gaelic League 161–3, 164, 180
Gentleman's Magazine 111
George IV, King 124
Germany, history and tradition in 154
Gladstone, William Ewart 160
Gonne, Maud 167, 168
Gothic architecture 109–10
 churches 109, 121–6, **125**, 129–31, **131**, **132**
 and modern towns 126–7
 see also Palace of Westminster; Pugin, Augustus
Gregory the Great, Pope 138
Gregory, Lady (Isabella) Augusta 163
 Yeats's letter to 166–7, 169, 182–3
Grindal, Edmund, archbishop of York, later archbishop of Canterbury
 injunctions to churchwardens 80–2, 84, 97, 100–2, 137
 portrait of **79**
Guadagnini violins 201–2, **202**
Gunn, Thom, 'Yoko' 69
Gunpowder Plot (1605) 82–3
Gurevich, Michael 215

Haig, Douglas (later Earl) 182
Hardman, John 141
Hardwick Hall, Derbyshire 113
Haydn, Joseph 200
Heaney, Seamus 55, 57
Heath Quartet 193, 201, 212, 213
Henry VIII, King 78, 79, 111, 127, 137
Herrick, Robert, 'The Captiv'd Bee' 50
Hinduism, and other religious traditions 82, 96
history vi
 and Irish cultural nationalism 160–4
 and tradition 153–4
  invented tradition 154–7, 170–1, 172–4, 176–80
 value judgements and reading historical material 168–9
 see also Ireland
Hitler, Adolf 154
Hobsbawm, Eric, 'Inventing traditions' 154–5, 157, 174, 176–80
Holub, Miroslav
 photograph of **52**
 'The Fly' 42, 51–4, 56
  and Lawrence's poems 58
  poetic timing 54
  translations of 53–4, 67–8
Holy Club, Oxford 85
Homer, *Iliad* 10
Hook, Walter, vicar of Leeds 91
Hooke, Robert, *Micrographia* 51

Hooker, Richard, *The Laws of Ecclesiastical Polity* 83
hoplites, and courage in Greek tradition **11**, 11
Hughes, Ted 55
 'Wodwo' 58
Hyde, Douglas 161, 163
hyperbolic sentiments, in Lawrence's poetry 61

Icarus, mythical son of Daedalus 20
iconoclasts, and Protestantism 82
imagery, poetic imagery in Blake's 'The Fly' 44
imitation
 and poetry 41–2, 45
 and popular music 41, 42
India, religion in nineteenth-century 96
individuals
 and tradition v
 and traditional beliefs 4, 5
Industrial Revolution, and English Christianity 89
intonation, performing Shostakovich's string quartets 216–17
invented tradition 154–7, 176–80
 in Ireland 156–7, 170–1, 172–4
invention of tradition 154–7
Ireland v, 148–90
 Act of Union with Britain 158
 Anglo-Irish landlords/land reform 151, 158–60, 173, 174
 Anglo-Irish literary revival 163–4
 Anglo-Irish peace treaty (1921) 170
 Church of 89–90
 civil war (1922–23) 170, 171–2
 DVD Video 'Ireland' 156, 160, 172–4
  Media notes 152, 157, 185–90
 Easter Rising (1916) 151, **152**, 152, **153**, 164–9
  aftermath of 169–72
  execution of rebels 151, 166, 169
  and political nationalism 158
  Proclamation of the Republic of Ireland 164–6, 181–2
  and Yeats's 'Easter 1916' 167–9, 183–5
  and Yeats's letter to Lady Gregory 166–7, 169, 182–3
 European Union membership 156, 173
 famine (1845–51) 158
 first Dáil Éireann (1919) 169–70
 Hill of Tara meetings 156, 158, **159**
 Home Rule movement 160, 164
 invented tradition in 156–7, 174–5
  and the built heritage 156–7, 172–4
  and the Irish Free State 156, 170–1, **172**
 Irish banknotes **172**
 National Museum of 161
 Roman Catholicism in eighteenth century 88
 unionist movement in 151–2
 War of Independence (1919–21) 169, 170
Irish Citizen Army 164, 165
Irish language 161–3, 170, 171, 174, 180
Irish nationalism 151, 157–64
 and Catholicism 151, 157, 158–60
 cultural 160–4
 and the First World War 164
 and invented tradition 156, 170–2
 and Northern Ireland 157
 political 157, 168–60
 and the Republic of Ireland 157
Irish Republican Brotherhood 158
Irish Times 166
Irish Volunteers (later Irish Republican Army) 164, 165, 169
Islam, and other religious traditions 82, 96–7
Italian Renaissance, and classical style 132–3

James I, King (James VI of Scotland) 83
James II (James VII of Scotland) 85
James, John Angell 90, 92
James, Paula 41
Jeffrey, K. 151
Jewishness in music
 and Shostakovich 204–5, 217–21
  klezmer **219**, 219–20, 221

Keats, John 64
Keble, John 89–90
key signatures, and sonata form 208
keys, and sonata form 208
klezmer music, and Shostakovich **219**, 219–20, 221
knowledge
 Plato's views on 20–5
  in *Laches* 17
  in *Meno* 20–2
  and moral rationalism 24–6
Krenek, E. 194
Krummendiek, Albert, bishop of Lübeck 133

La Fontaine, Jean de 45
 'The Grasshopper and the Ant' 68
Laches, Athenian soldier and politician 9
 see also Plato
Larkin, Philip, 'The Mower' 69
Lattimore, R. 12
Laud, William, archbishop of Canterbury 84
Lavery, Sir John, *Lady Lavery as Cathleen Ní Houlihan* **171**, **172**
Lawrence, D.H. v, 57, 58–65
 and artistic traditions 41, 63–5
 'Bat' 59
 Birds, Beasts and Flowers 61
 hyperbolic sentiments in 61
 Lady Chatterley's Lover 61
 life and work 61
 'Lizard' (poem) 62, 63
 'Mountain Lion' 58, 60, 61
 paintings 61–2
 'Poetry of the present' (essay) 64–5
 The Rainbow 61

rhetorical repetitions in 59–60
Self-portrait **62**
'Snake' 41, 60, 63, 64–5
Sons and Lovers 61
'The Lizard' (watercolour) 62
'Tortoise' 59

literature, Anglo-Irish literary revival 163–4

liturgical calendar, in pre-Reformation Christianity 76–7

Long Melford Church, Suffolk **76**
interior **77**
pre-Reformation account of 75–8, 99–100, 138, 139

love poetry, and Donne's 'The Flea' 50–1

Lübeck, northern Germany
cathedral 110, 133–4, **134**, 135, 138, 139, **140**
Church of Our Lady 139

MacCaig, Norman, 'Toad' 69

McLaren, Colin 57

MacNeice, Louis 42, 45, 51
'Dogs in the Park' 68

madrigals, and chamber music 197

Marlowe, Christopher, *Dr Faustus* 53, 82

Martyn, Roger, on pre-Reformation Long Melford Church, Suffolk 75–8, 82, 97, 138, 139

Marvell, Andrew, 'The Mower to the Glowworms' 50

Mary I, Queen 78, 80, 82

Mary II, Queen 85

medieval bestiaries 57

Methodist movement, and English Christianity 83, 85–8, 89, 91

Modern Movement 120, 130

moral beliefs 4–5

moral rationalism 5
Plato on 24–6

moral traditionalism 5
Plato on 24–6

Mozart, Wolfgang Amadeus, wind octet 200–1, 214

Muldoon, Paul (editor)
The Faber Book of Beasts 41
on Blake's 'The Fly' 43
on Donne's 'The Flea' 48
introduction to 55–7
and Lawrence's poetry 60, 63
and Whitman 65
The Faber Book of Contemporary Irish Poetry 55

music vi
anthologies 55
New Grove Dictionary of Music and Musicians online 207
tradition and dissent in 193–5
see also Shostakovich, Dmitri; string quartets

musical instruments
chamber music 197
klezmer music **219**, 219–20
string quartets 196, 201–2, **202**, **203**

mutes for violins 212, **213**

Myrios Quartet 193

Nash, John 121

The Nation newspaper 160

National Gallery, London 114, 121

nationalism *see* Irish nationalism

Navarra Quartet 193, 201–2, 216–17

Neurath, Otto, and 'Neurath's ship' 36

Newman, John Henry 90
sermon at St Mary's College, Oscott 95, 97, 104–6

Nicias, Athenian soldier and statesman 9
definition of courage in Plato's *Laches* 16–17, 19, 20, 23, 25

Northern Ireland, and Irish nationalism 157

Notke, Bernt, wooden screen in Lübeck's cathedral 133–4, **134**, 135, 138

nursery rhymes, and Blake's 'The Fly' 43, 48

O'Connell, Daniel 158, 160
round tower built to commemorate 156, 160–1

O'Day, A. 161

O'Hickey, M.P., on the ideals of the Gaelic League 162–3, 180

opera
and chamber music 197
and musical tradition 194

opinion, and knowledge, in Plato's the *Meno* 20–2

Ovide Moralisé, painting of a philosophy lesson **27**

Oxford Dictionary of National Biography (ODNB) 160

Oxford English Dictionary (OED) online 41

Oxford Movement 90–1, 141

Oxford Reference Online 5

Palace of Westminster 109, 110, 111–19
aerial view of 117–18, **119**
Clock Tower (Big Ben) 111, 114, 117, **119**
and English kings 111
Gothic revival character 111
House of Commons 113, 116, 118
House of Lords 113, 116, 118
old Palace **112**
destruction by fire 111
plan **115**, 116
rebuilding in Gothic style 111–14
plan 114–19, **115**, 116
St Stephen's Hall **115**, 116
view from the Thames 117, **118**
Westminster Hall 111, **115**, 116

panopticons 127

Parnell, Charles Stewart 160

Pearse, Patrick/Pádraig 151, 167
Proclamation of the Republic of Ireland 164–6, 181–2

Perpendicular Gothic architecture 113, 114

personal experience
and knowledge 22
and traditional beliefs 4, 5

personification, in Blake's 'The Fly' 44

Petrie, George 160–1

Philip, R. 221

Phillips, Thomas, portrait of William Blake *47*

philosophy v, vi
- and background assumptions 10–11
- painting of a philosophy lesson **27**
- philosophical arguments 13–16
  - and the Socratic method of teaching and learning 26–8
- reading a philosophical text 9–10
- *see also* Plato; Socrates

picturesque architecture, and the Palace of Westminster 117–18

Pius IX, Pope, restoration of Catholic bishoprics in England 94–5

Plath, Sylvia 55
- 'Blue Moles' 68

Plato v, vi, 1–37
- and the Academy 6, 24, **25**
- *Apology* 36
- in Athens 5–6
- bust of **3**
- *Laches* 3, 6–7, 8, 9–20
  - ending of 23, 26–7
  - and Greek tradition 11–12
  - interview with Tim Chappell on 17, 28, 36–7
  - Nicias' definition of courage in 16–17, 19, 20, 23, 25
  - readings from 29–34
  - Socrates' argument in 13–16, 18–19, 20, 23, 27
  - Socrates' question in 9–11
- *Meno* 20–2, 36
  - readings from 35–6
- *Protagoras* 36
- rejection of tradition 24–6
- and Socratic dialogues 6–8, 24, 25–6
- the *Symposium* 8, 22

Plunkett, Count George 183

poetry v–vi
- blank verse and free verse 53
- published by Faber and Faber 55
- technical terms 41
- tradition and dissent in 41–2
- traditions in animal poetry 42–54
- Yeats's 'Easter 1916' 167–9, 183–5
- *see also The Faber Book of Beasts*

political Irish nationalism 157, 168–60

Pope, Alexander, 'Imitation...of Horace' 45

popular music, and imitation 41, 42

Pranker, Robert (after John Griffiths), *Enthusiasm Displayed* **86**

premises of an argument 13–14
- and the foolish fire-fighter case 15–16
- Socrates' argument in Plato's *Laches* 19

prodigy houses, Elizabethan 113, 114

Protestantism
- and church buildings 124
- and English Christianity 78, 79–88
  - Evangelicals 83, 85–8, 91, 97
  - Methodists 83, 85–8, 89, 91
  - and the nineteenth-century Catholic revival 94–5
  - the Protestant Reformation 75, 78–83, 137
  - Puritans 79, 82
  - religious dissent 83, 84, 85–8, 89, 91–2
- and Irish nationalism 152, 158, 171
- and other religious traditions 82
- Pugin on architecture and 120
- *see also* Church of England

Pugin, Augustus Welby Northmore vi, 107–47
- architectural career 110–11
- on architecture and society 126–7, 131
- and the Camden Society 141–2
- and churches
  - church architecture 121–6, 129–30, **131**
  - furnishings of Catholic churches 132–41
- *Contrasts* 110, 114, 119
  - and church buildings 121–6
  - 'Contrasted residences for the poor' 126, 127
  - 'Contrasted towns' 126–7
  - frontispieces 120–1, **122**, **123**
- DVD ROM material on 109–10
- and the Palace of Westminster 110, 111–19
  - contribution to interior design 118
- St Chad's Cathedral vi, 93–4, **94**
- A Treatise on Chancel Screens and Rood Lofts 133–5
- True Principles of Pointed or Christian Architecture 110, 119, **128**, 128–31, **129**
  - and church buildings 129–30
  - flying buttresses 130, **131**
  - 'On the present degraded state of ecclesiastical buildings' 125, 144–5
  - roof structures 130, **132**
  - 'The Commissioners' churches 126, 146–7
- writings 110, 119–31
- *see also* Gothic architecture

Pugin, Cuthbert 111

Pugin, Edward Welby 111

Pugin, Peter Paul 111

Pugin Society 111

purgatory, and English Christianity 75, 78

Quakers (Society of Friends) 84, 91–2

Ranger, Terence 154

reasoning
- and knowledge 22
- and traditional beliefs 4, 5

reflection
- and knowledge 22, 23
- and traditional beliefs 4, 5

religion v, vi
- different meanings of being 'religious' 73–4
- 'phenomenological' similarities in different religions 82
- present-day religious fundamentalism 96–7
- and tradition 154
- *see also* Catholicism; English Christianity; Protestantism

Republic of Ireland, and Irish nationalism 157

rhetorical repetitions, in Lawrence's poetry 59–60
Richthofen, Frieda von 61
Robson, George F., *View of the Palace of Westminster from the River* **112**
Roman Catholicism *see* Catholicism
rood lofts, in Catholic churches 135–7, **136**, 141–2
Russell, Lord John 95

St Giles, Cheadle, Lady Chapel altarpiece 139
St Paul's Cathedral, London 112, 130, **131**
Schoenberg, Arnold 194
Scottish Parliament building 113
Scythians, nomadic people 10, **11**
Second World War, and Shostakovich 204
Serenus, bishop of Marseille 138
sexuality
  in Donne's 'The Flea' 49–51
  and Lawrence 61
Shelley, Percy Bysshe, 'To a Sky-Lark' 64
Shostakovich, Dmitri vi, 193, 203–22
  and atonal music 205
  in context 203–7
  From Jewish Folk Poetry (song cycle) 218
  and Jewishness in music 204–5, 217–21, 224–5
    klezmer music **219**, 219–20, 221
  music for the stage 204
  photographs of **205**, **206**
  Piano Quintet 204
  Piano Trio No. 2 204, 217–18, 220–1
  and the Second World War 204
  and the Stalin regime 203, 205, 216, 218, 221–2
  string quartets 193, 195–6, 207–17
    No. 2 204, 207–9, 213
    No. 3 195–6, 209, 214–15, 216–17
    No. 7 206, 212–14
    No. 9 215
    rehearsing and performing 216–17
  symphonies 203, 204, 205, 216
    No. 13 218
  Testimony 206–7, 209–12, 217, 224–5
simile, in Blake's 'The Fly' 44
Sinn Féin, and the 1918 general election 169
Smirke, Sir Robert 121
Soane, Sir John 121
Socrates
  the historical Socrates 7, 8
  life 6
  in Plato's dialogues 6–8, 23–4, 25–6
    Laches 9–11, 13–16, 18–19, 20, 23, 27
    Meno 20–2
  portrait statuette of **7**
  the Socratic method of teaching and learning 26–7
Sollertinsky, Ivan 218
sonata form, and Shostakovich's string quartets 207–8, 209
Sophocles 36
sound arguments 14
Spanish Armada, and Catholicism 82
Sparta, war with Athens 6, 9
Stalinism, and Shostakovich's music 203, 205, 216, 218, 221–2
Stephanus *see* Estienne, Henri
Stevenson, J. 161
Storer, J. and H.S. (after Petrie), *Mount Cashell, Co. of Tipperary* **162**
Stravinsky, I. 194
string quartets 193, 195–202
  and chamber music 196–9
  and the classical period of music 199–201, 214, 215
  composers of 200
  DVD Video of 193, 195–6, 201–2, 207–17
  instruments 196, 201–2, **202**, **203**
  players 196, 201–2
  see also Shostakovich, Dmitri
Synge, John Millington
  In the Shadow of the Glen 163
  The Playboy of the Western World 163–4

Taruskin, Richard 209
Tchaikovsky, Pyotr Il'yich 202, 218
Theiner, George, translation of Holub's 'The Fly' 53
time signatures in music 208, 214
Tomes, Susan
  'C is for chamber music' 198–9, 223–4
  'R is for Rehearsal and Repetition' 216
Toscanini, Arturo 204
trabeated architecture 128
traditional beliefs
  questioning 3–5
    in Athens 6
    Plato and moral traditionalism 24–6, 41
traditions v–vi, 226
  see also invented tradition
Turner, J.M.W. 111
Tyrtaeus, Spartan poet 12

Ullathorne, Bernard, bishop of Birmingham 94
urban growth, and English Christianity 88–9
utilitarianism 127

validity, and deductive arguments 14–15
values
  and courage, in Plato's *Laches* 17
  and philosophical arguments 16
Vienna, New Year's Day concert *195*
violas, and string quartets 196, 201

violins
  mutes 212, **213**
  and string quartets 196, 201–2, 202, 203

virtue, courage as the whole of, in Plato's *Laches* 19

Volkov, Solomon 206

Walsh, Thomas, vicar-apostolic 93, 94

Waterloo, battle of (1815), and new church buildings 126

Welsh Assembly building 113

Wesley, John 85–6, 88, 91

Westminster *see* Palace of Westminster

Westminster Abbey 113

Whitefield, George 85–8
  evangelical preaching **86**, 86–7, 97, 102–4
    criticisms of the Anglican clergy 87–8, 97

Whitman, Walt 41, 42
  'A Noiseless Patient Spider' 65
  and Lawrence 65

Wilkins, William 121

William III, King 85

William of Wykeham, Bishop 121

Windsor Castle, St George's Chapel 121–4

Wiseman, Nicholas, cardinal and archbishop of Westminster 94, 104

Wolsey, Cardinal 111

workhouses, Pugin on Gothic architecture and 127

Worthern, John 61

Wright, James, 'A Blessing' 68, 69

Wyatt, James 117

Yeats, W.B. 161, 163
  The Countess Cathleen 163
  'Easter 1916' 167–9, 183–5
  letter to Lady Gregory 166–7, 169

Yevtushenko, Yevgeny, 'Babi Yar' 218

York
  Centenary Chapel 91, **92**
  Holy Trinity Church, Goodramgate **81**
  St Wilfrid's Roman Catholic Church 91, **93**
  York Minster 91, **93**

Young Ireland 160